This Sketchbook Belong to:

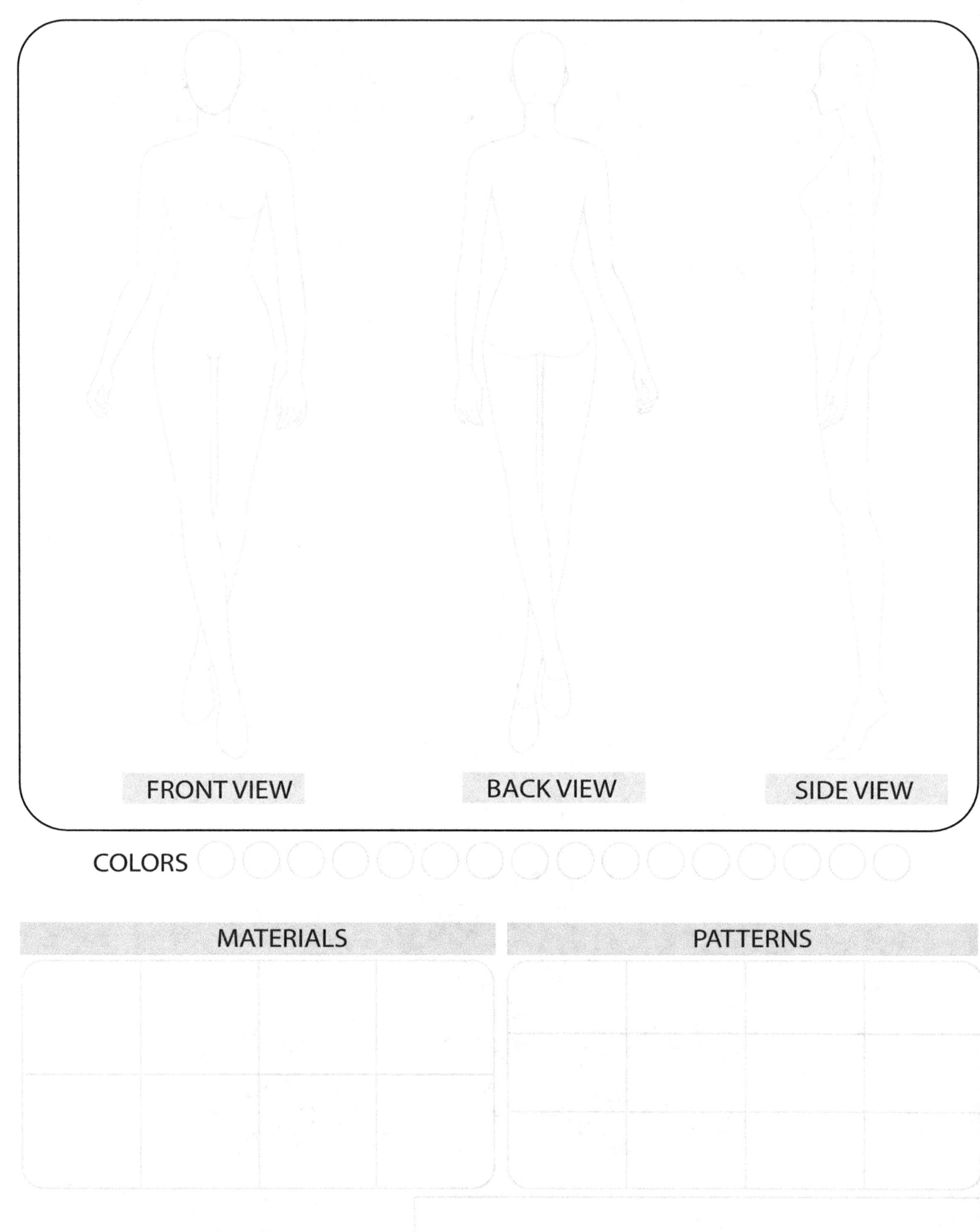

FRONT VIEW
BACK VIEW
SIDE VIEW
COLORS
MATERIALS
PATTERNS
ACCESSORIES

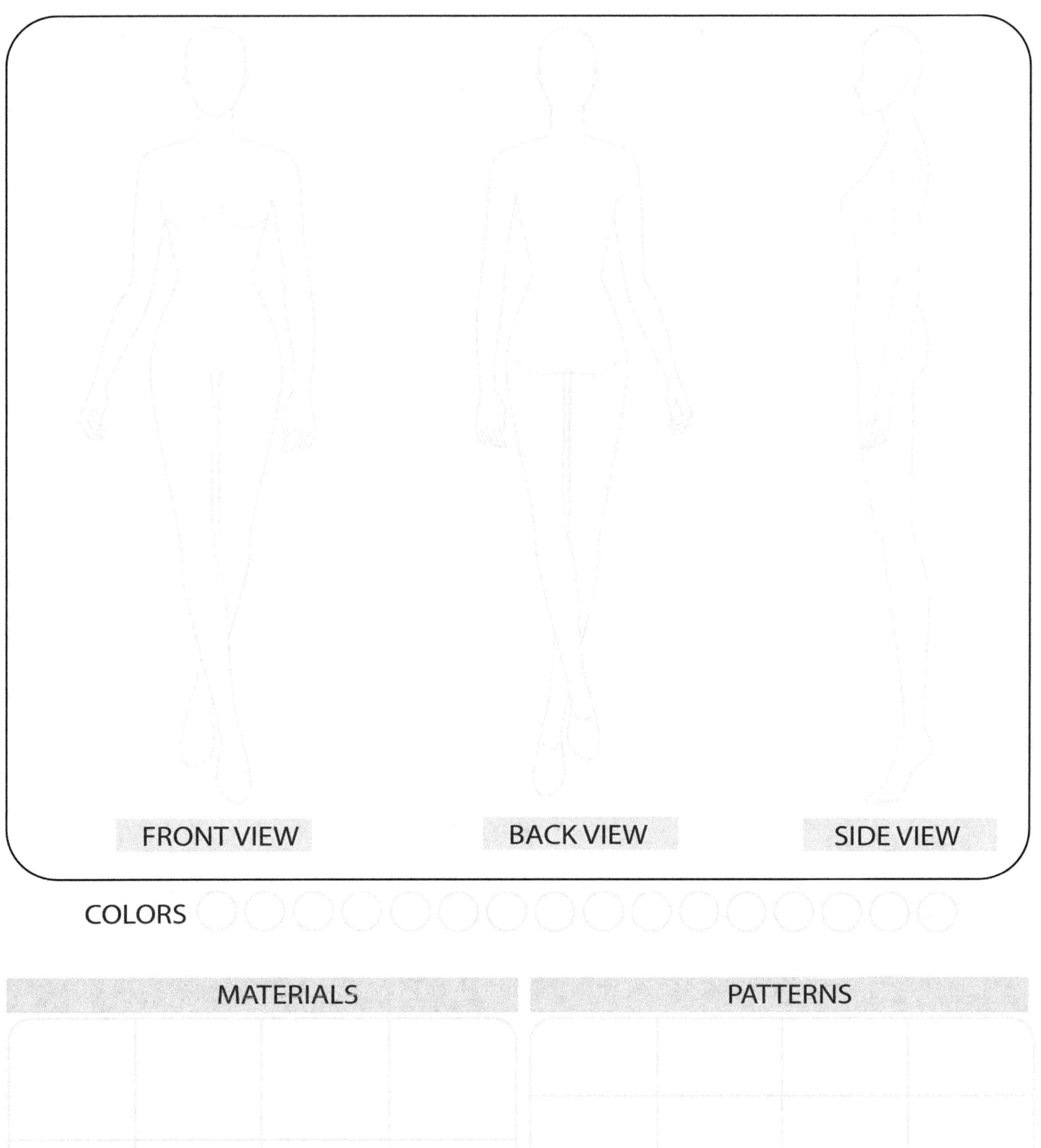

FRONT VIEW
BACK VIEW
SIDE VIEW
COLORS
MATERIALS
PATTERNS
ACCESSORIES

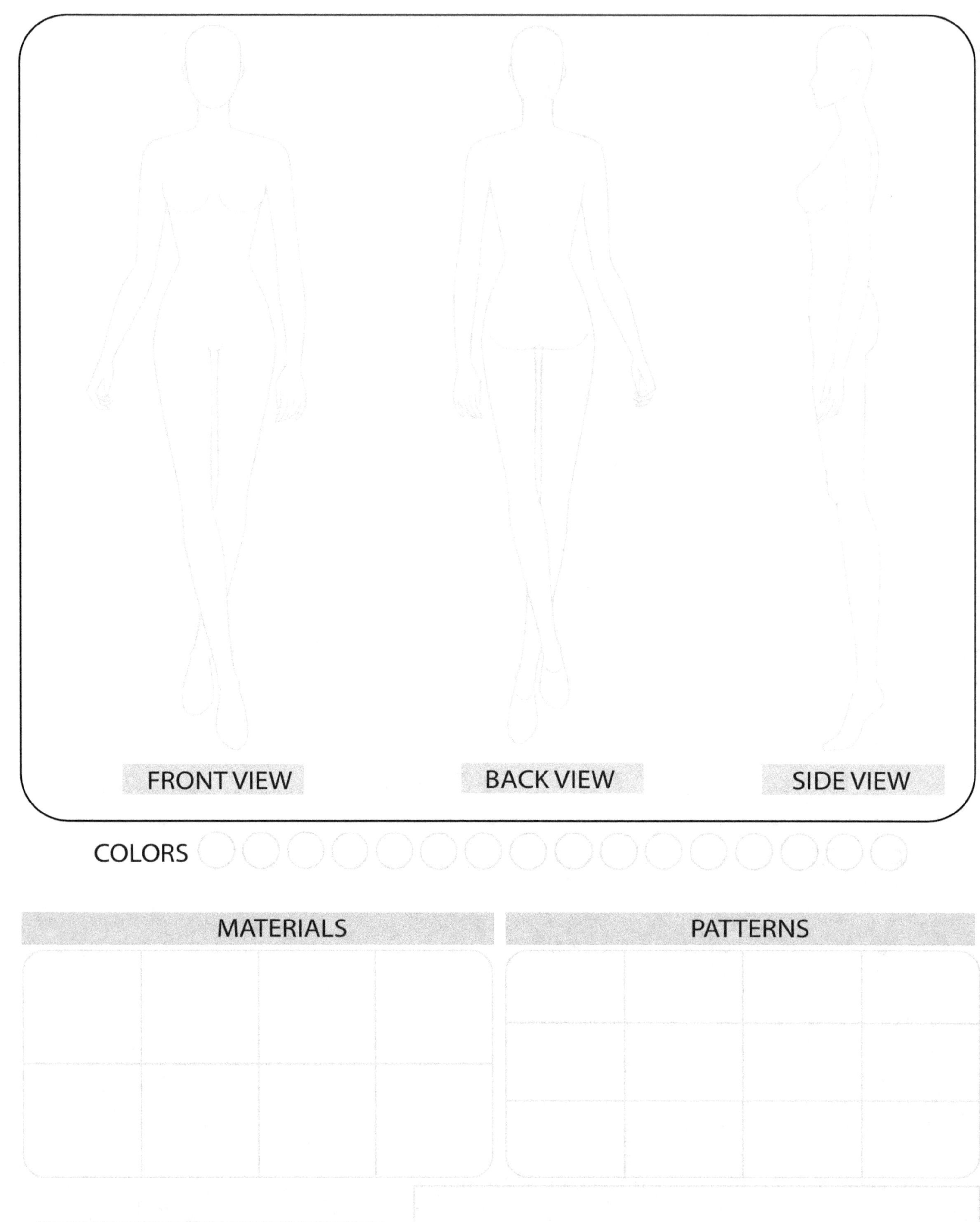

FRONT VIEW
BACK VIEW
SIDE VIEW
COLORS
MATERIALS
PATTERNS
ACCESSORIES

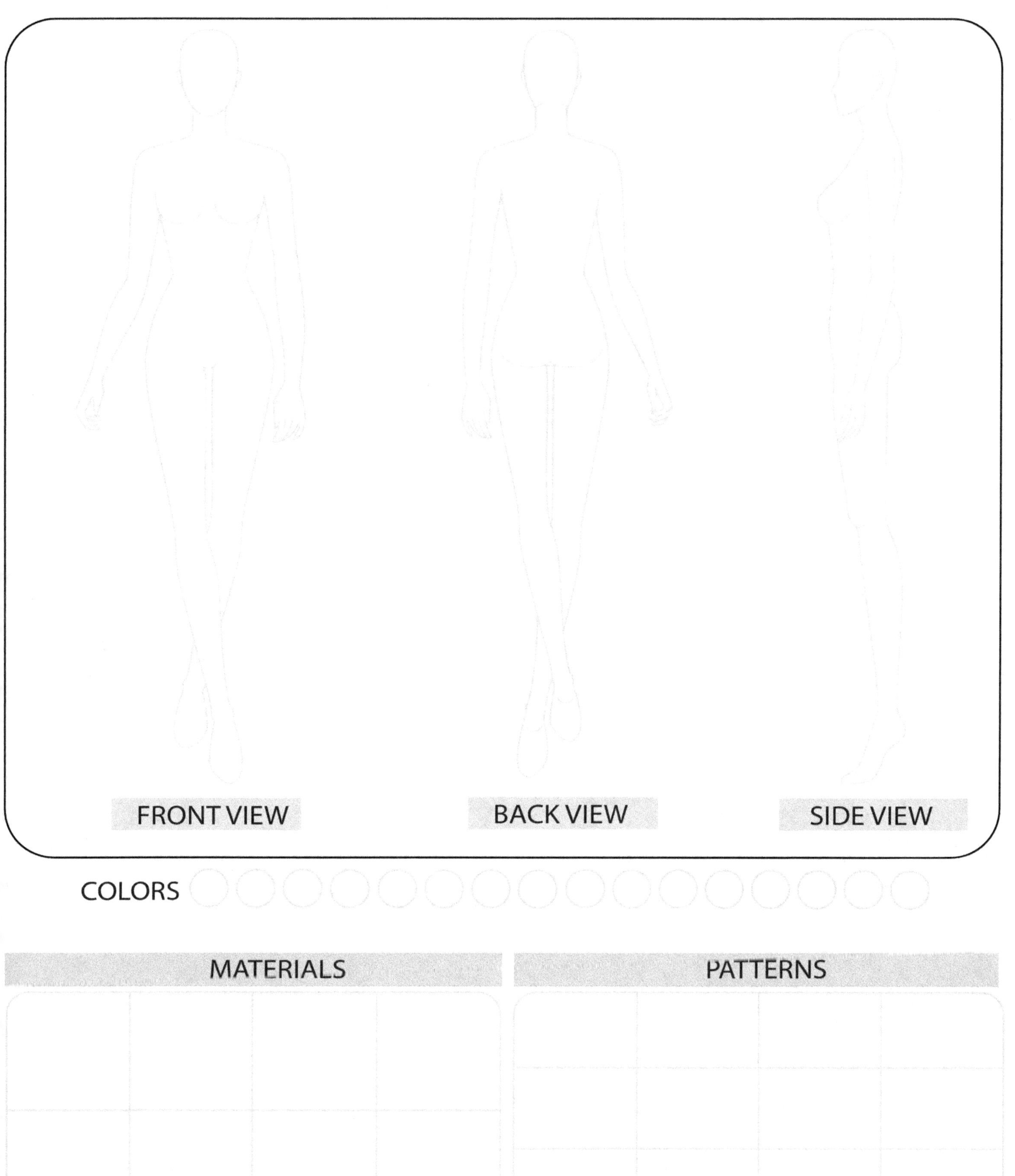

FRONT VIEW
BACK VIEW
SIDE VIEW
COLORS
MATERIALS
PATTERNS
ACCESSORIES

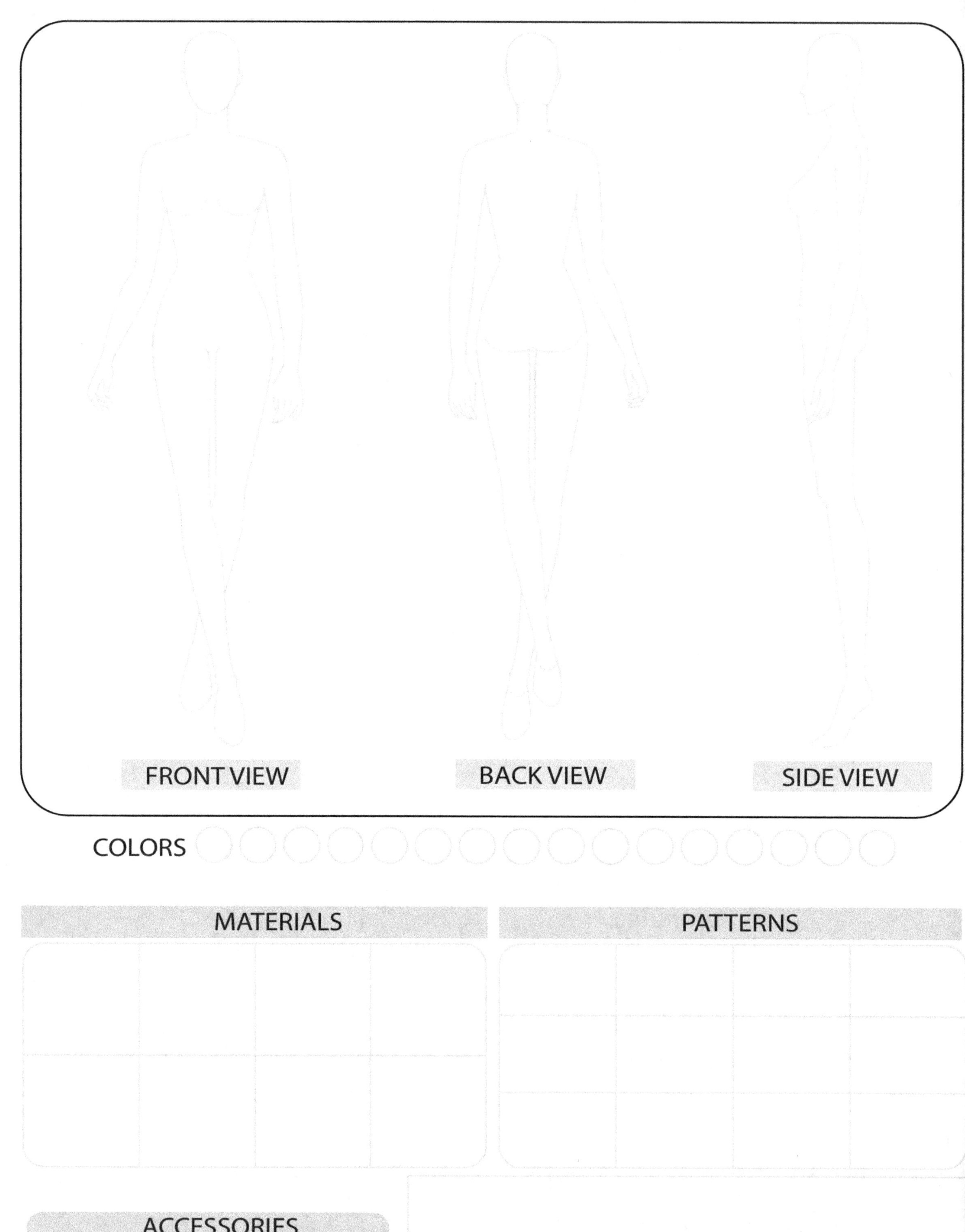

FRONT VIEW
BACK VIEW
SIDE VIEW
COLORS
MATERIALS
PATTERNS
ACCESSORIES

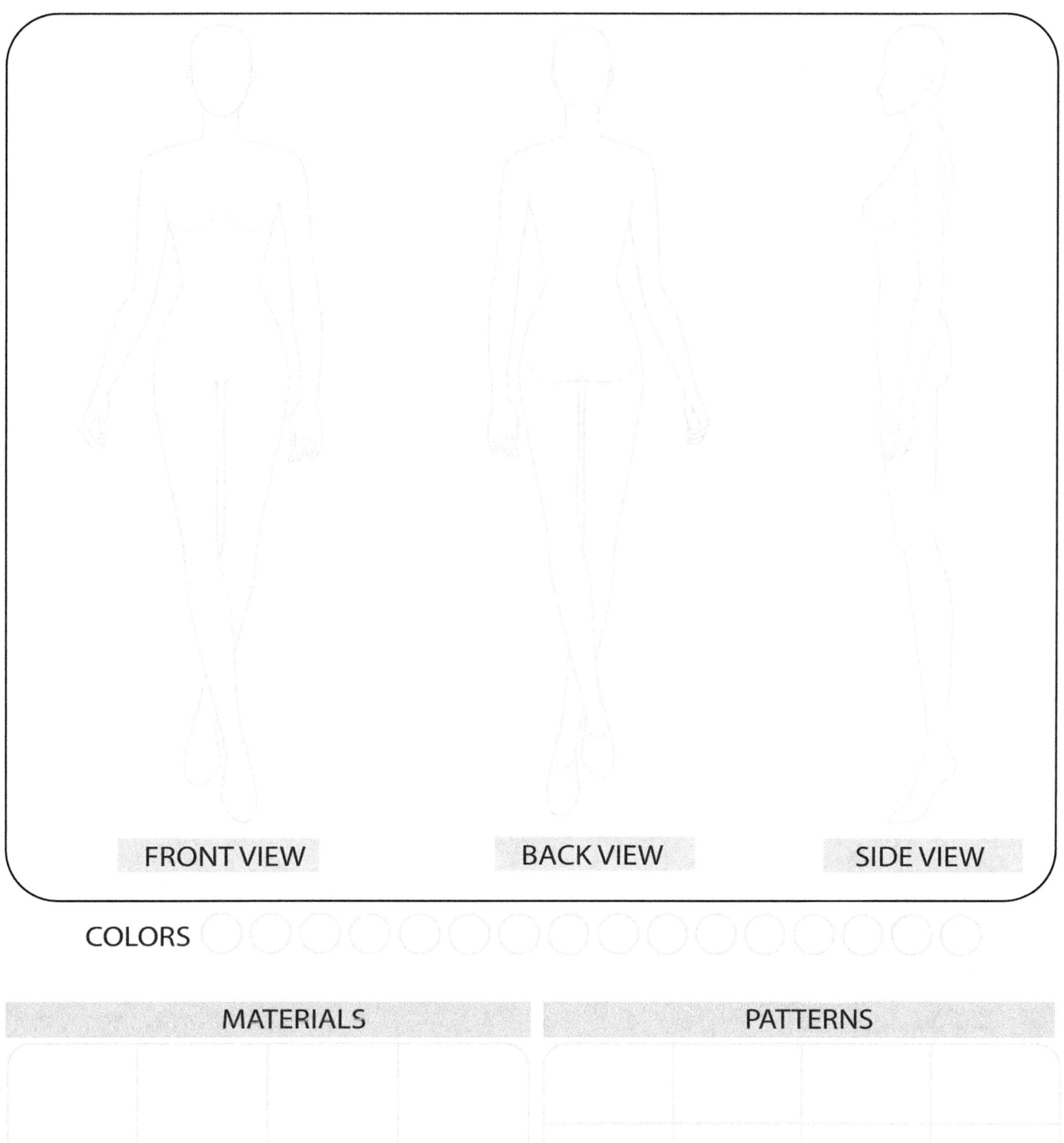

COLORS

MATERIALS

PATTERNS

ACCESSORIES

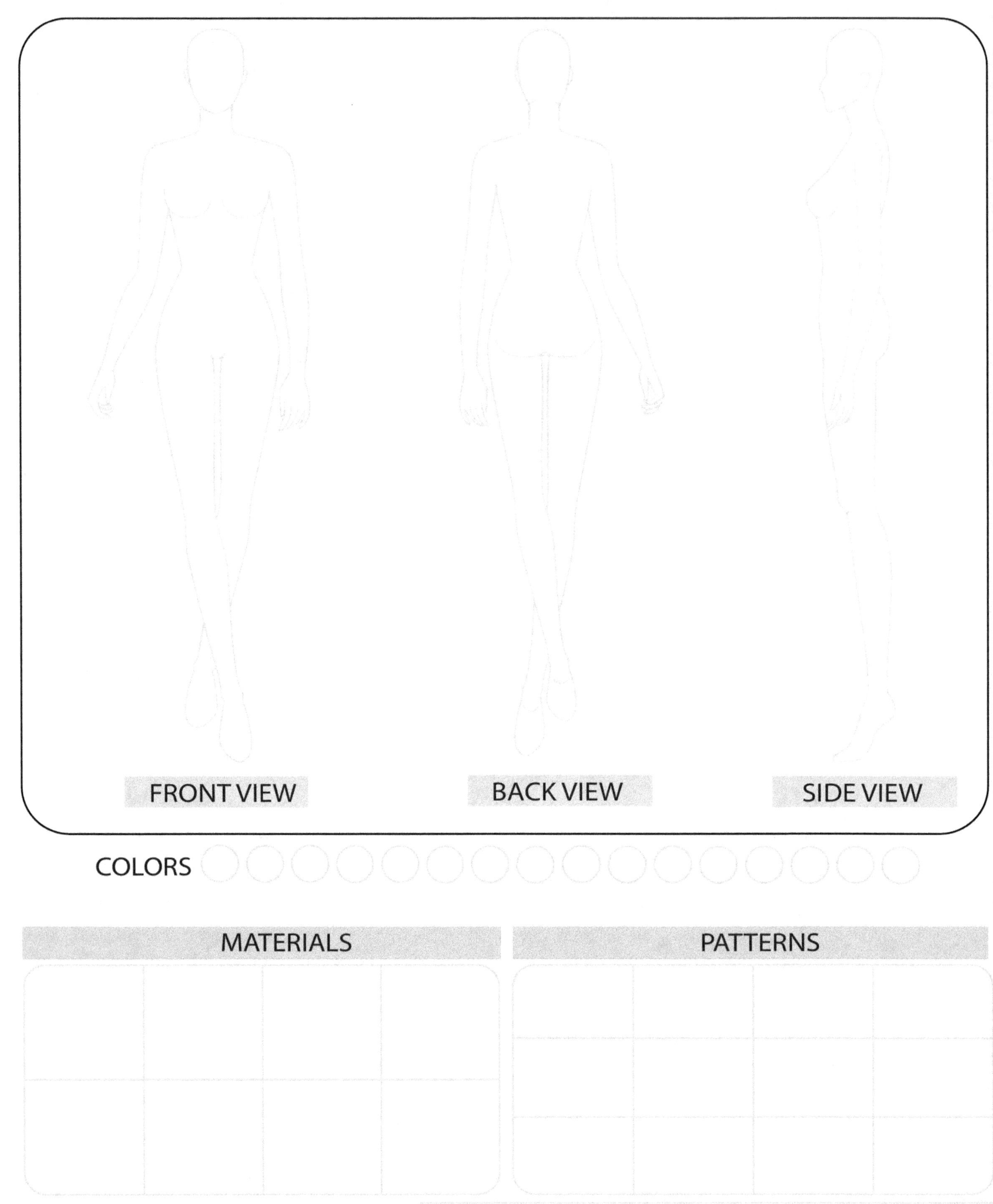

FRONT VIEW
BACK VIEW
SIDE VIEW
COLORS
MATERIALS
PATTERNS
ACCESSORIES

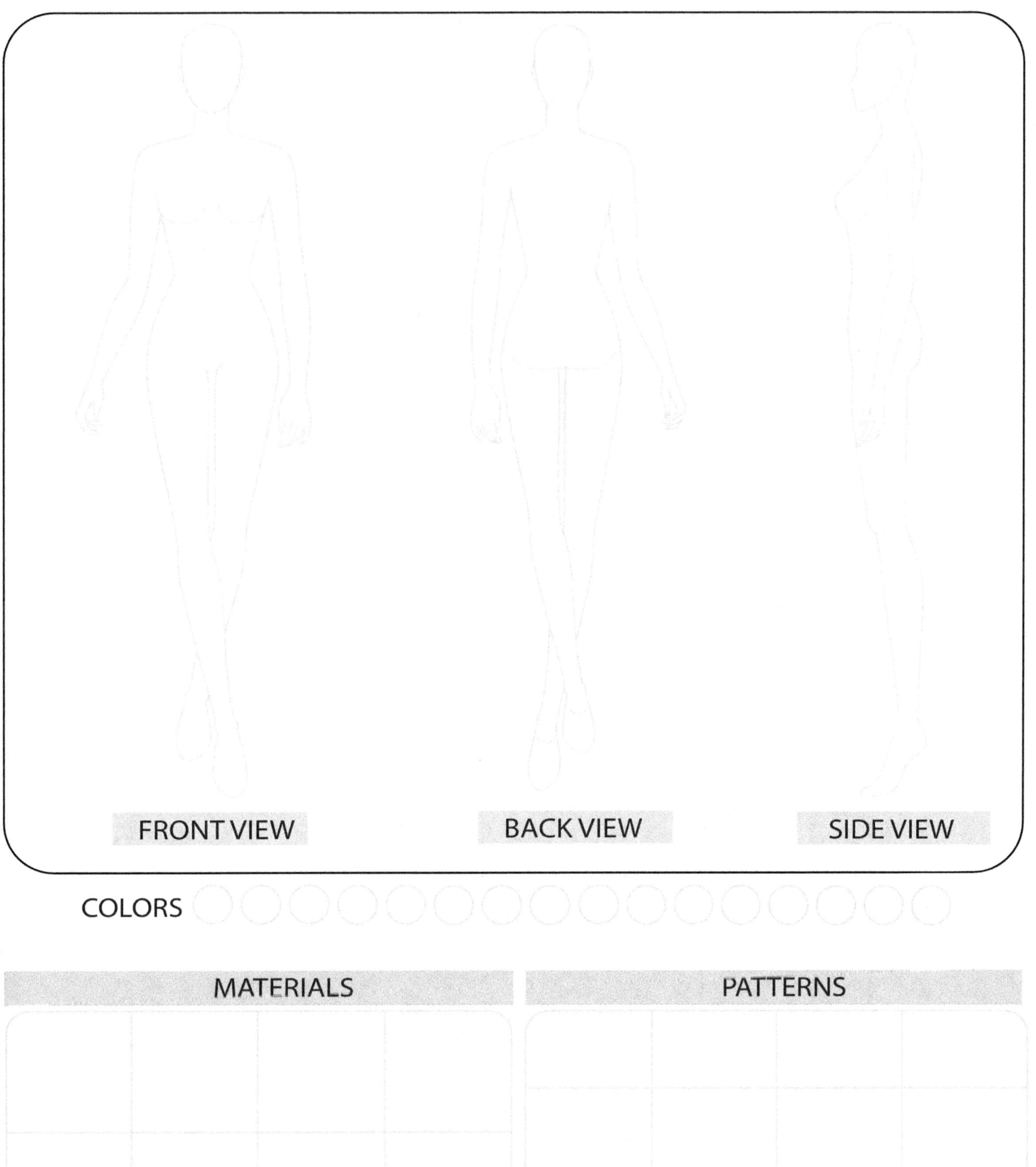

FRONT VIEW
BACK VIEW
SIDE VIEW
COLORS
MATERIALS
PATTERNS
ACCESSORIES

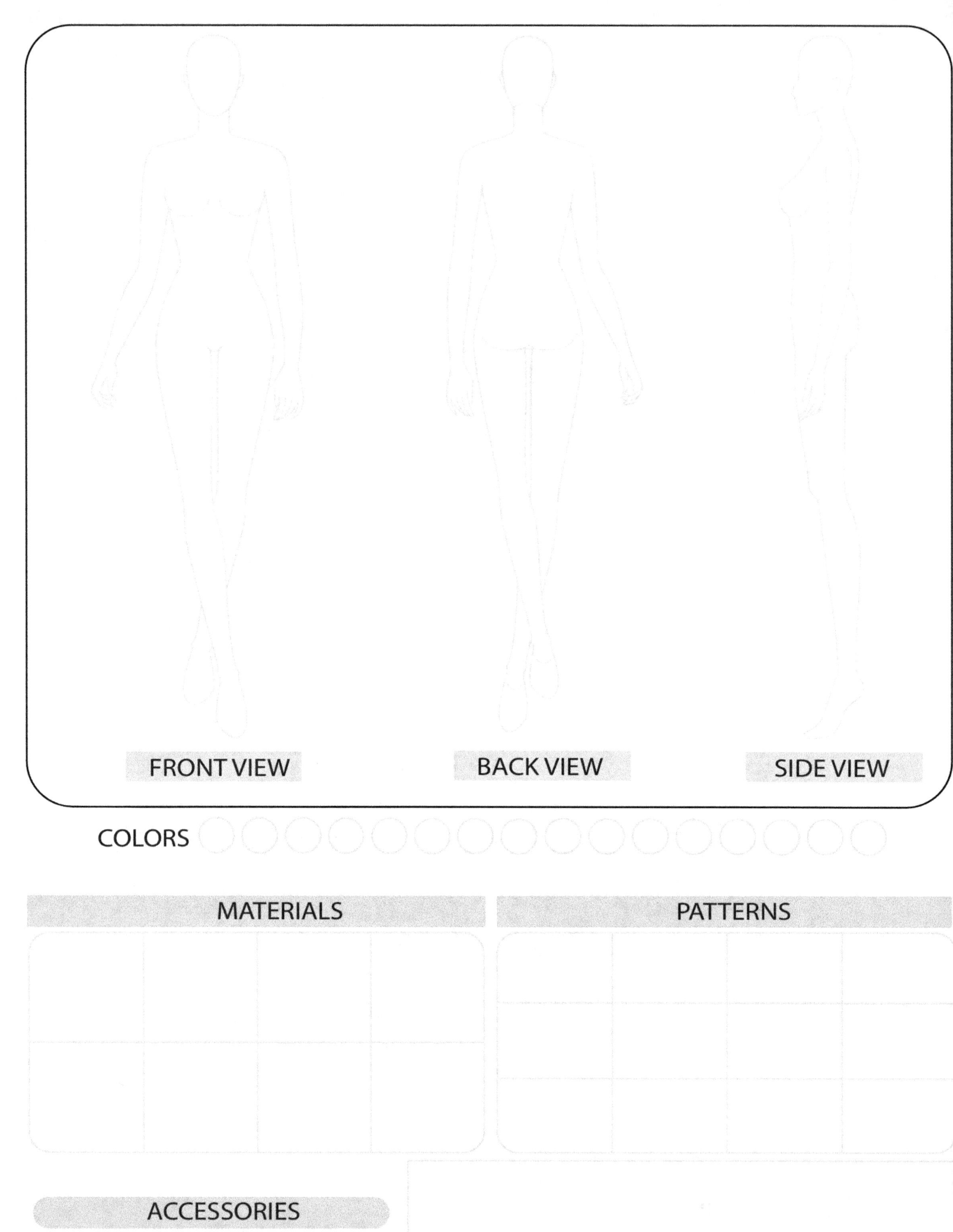

FRONT VIEW
BACK VIEW
SIDE VIEW
COLORS
MATERIALS
PATTERNS
ACCESSORIES

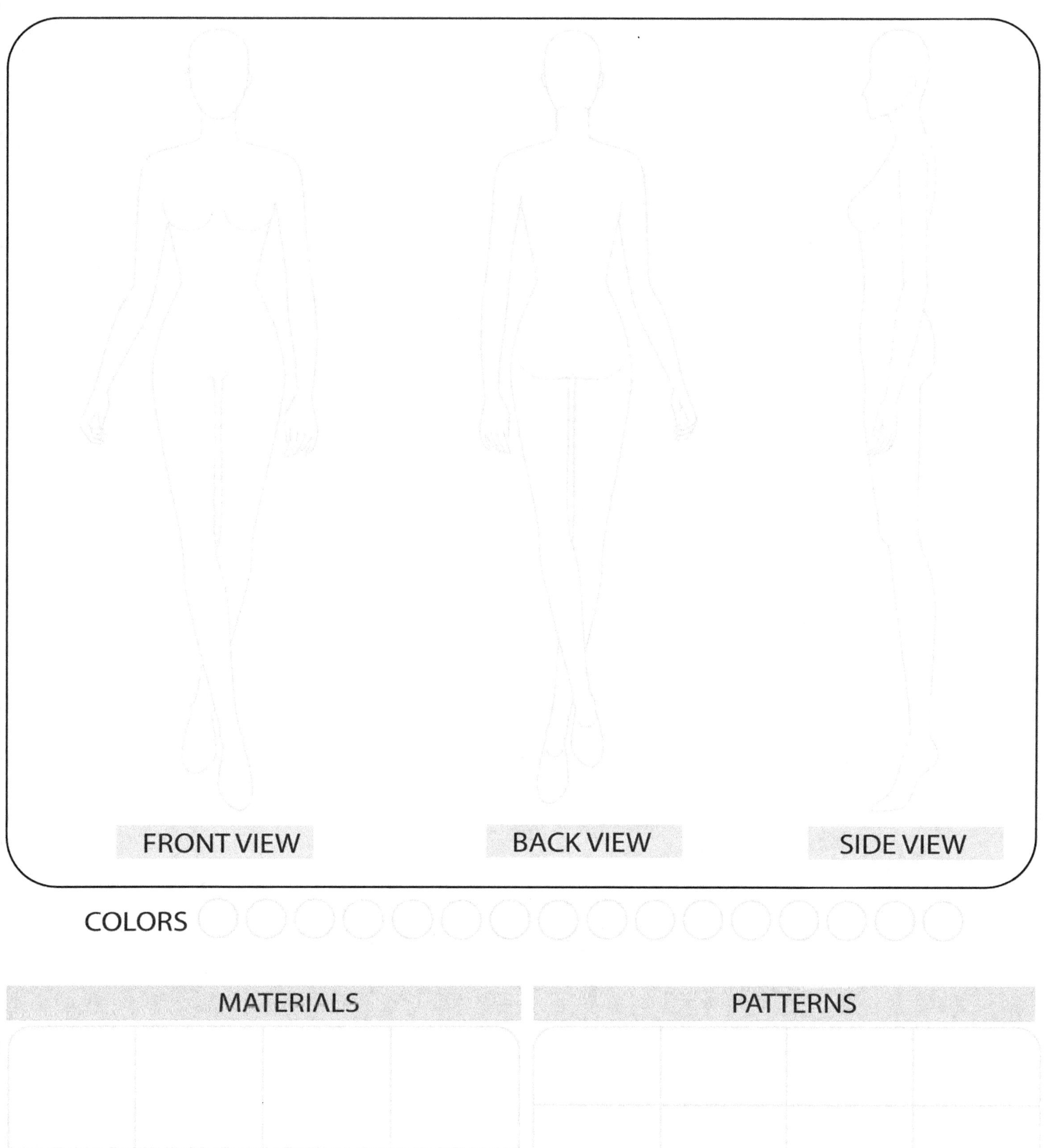

COLORS

MATERIALS

PATTERNS

ACCESSORIES

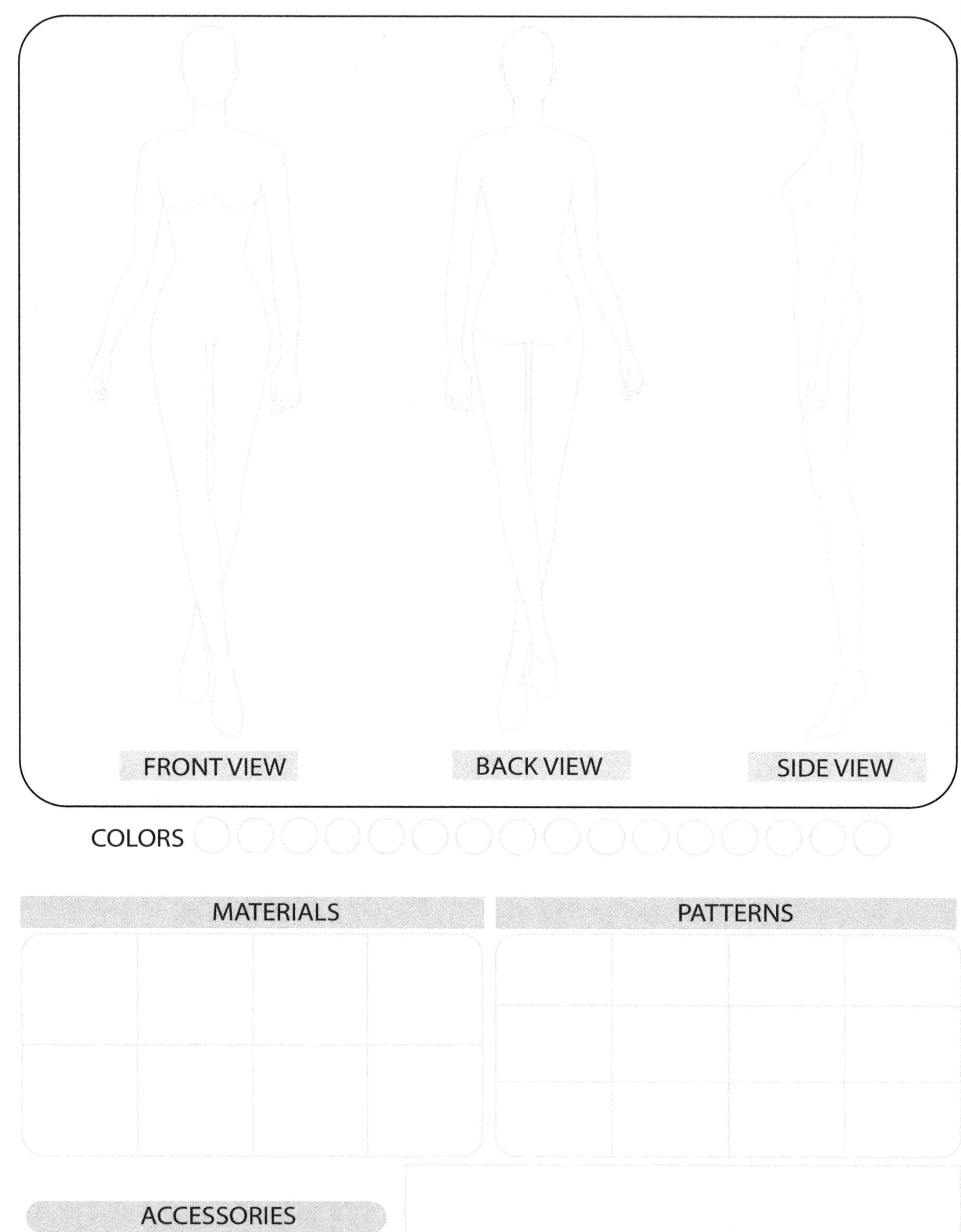
FRONT VIEW
BACK VIEW
SIDE VIEW
COLORS
MATERIALS
PATTERNS
ACCESSORIES

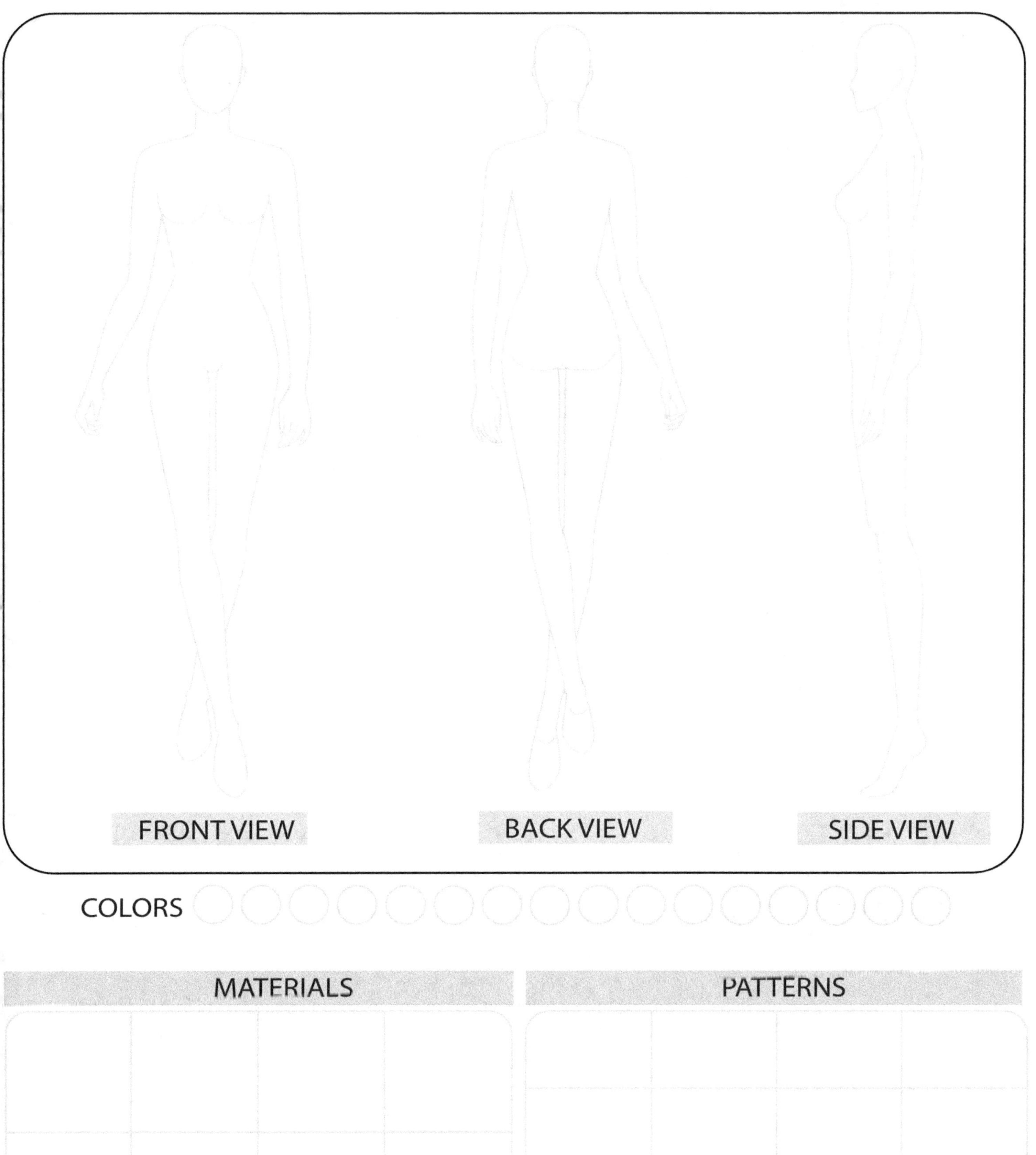

FRONT VIEW

BACK VIEW

SIDE VIEW

COLORS

MATERIALS

PATTERNS

ACCESSORIES

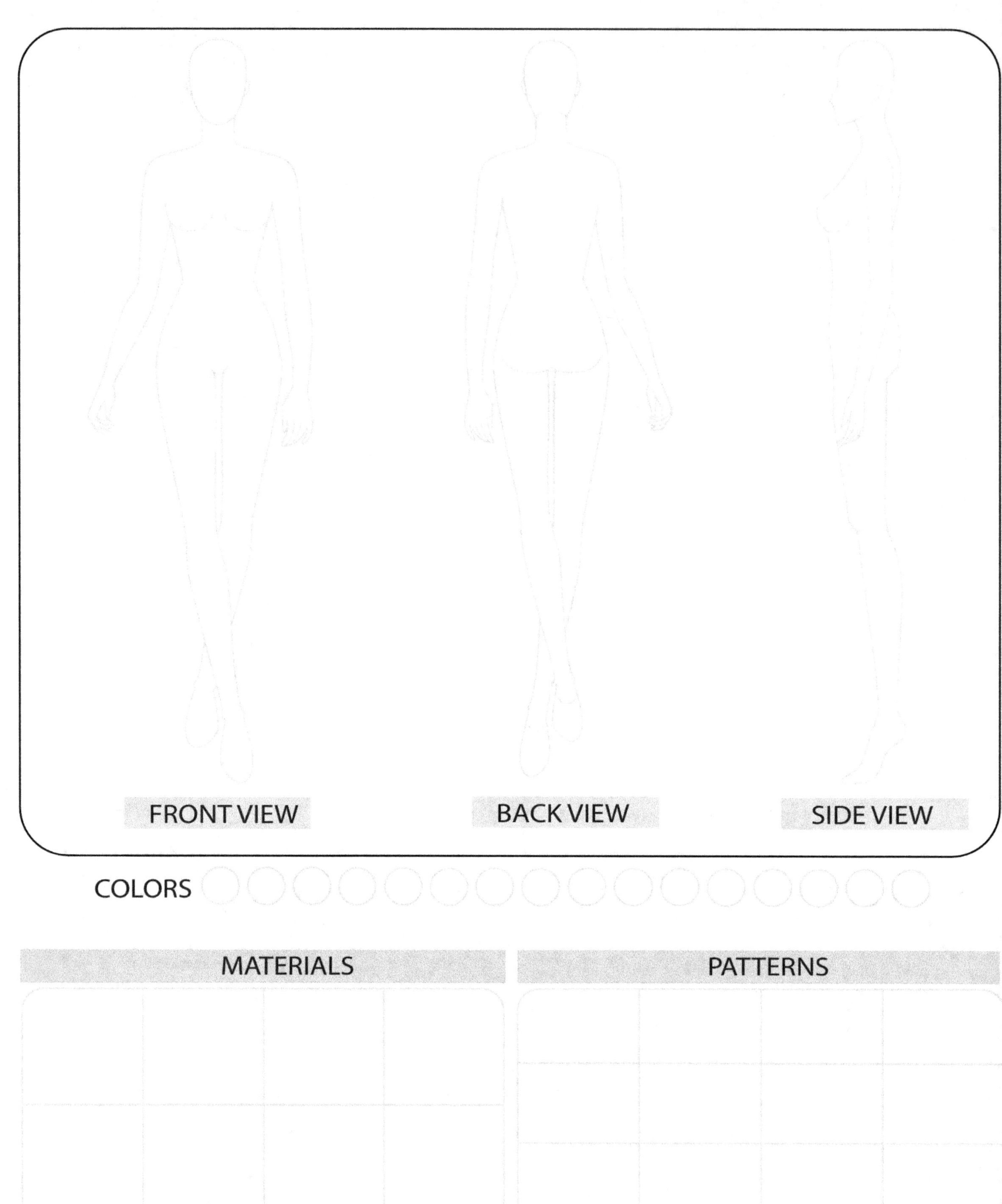

FRONT VIEW
BACK VIEW
SIDE VIEW
COLORS
MATERIALS
PATTERNS
ACCESSORIES

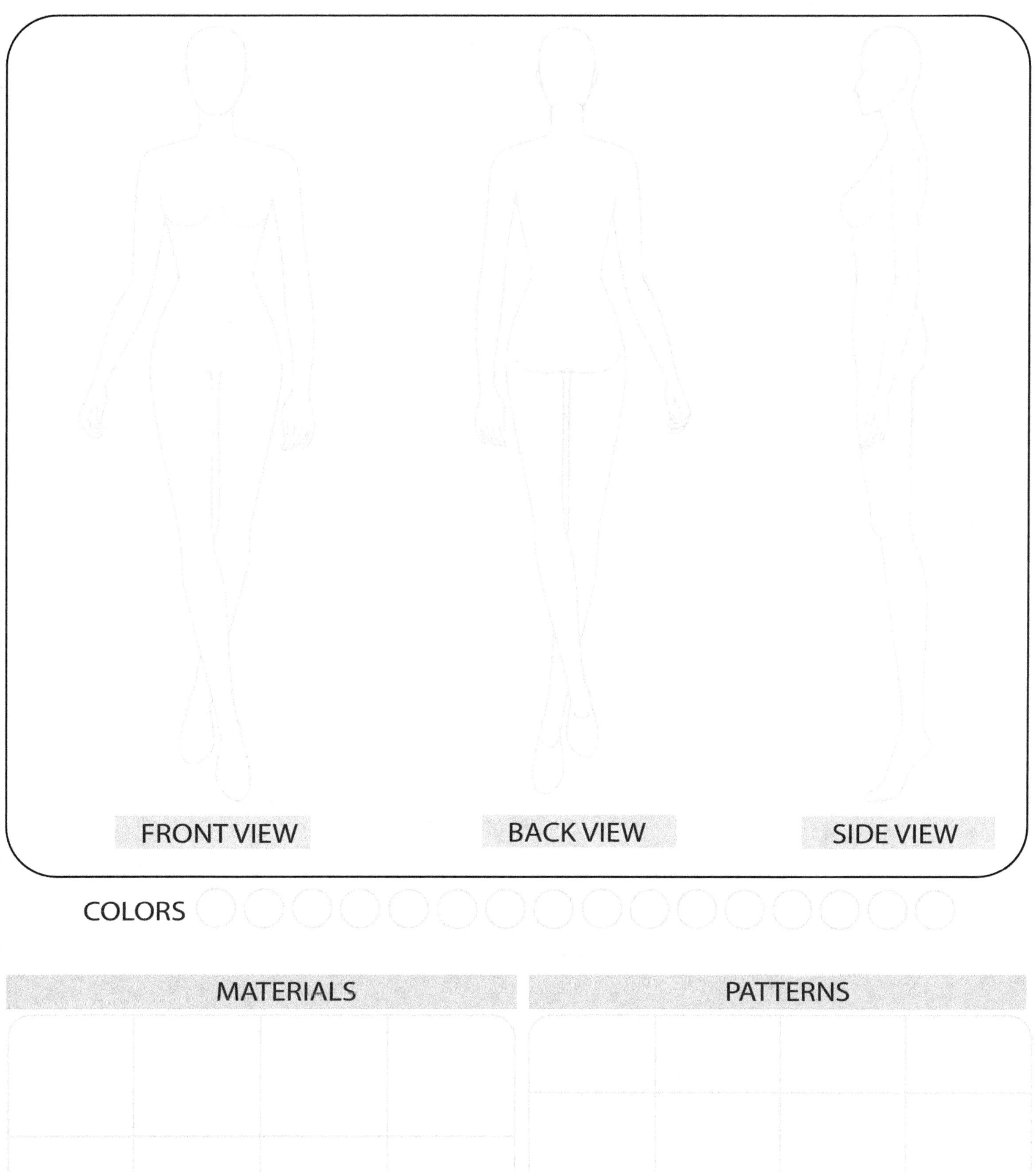

COLORS

MATERIALS

PATTERNS

ACCESSORIES

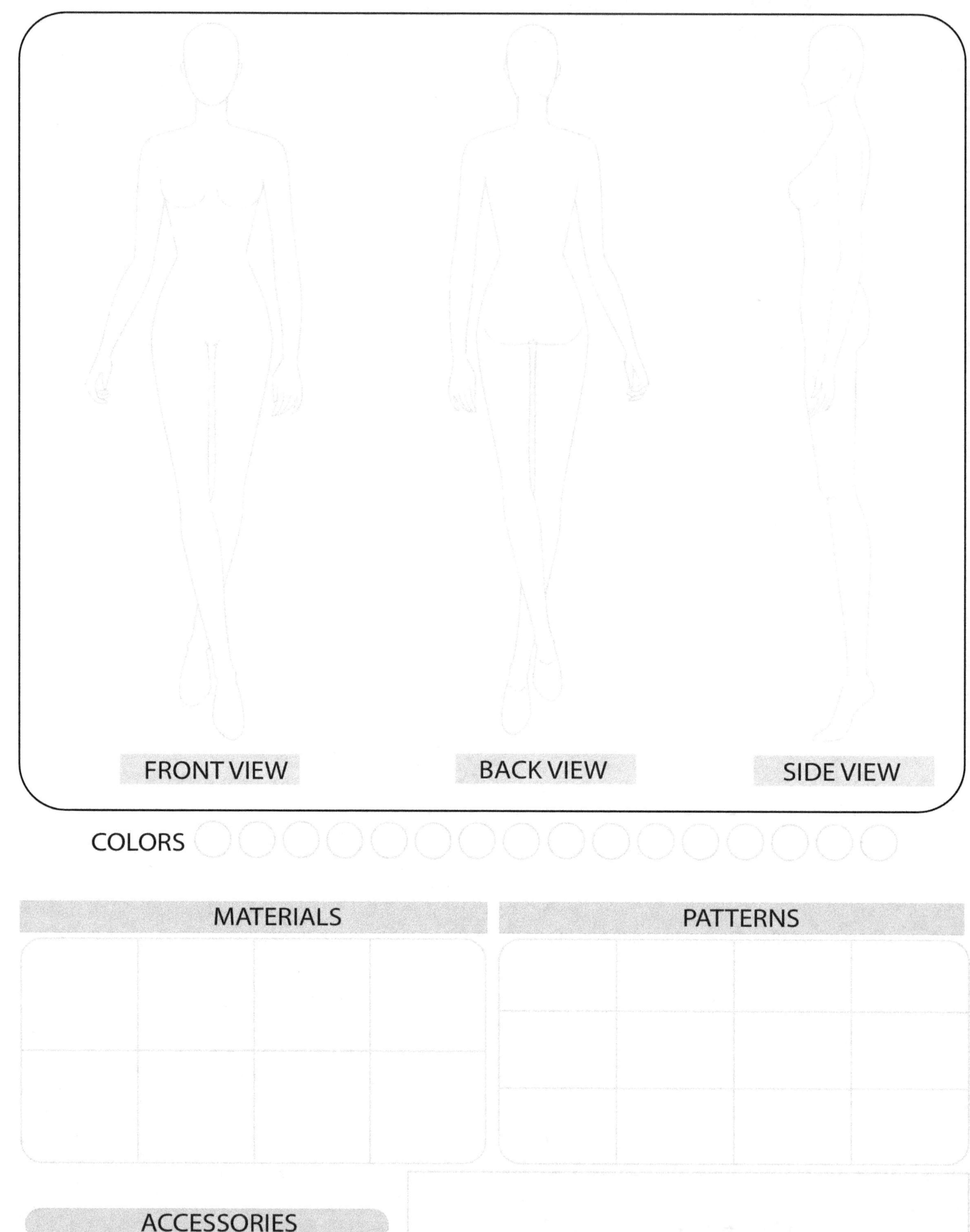

FRONT VIEW

BACK VIEW

SIDE VIEW

COLORS

MATERIALS

PATTERNS

ACCESSORIES

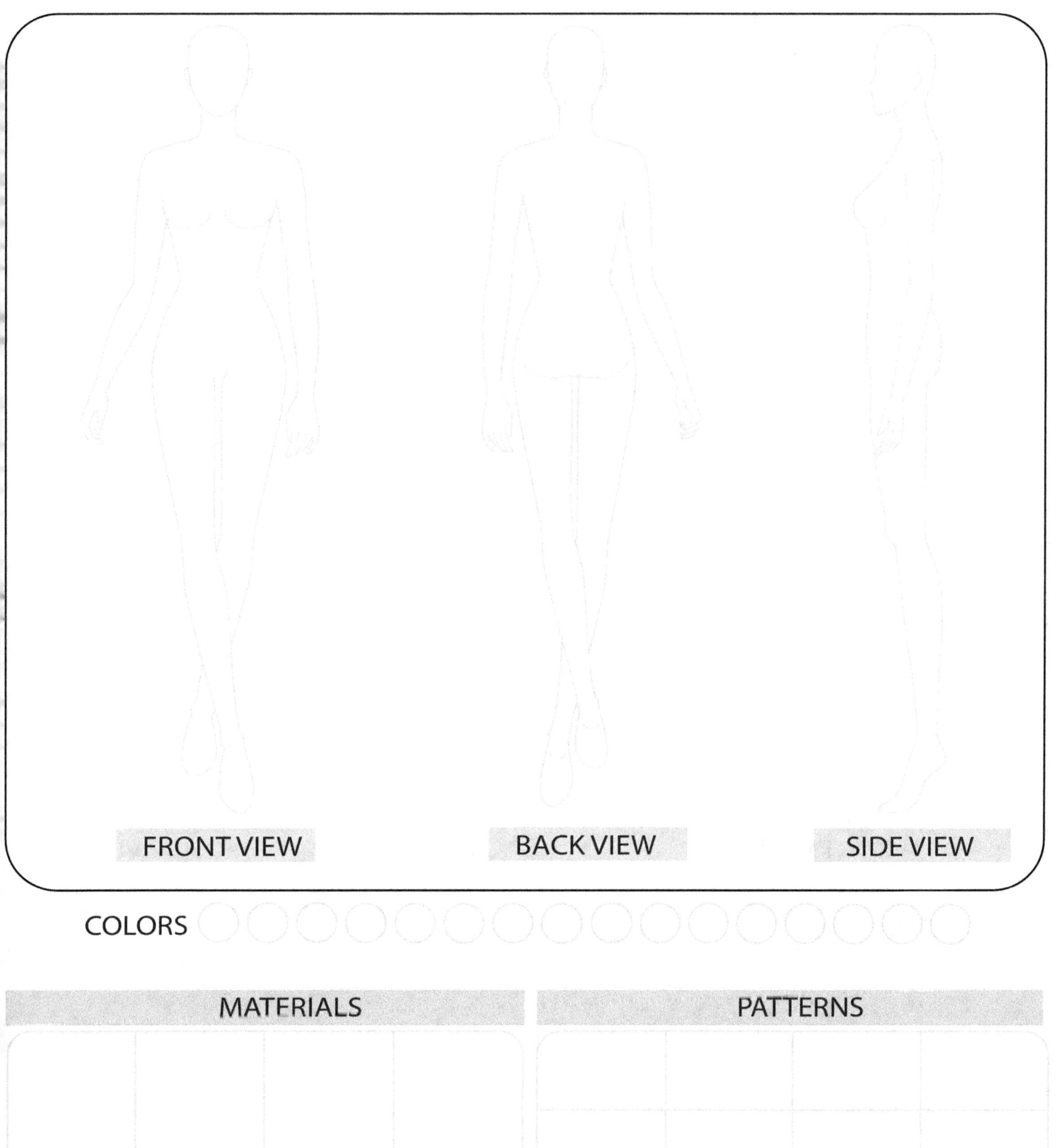

FRONT VIEW

BACK VIEW

SIDE VIEW

COLORS

MATERIALS

PATTERNS

ACCESSORIES

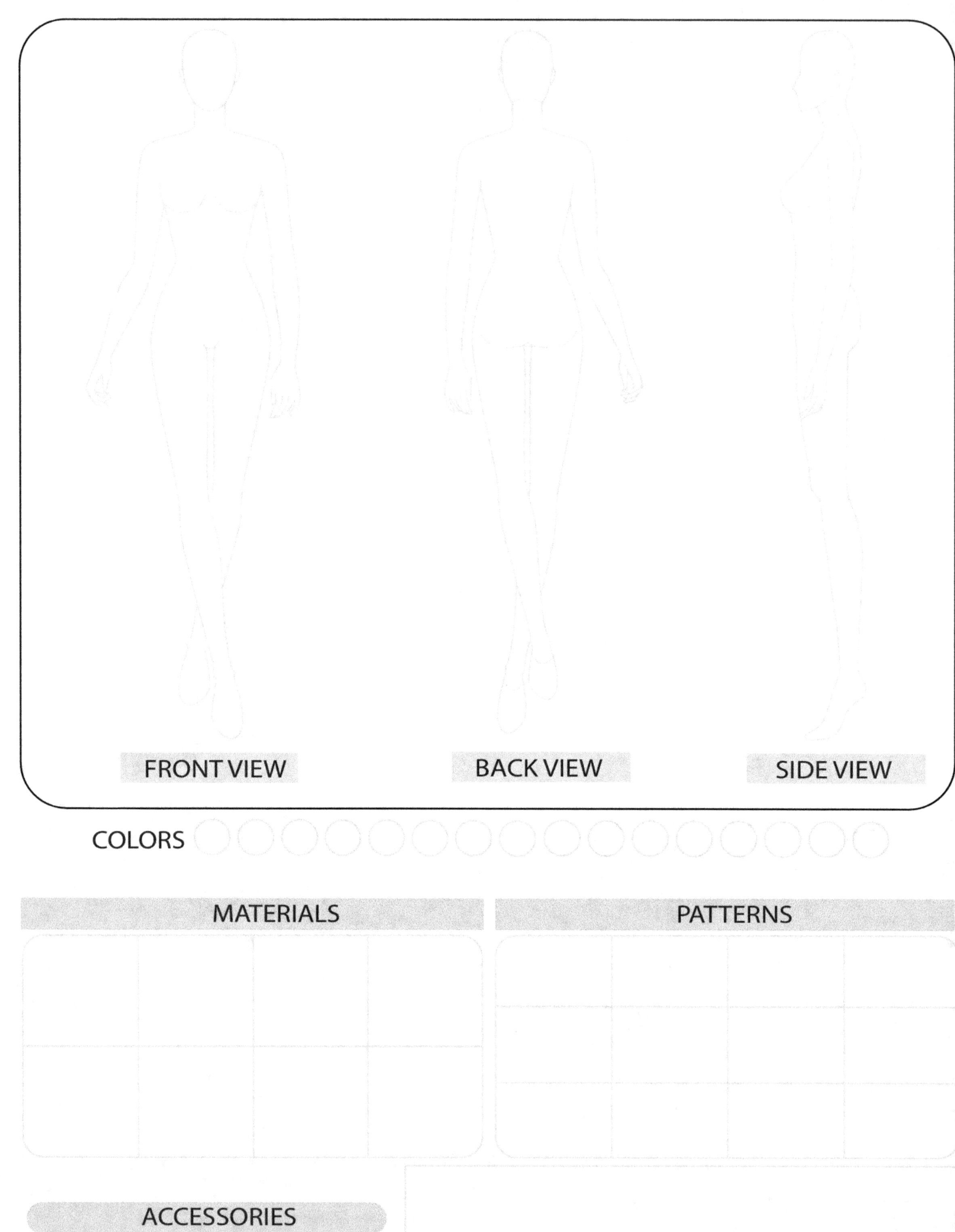

FRONT VIEW
BACK VIEW
SIDE VIEW
COLORS
MATERIALS
PATTERNS
ACCESSORIES

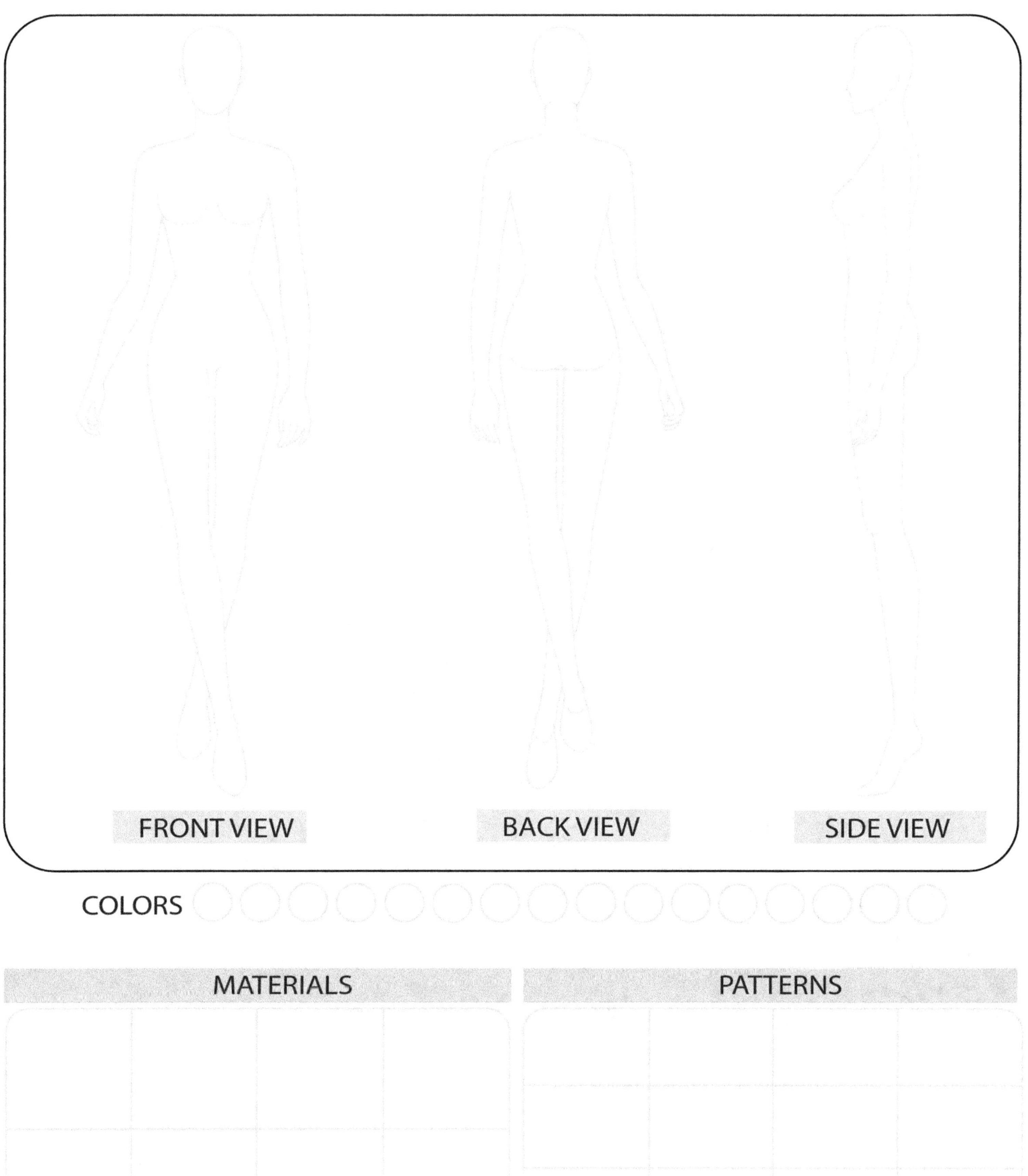

FRONT VIEW   BACK VIEW   SIDE VIEW

COLORS

MATERIALS   PATTERNS

ACCESSORIES

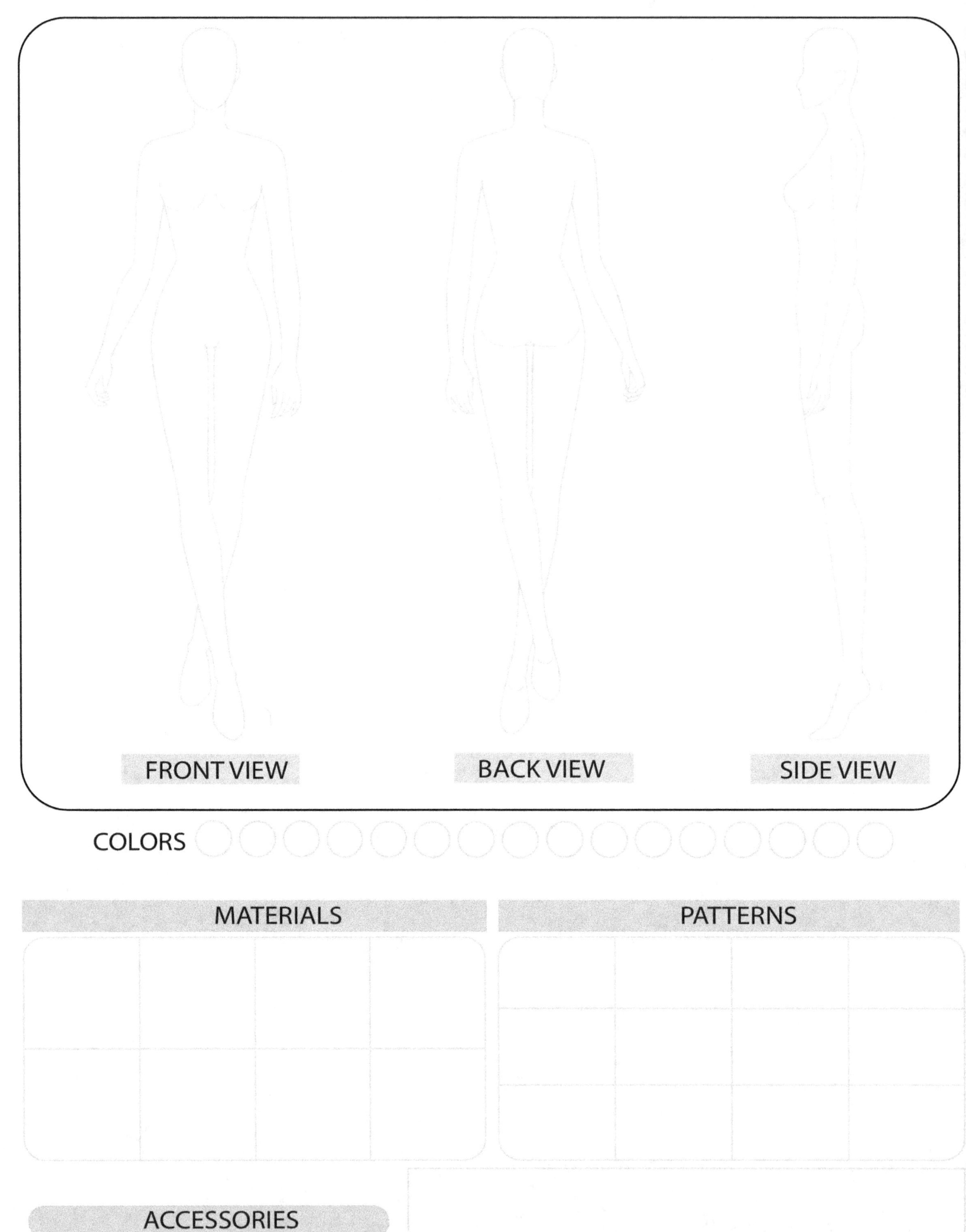

FRONT VIEW
BACK VIEW
SIDE VIEW
COLORS
MATERIALS
PATTERNS
ACCESSORIES

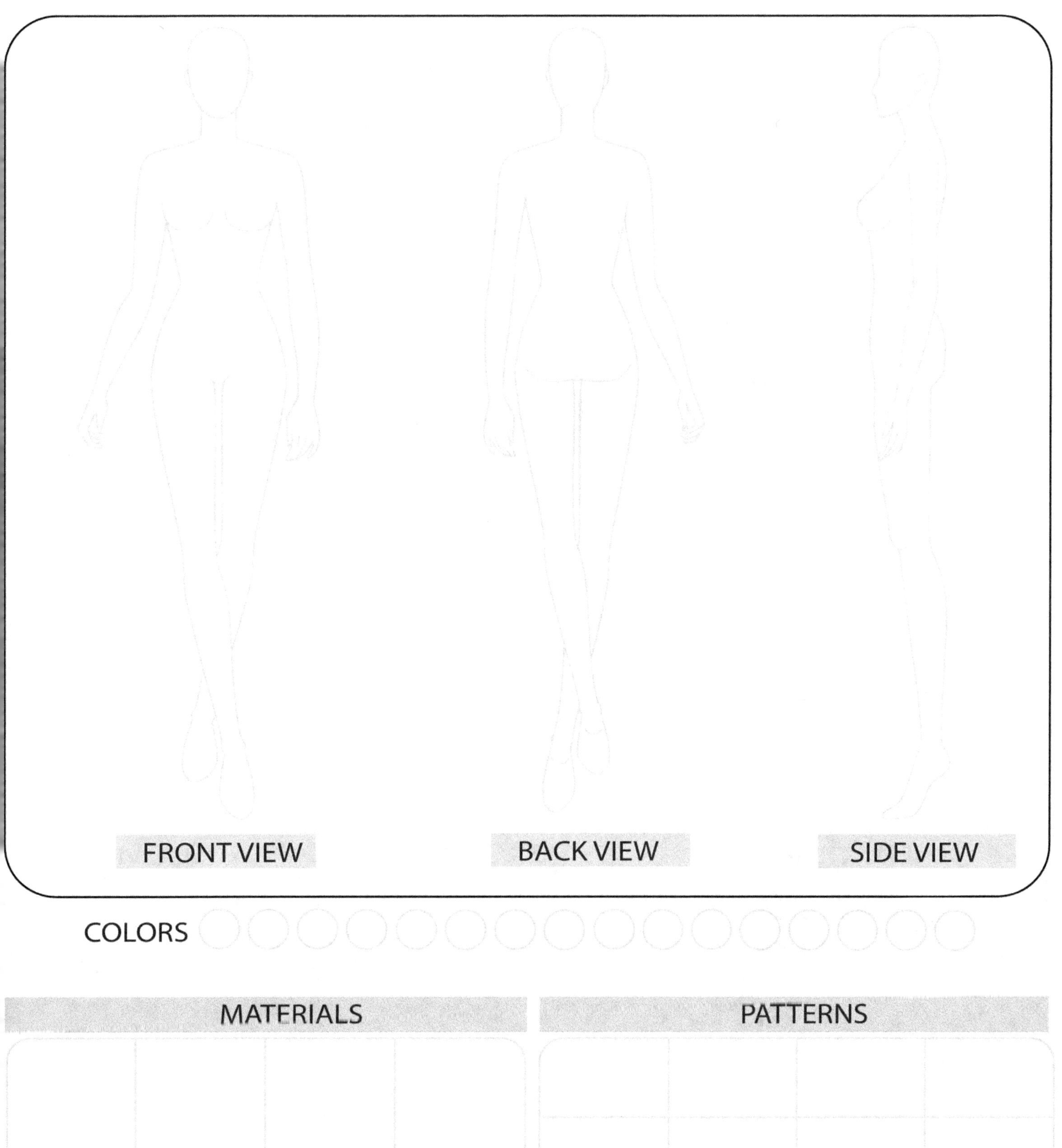

FRONT VIEW

BACK VIEW

SIDE VIEW

COLORS

MATERIALS

PATTERNS

ACCESSORIES

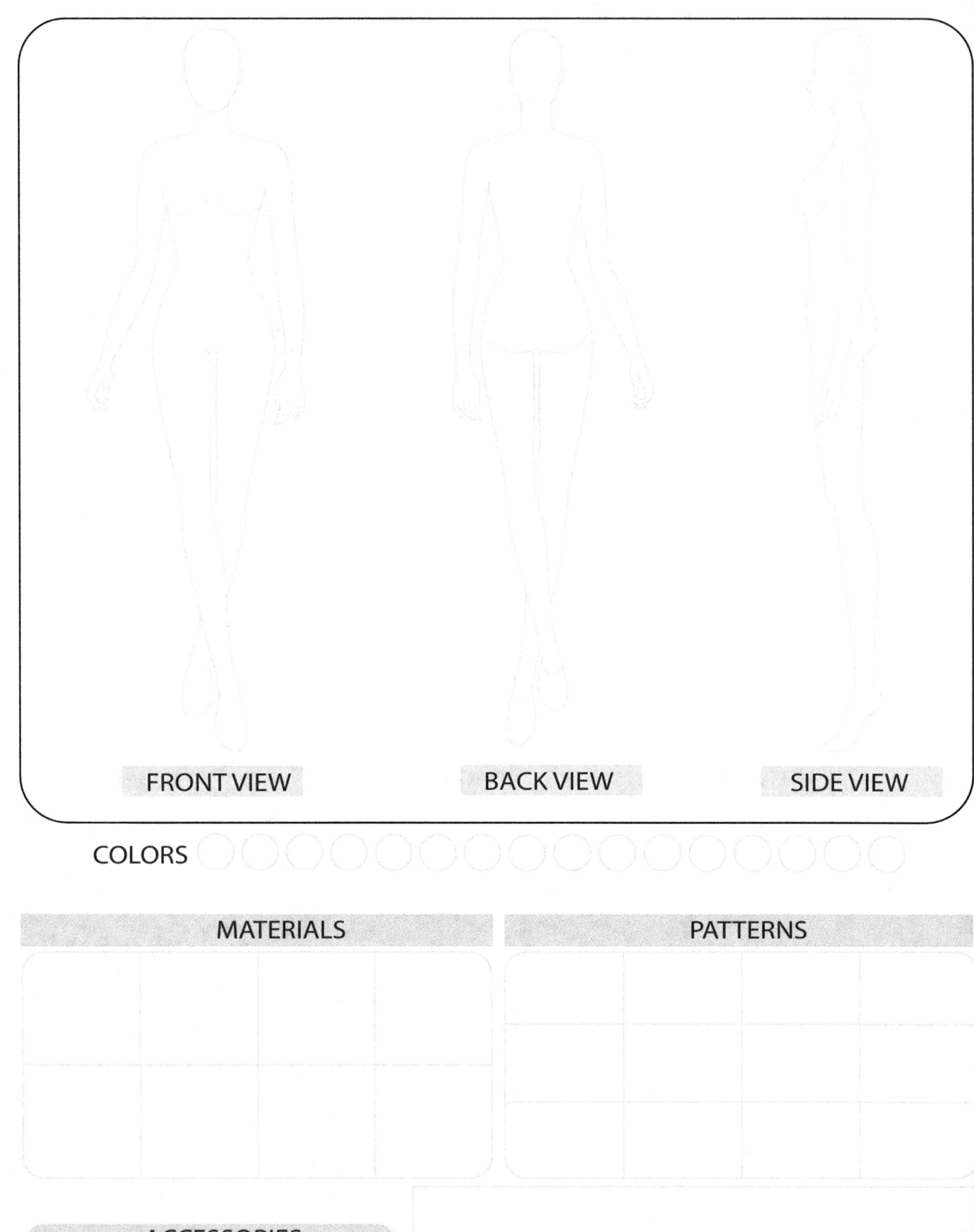

FRONT VIEW
BACK VIEW
SIDE VIEW
COLORS
MATERIALS
PATTERNS
ACCESSORIES

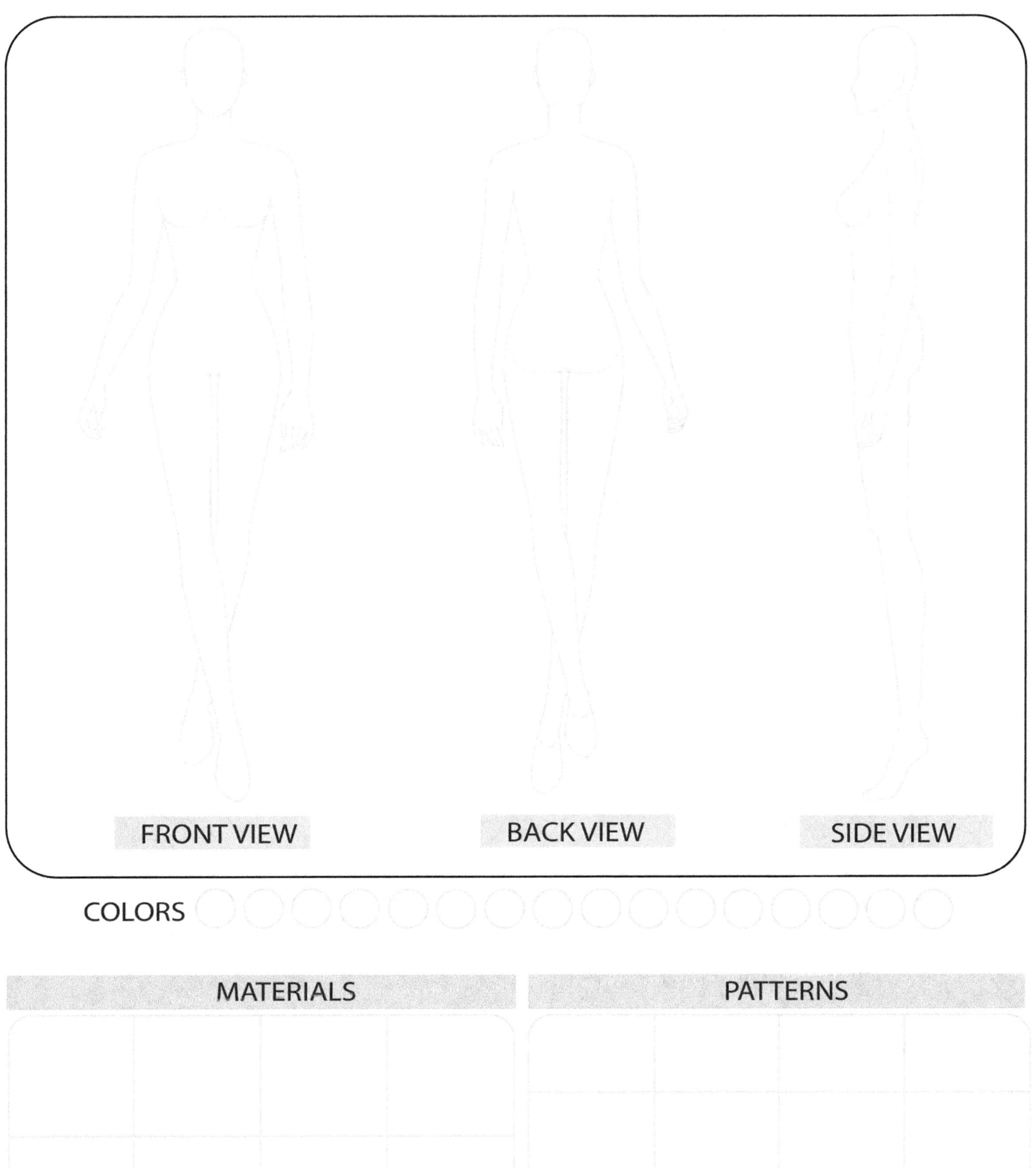

FRONT VIEW
BACK VIEW
SIDE VIEW
COLORS
MATERIALS
PATTERNS
ACCESSORIES

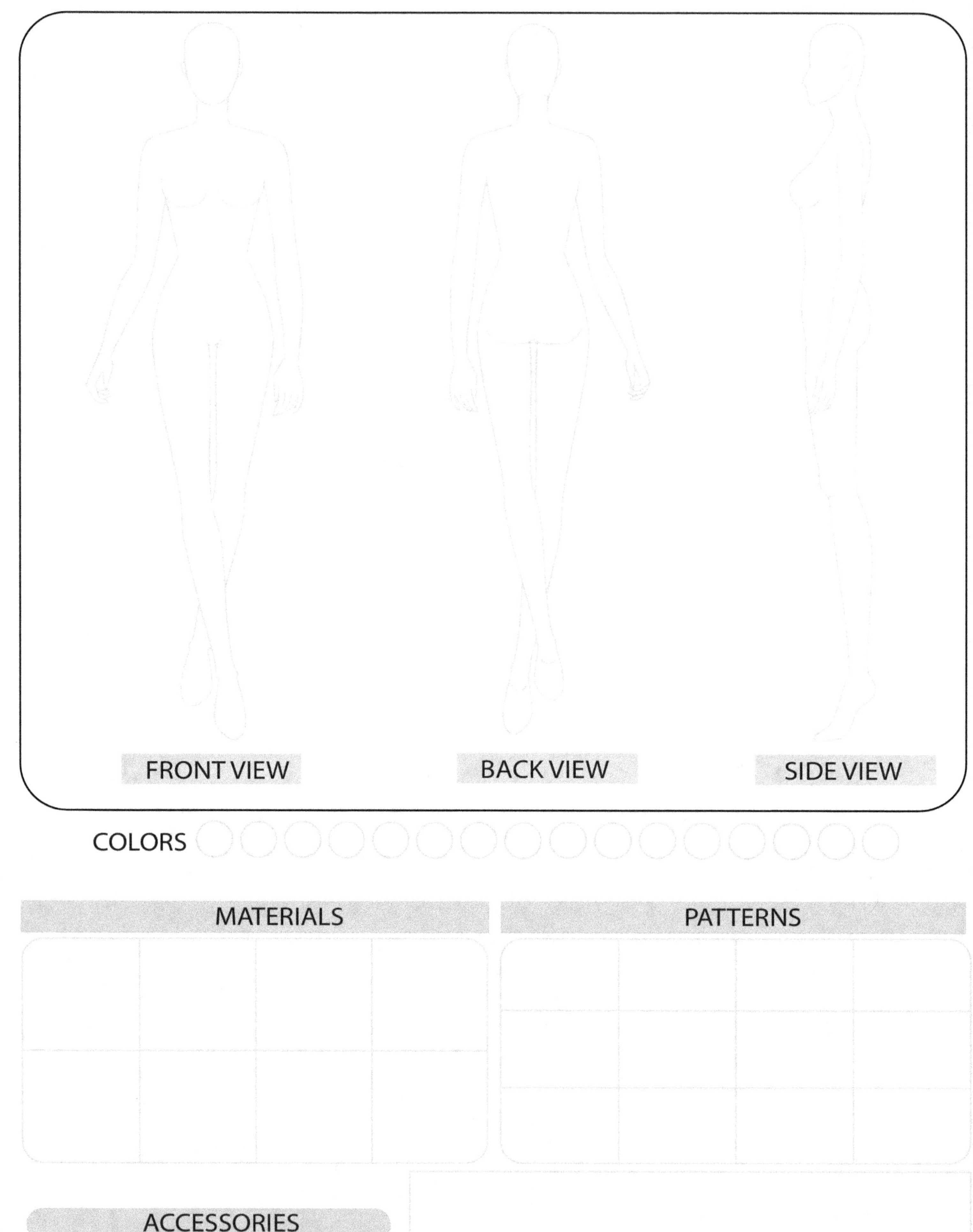

FRONT VIEW
BACK VIEW
SIDE VIEW
COLORS
MATERIALS
PATTERNS
ACCESSORIES

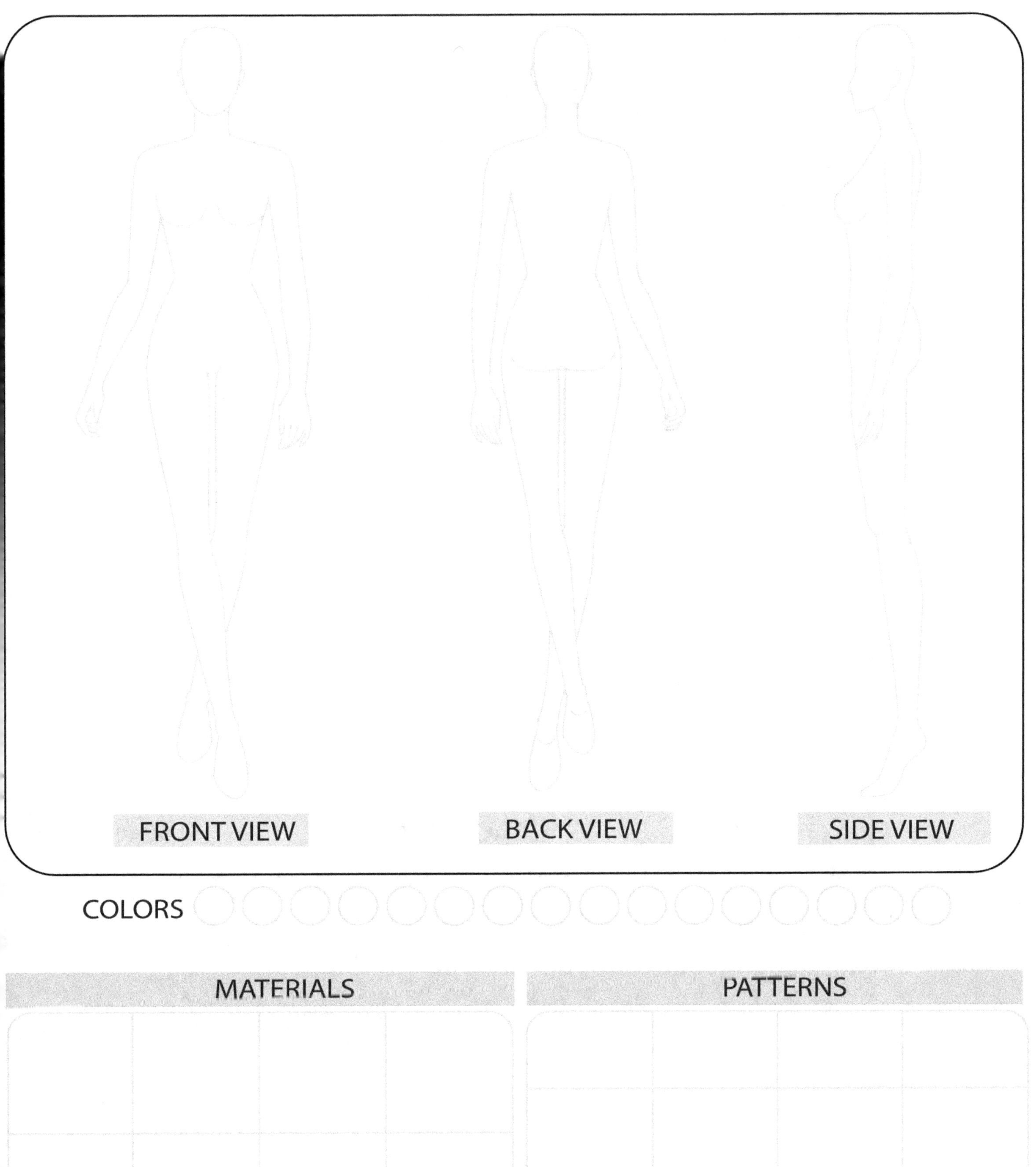

FRONT VIEW

BACK VIEW

SIDE VIEW

COLORS

MATERIALS

PATTERNS

ACCESSORIES

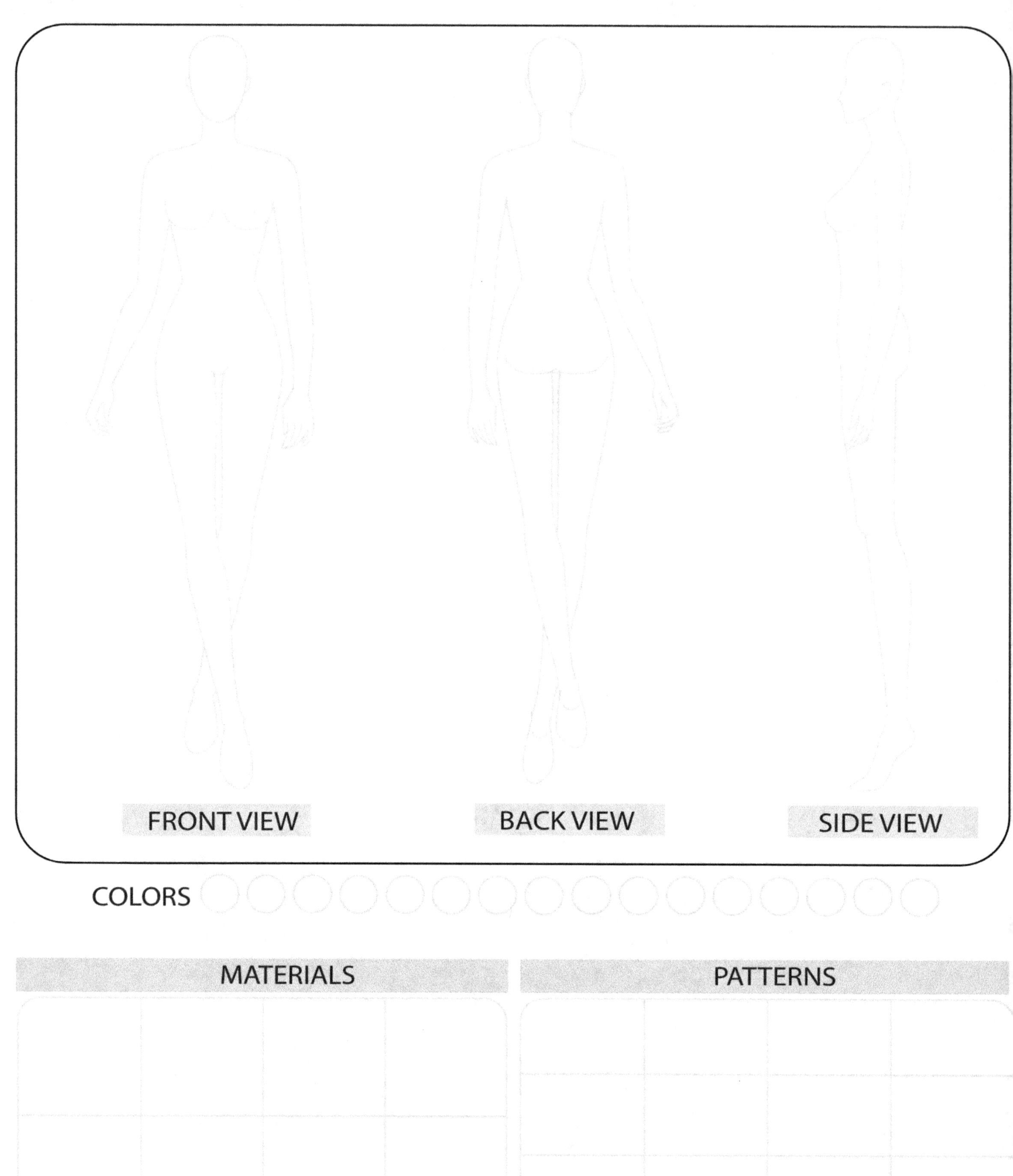

FRONT VIEW

BACK VIEW

SIDE VIEW

COLORS

MATERIALS

PATTERNS

ACCESSORIES

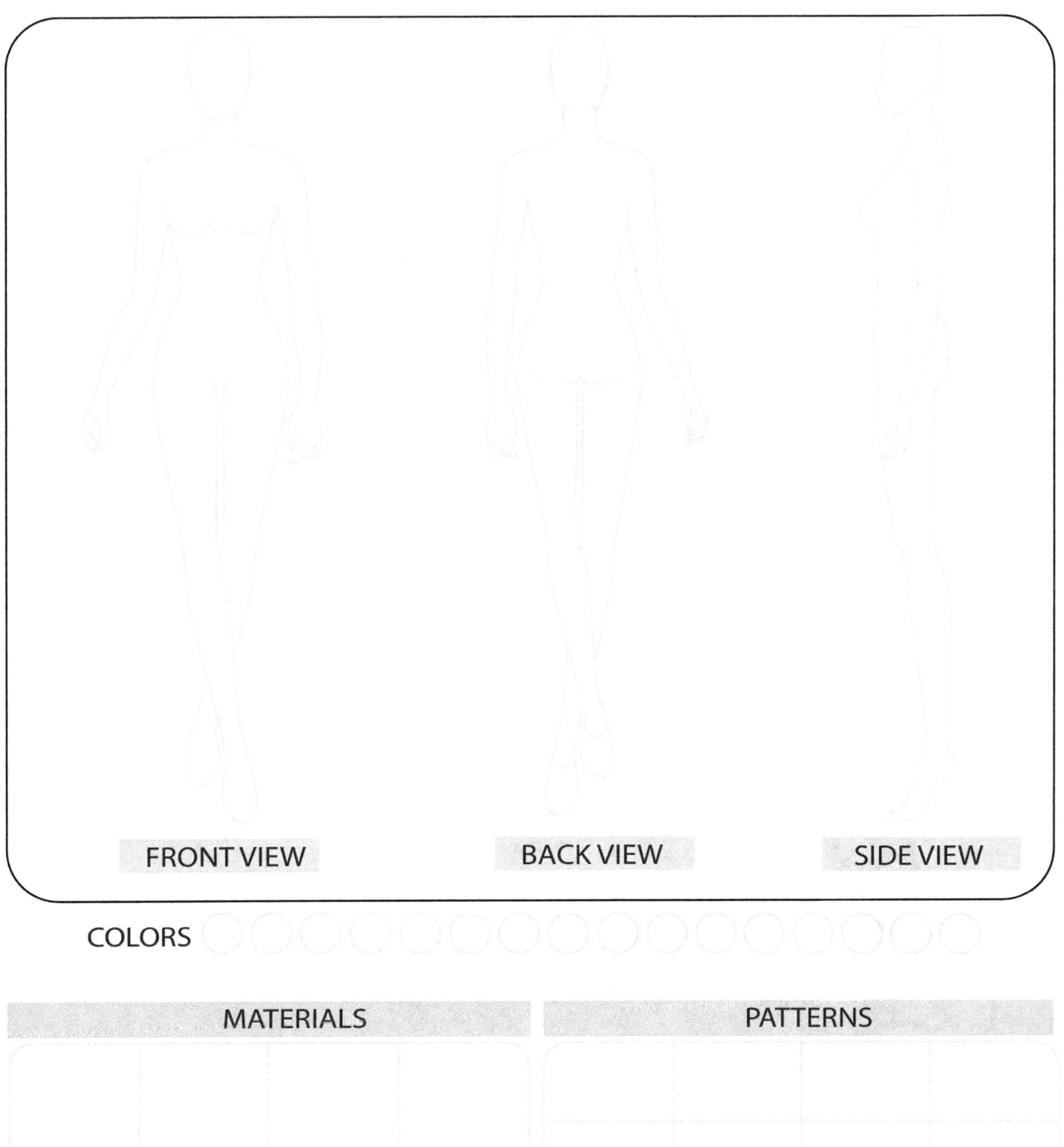

FRONT VIEW

BACK VIEW

SIDE VIEW

COLORS

MATERIALS

PATTERNS

ACCESSORIES

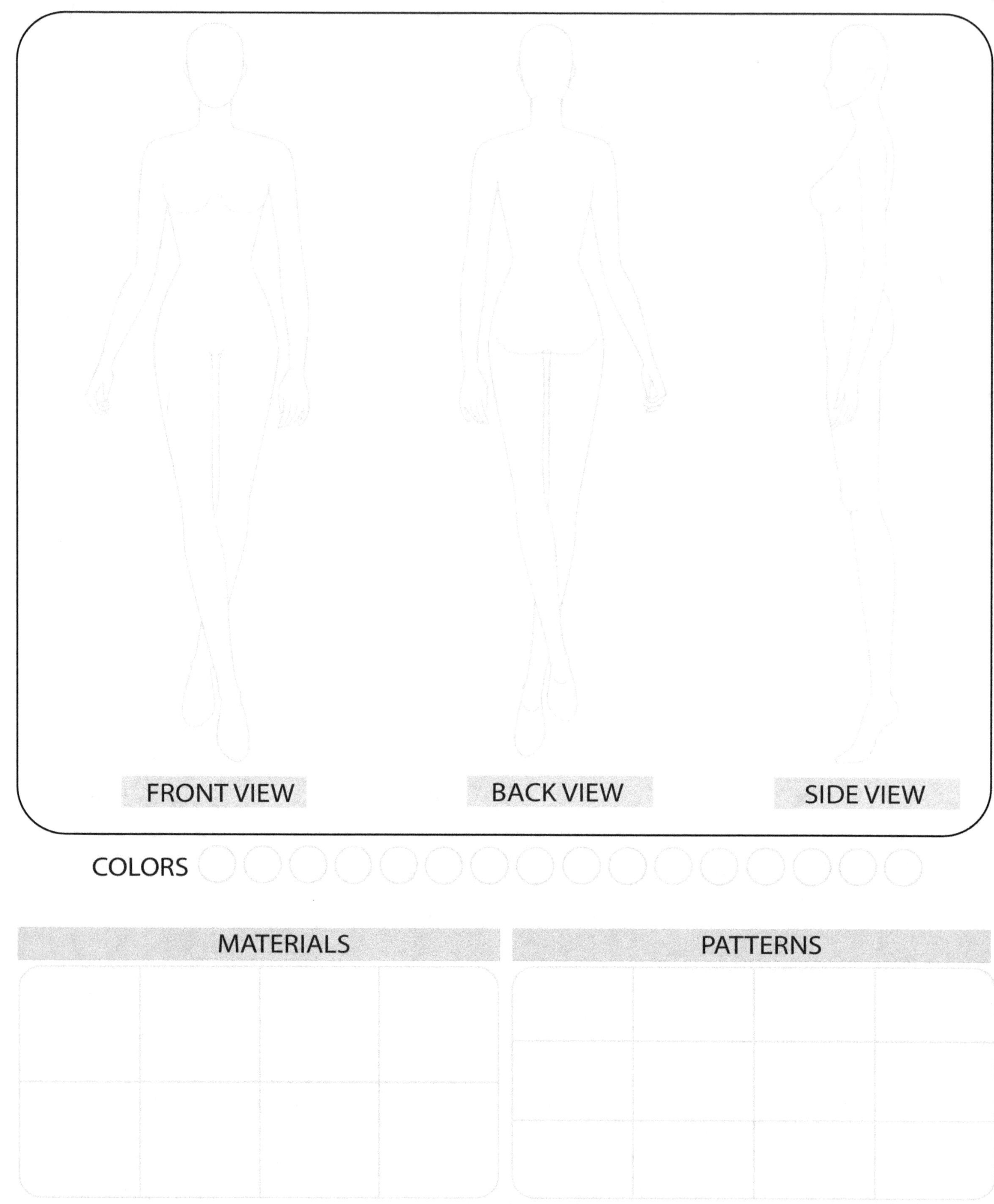

COLORS

MATERIALS

PATTERNS

ACCESSORIES

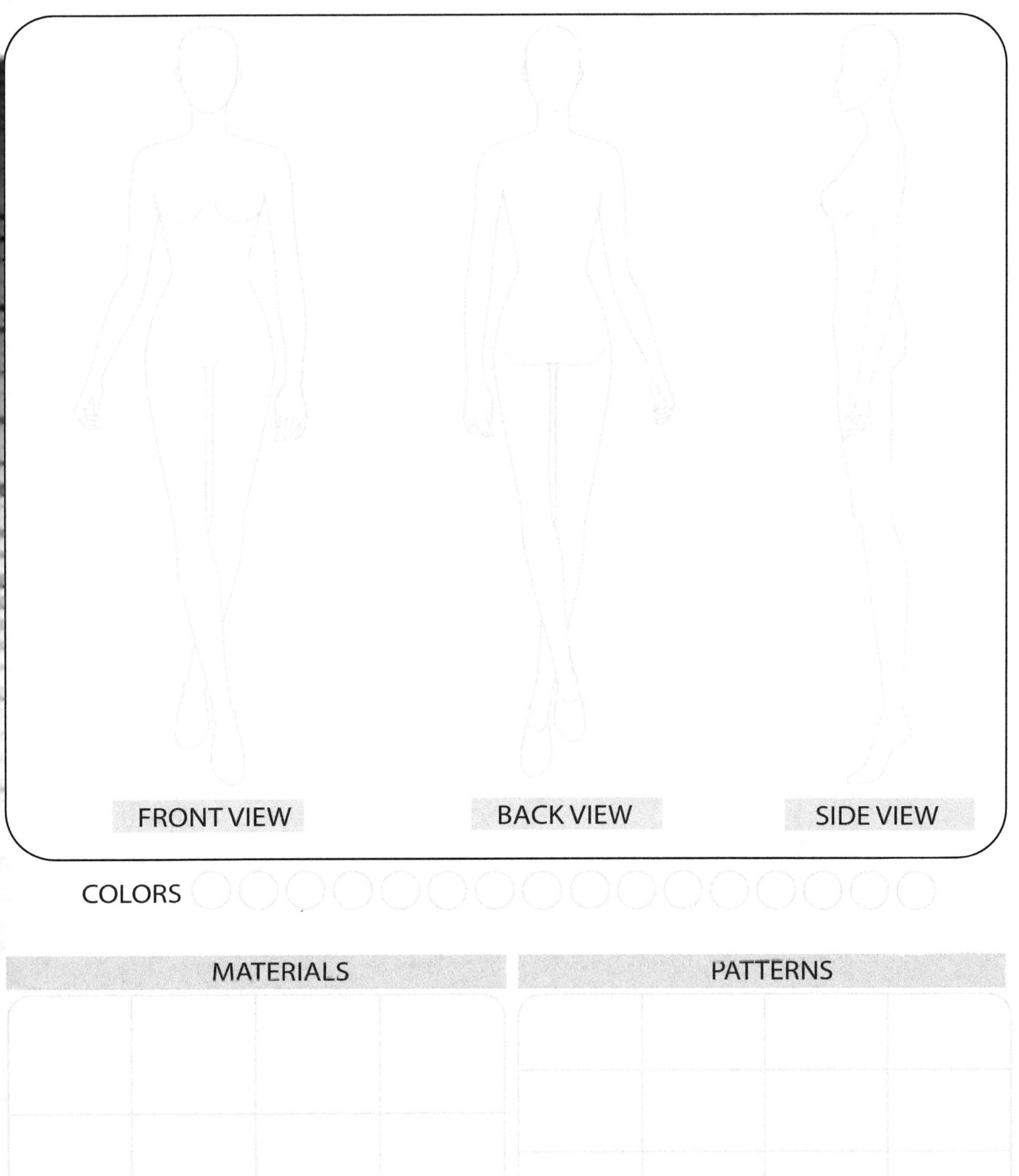

FRONT VIEW
BACK VIEW
SIDE VIEW
COLORS
MATERIALS
PATTERNS
ACCESSORIES

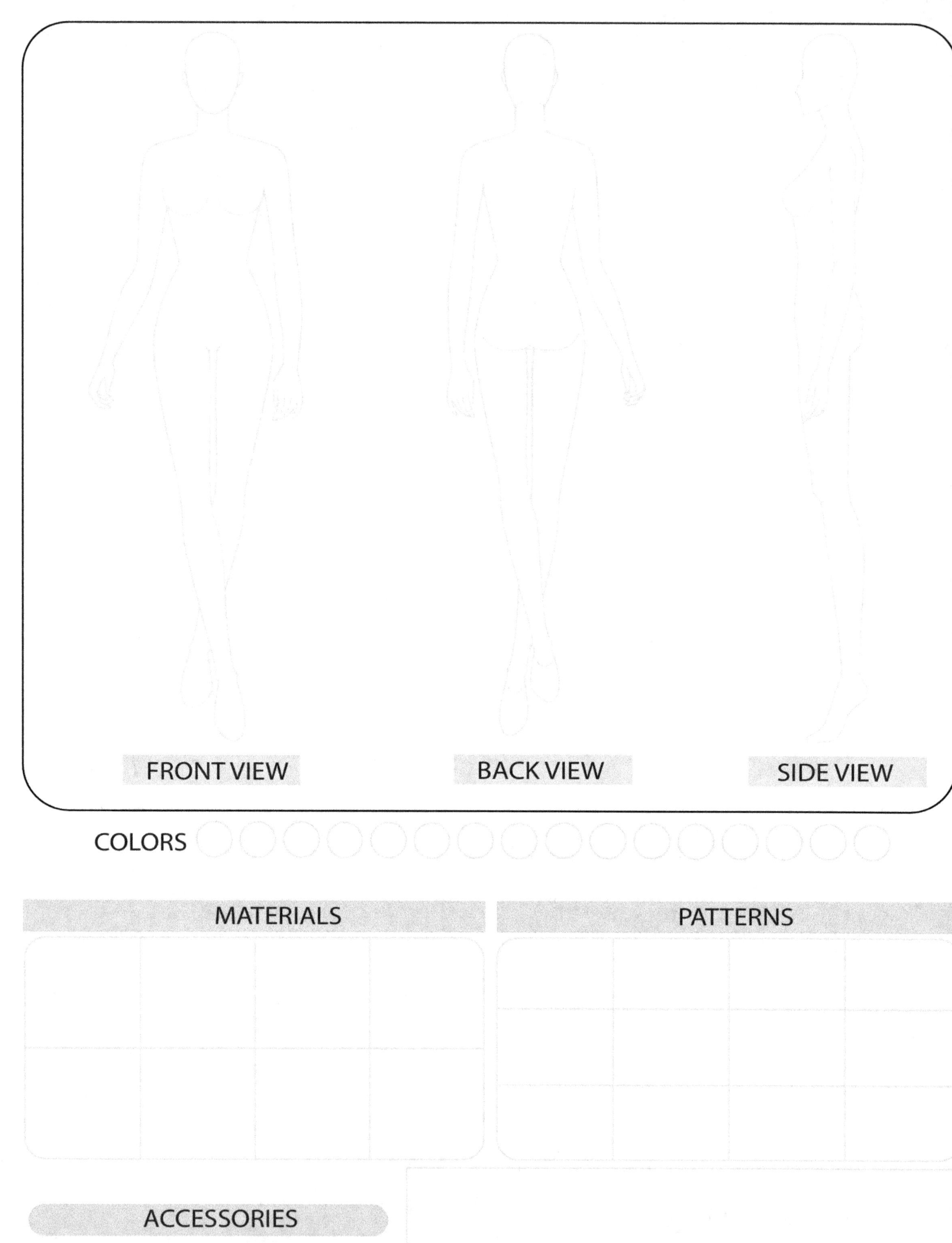

FRONT VIEW
BACK VIEW
SIDE VIEW
COLORS
MATERIALS
PATTERNS
ACCESSORIES

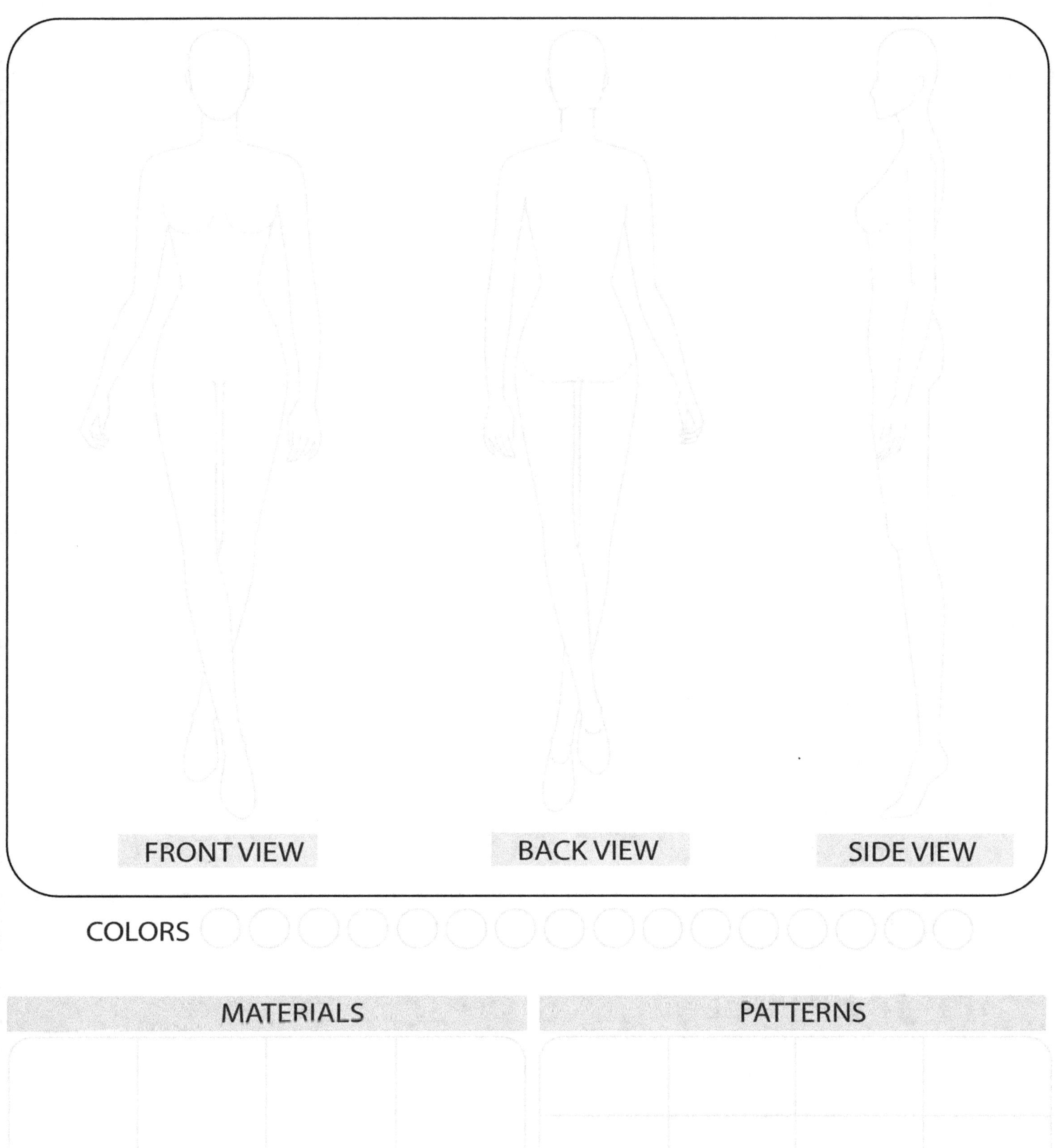

FRONT VIEW
BACK VIEW
SIDE VIEW
COLORS
MATERIALS
PATTERNS
ACCESSORIES

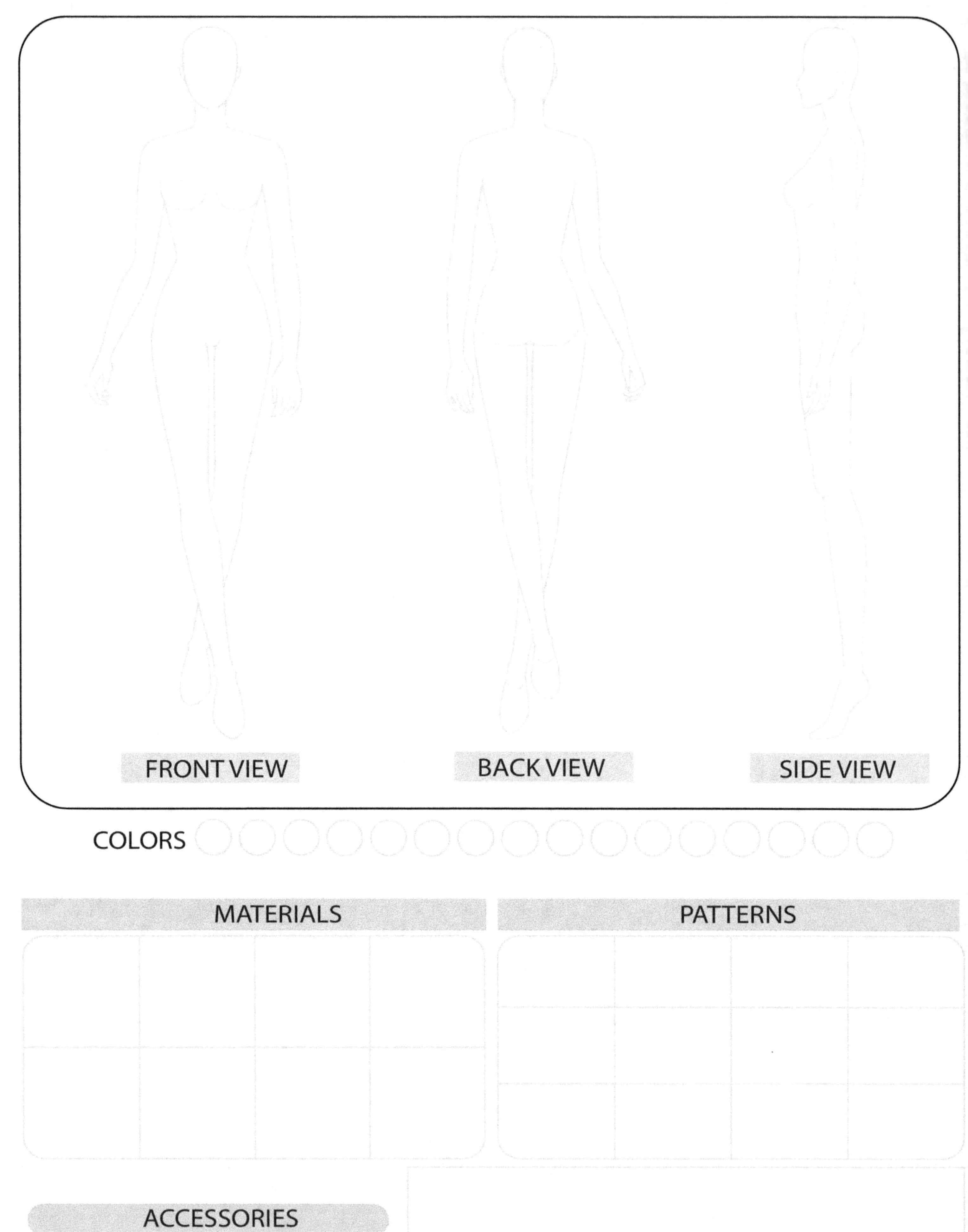

FRONT VIEW
BACK VIEW
SIDE VIEW
COLORS
MATERIALS
PATTERNS
ACCESSORIES

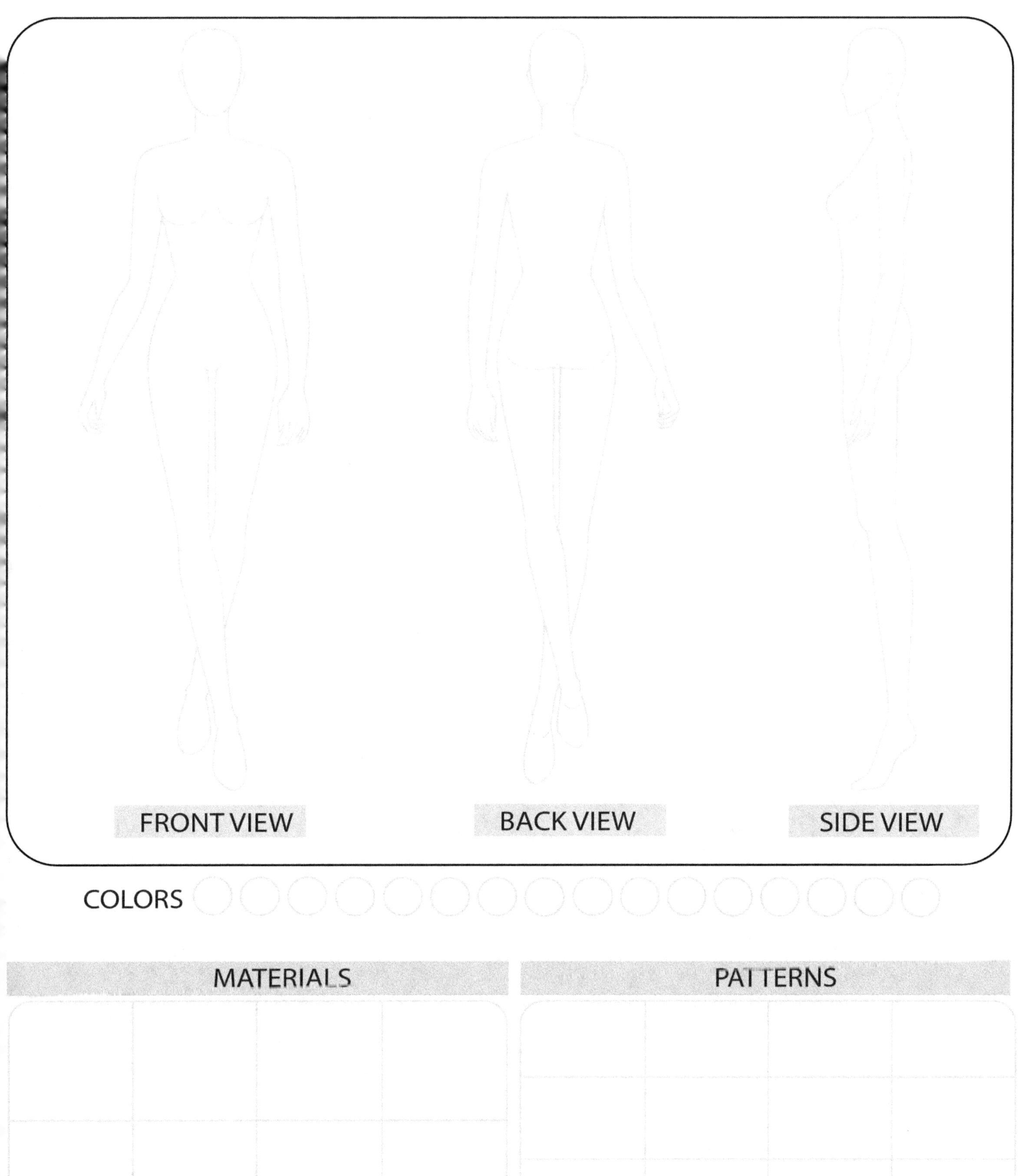

FRONT VIEW

BACK VIEW

SIDE VIEW

COLORS

MATERIALS

PATTERNS

ACCESSORIES

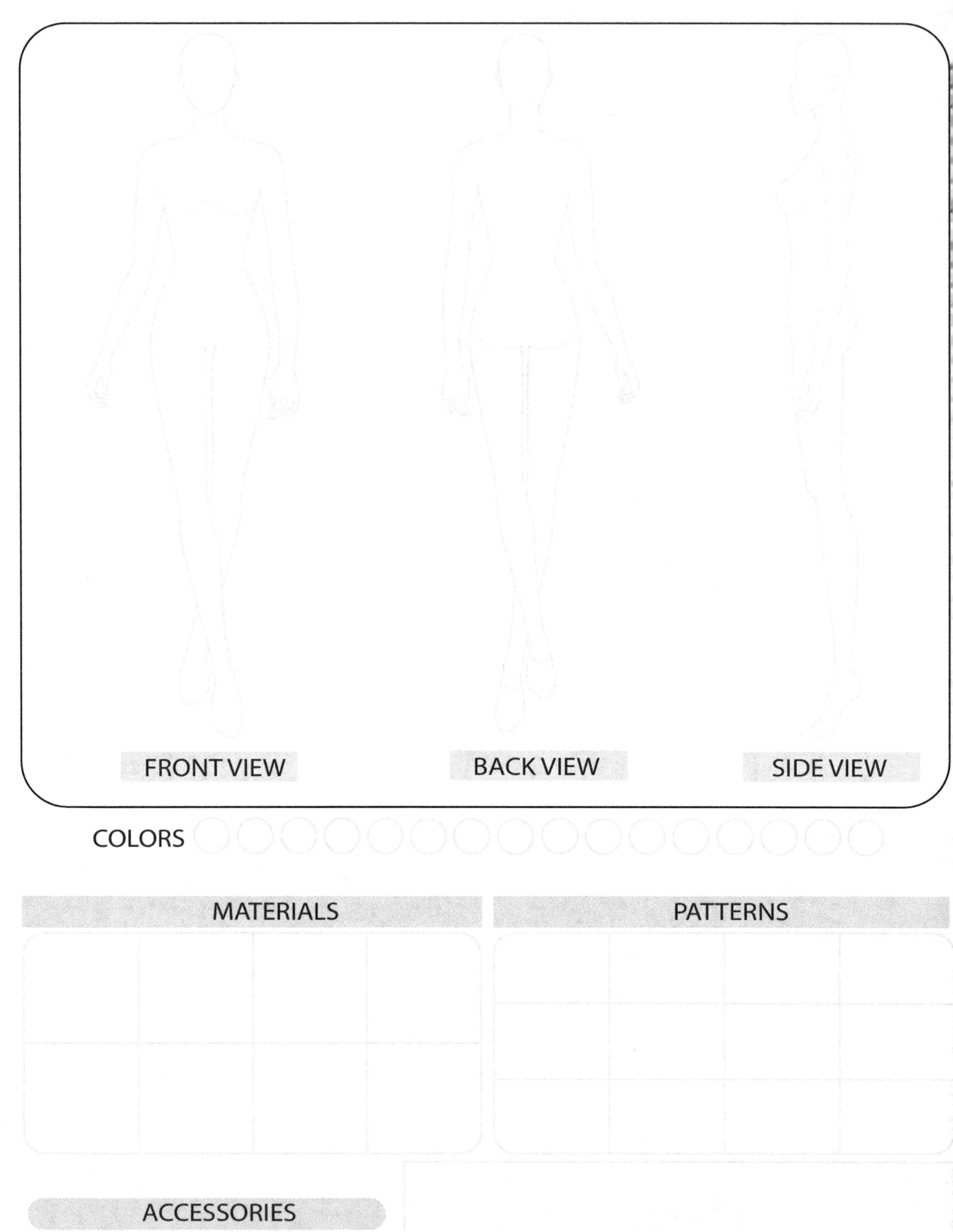

FRONT VIEW
BACK VIEW
SIDE VIEW
COLORS
MATERIALS
PATTERNS
ACCESSORIES

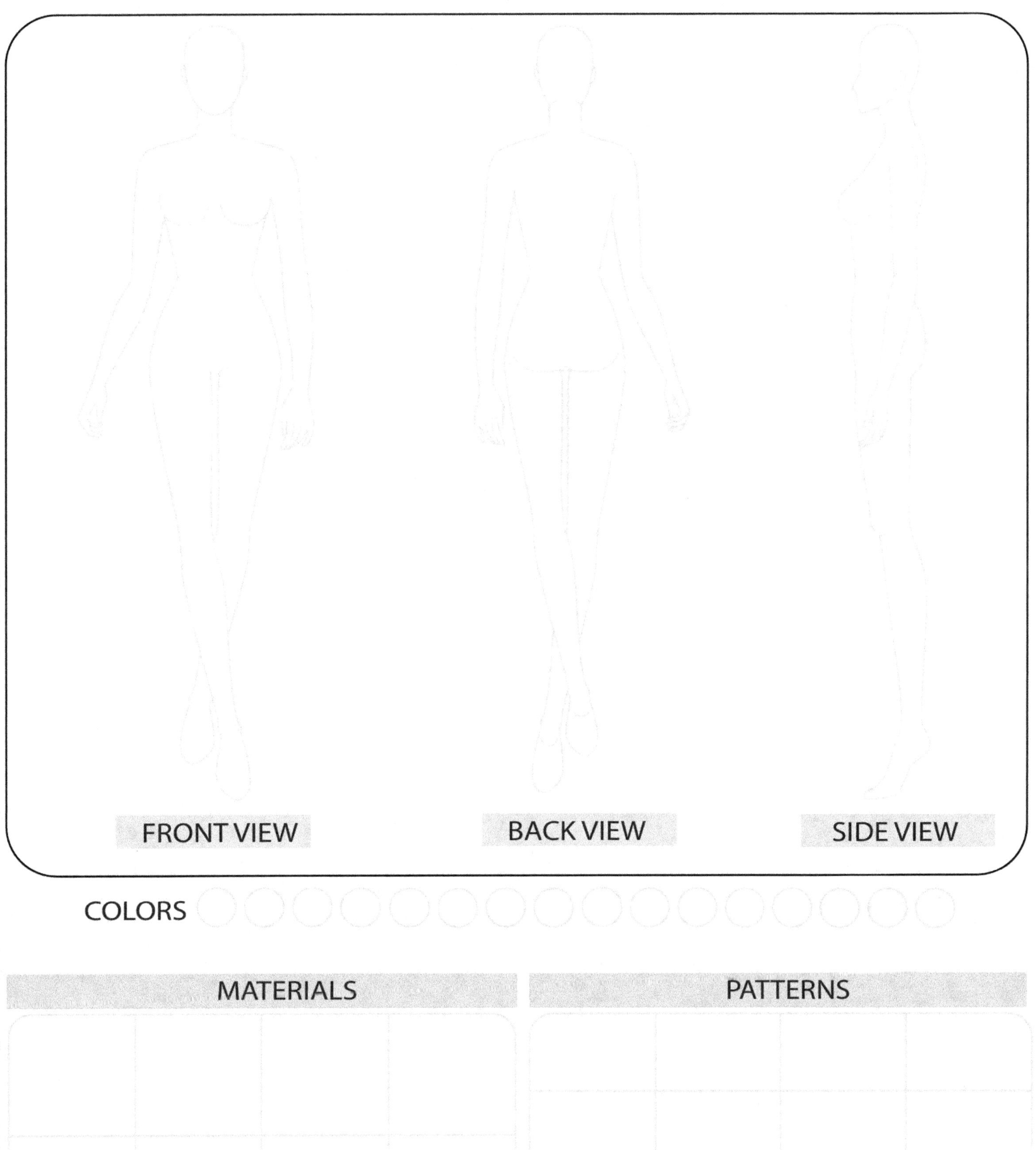

FRONT VIEW
BACK VIEW
SIDE VIEW
COLORS
MATERIALS
PATTERNS
ACCESSORIES

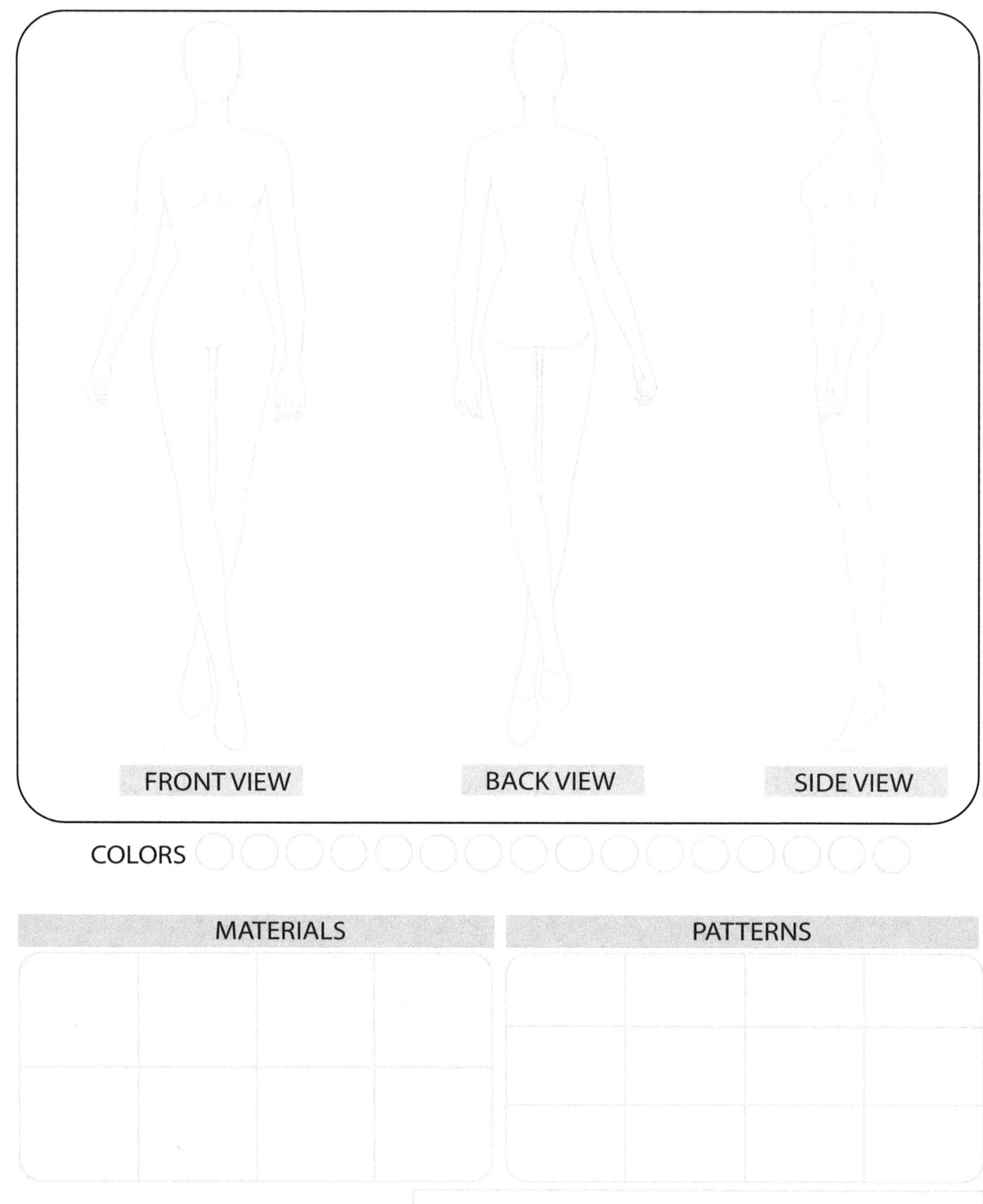

FRONT VIEW
BACK VIEW
SIDE VIEW
COLORS
MATERIALS
PATTERNS
ACCESSORIES

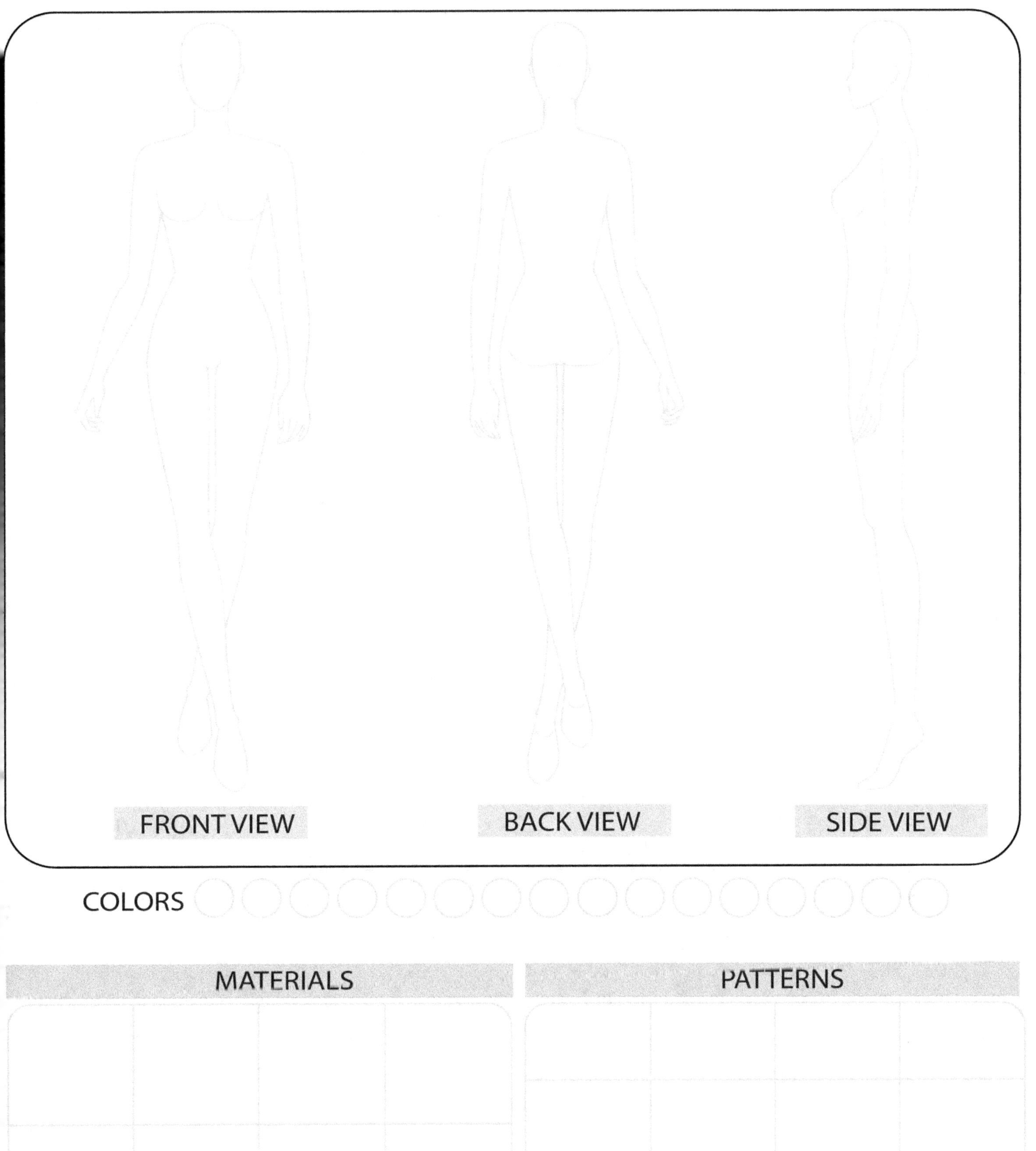

COLORS

MATERIALS

PATTERNS

ACCESSORIES

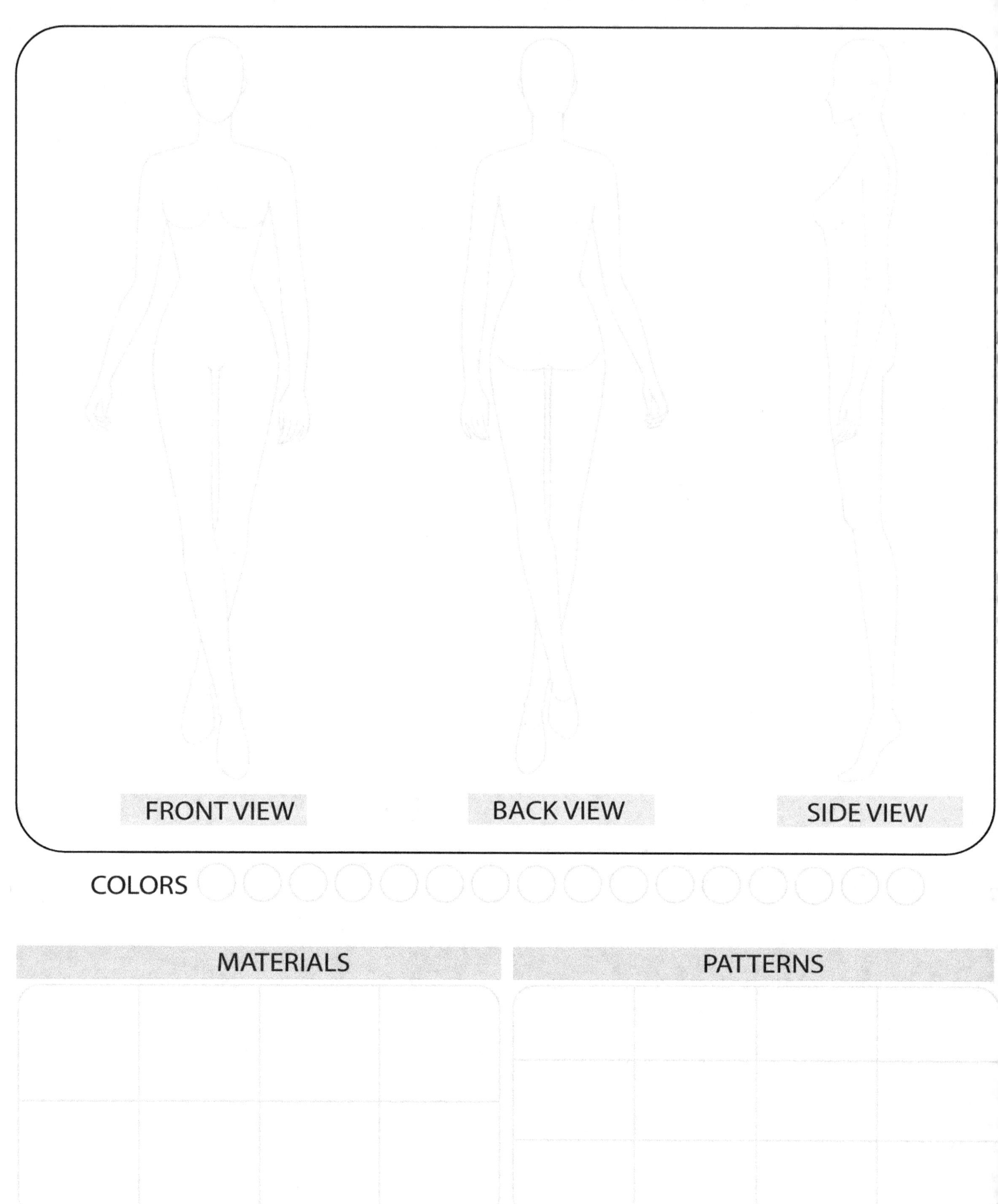

FRONT VIEW
BACK VIEW
SIDE VIEW
COLORS
MATERIALS
PATTERNS
ACCESSORIES

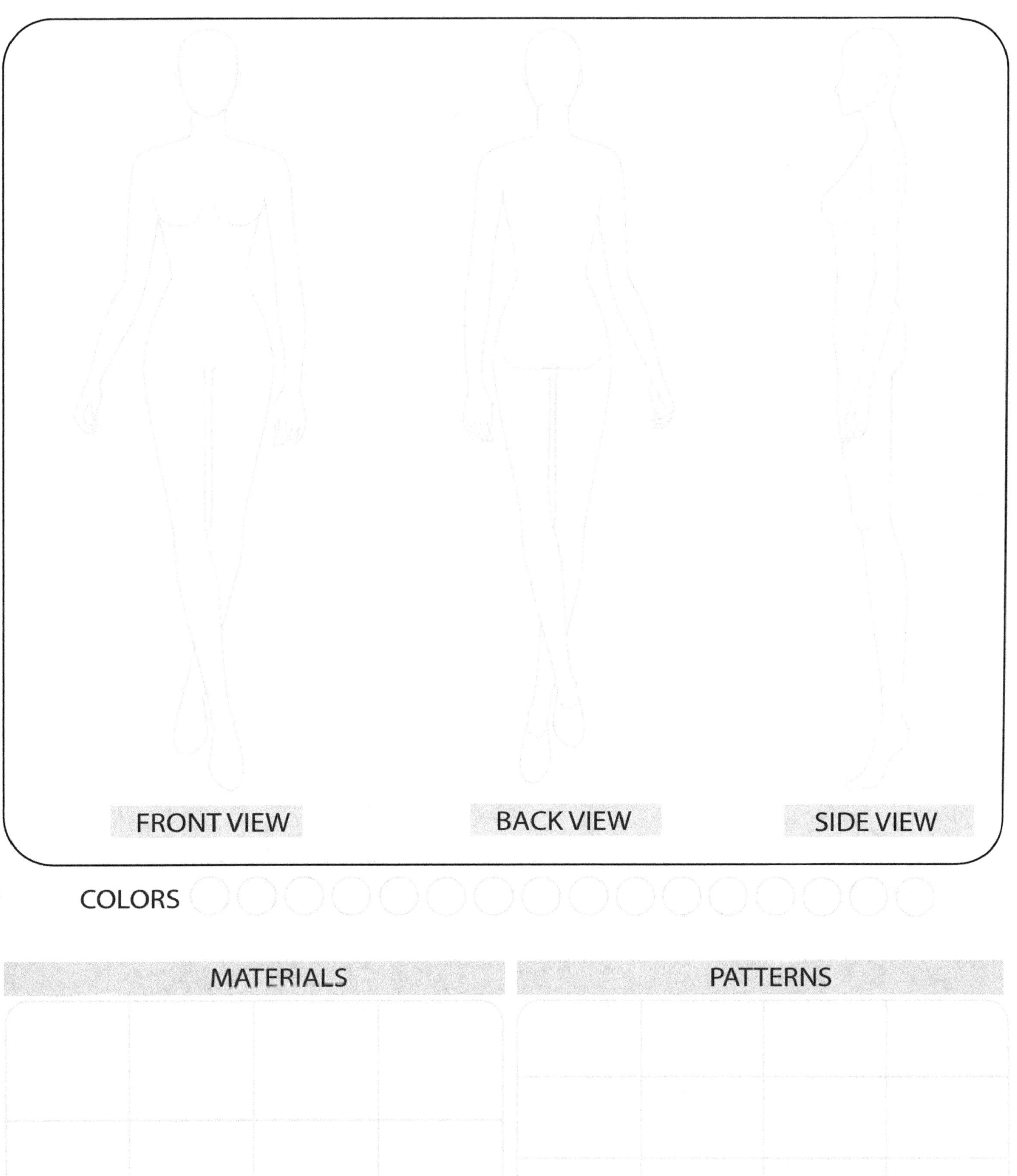

FRONT VIEW
BACK VIEW
SIDE VIEW
COLORS
MATERIALS
PATTERNS
ACCESSORIES

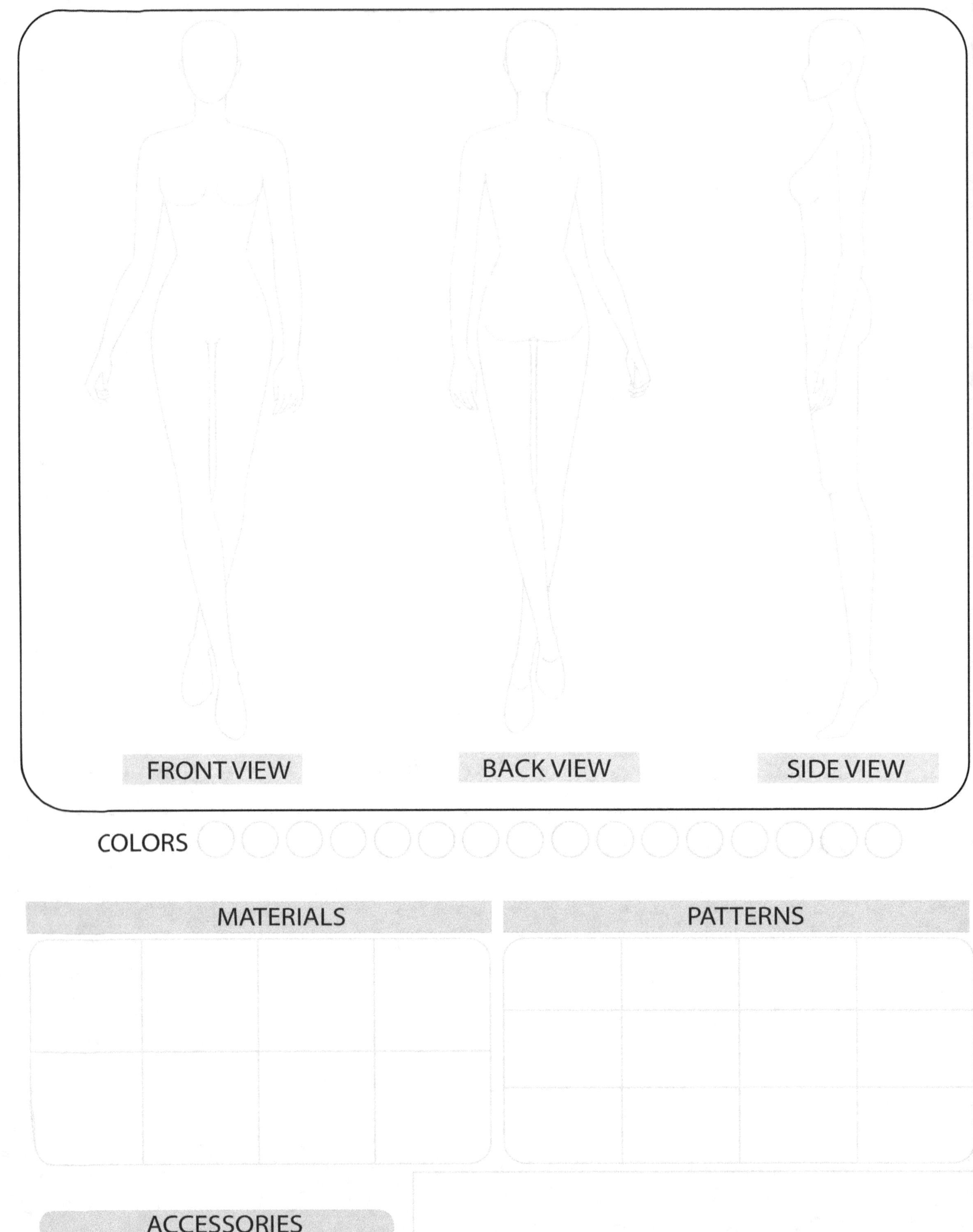

FRONT VIEW
BACK VIEW
SIDE VIEW
COLORS
MATERIALS
PATTERNS
ACCESSORIES

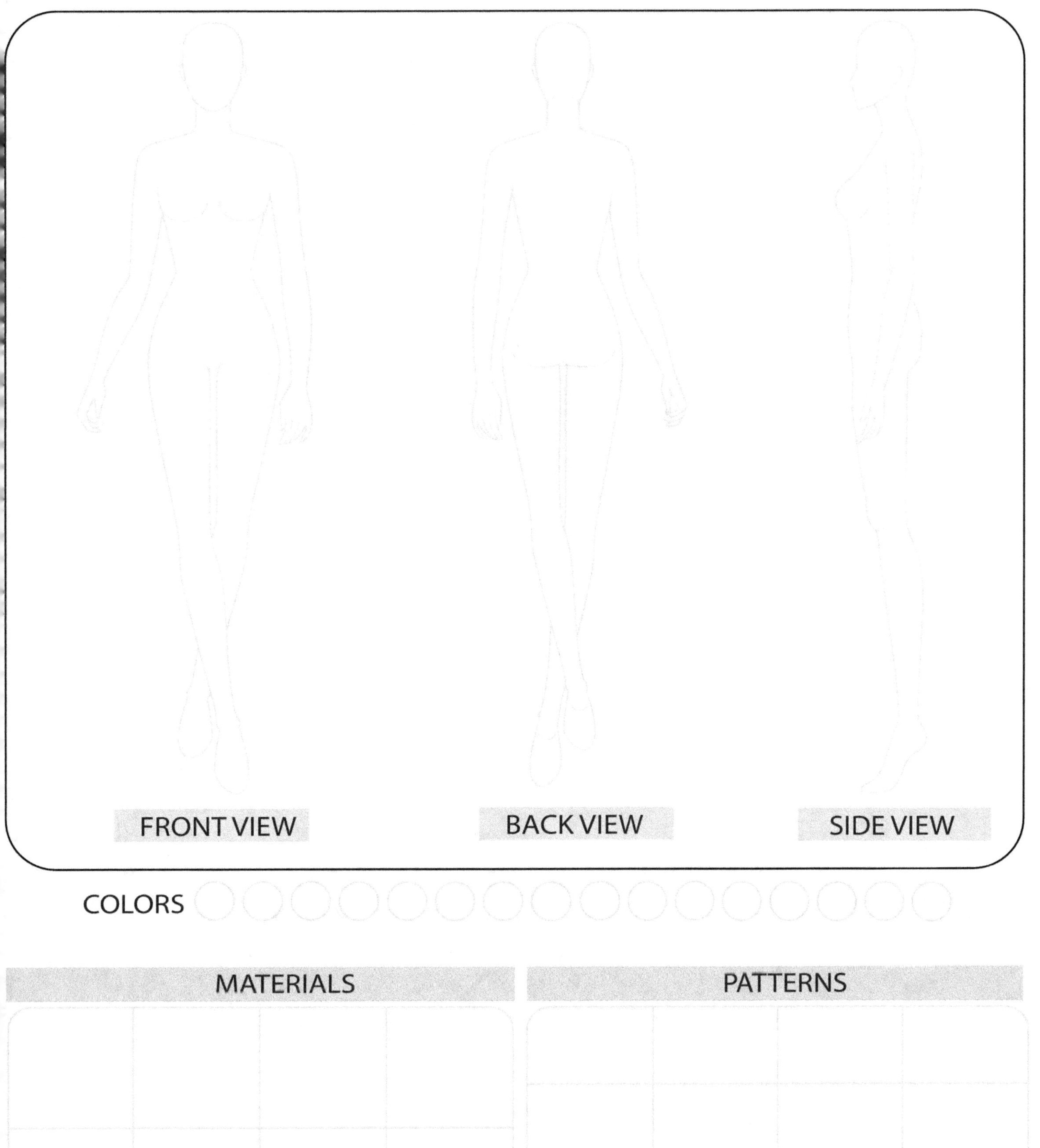

FRONT VIEW
BACK VIEW
SIDE VIEW
COLORS
MATERIALS
PATTERNS
ACCESSORIES

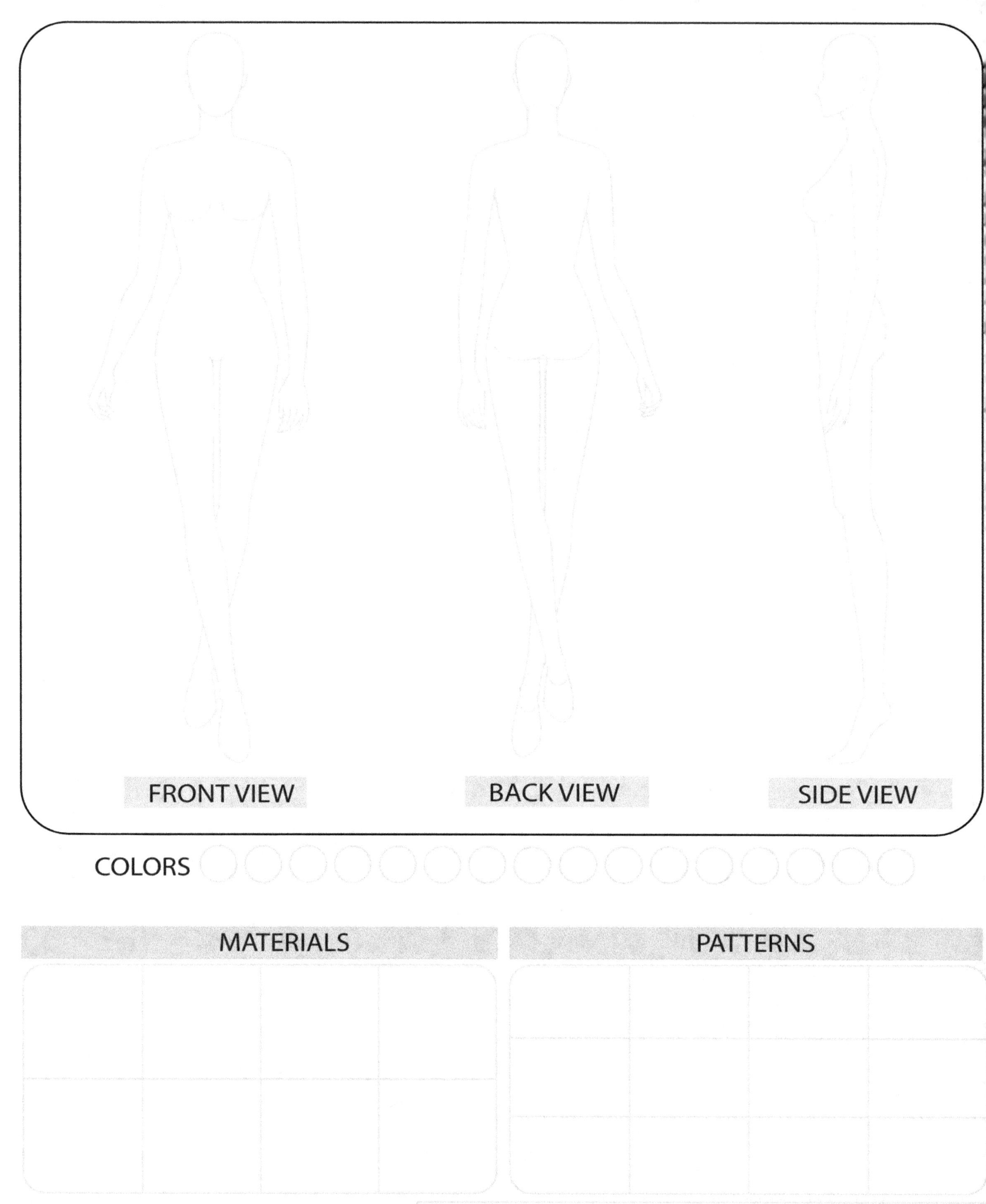

COLORS

MATERIALS

PATTERNS

ACCESSORIES

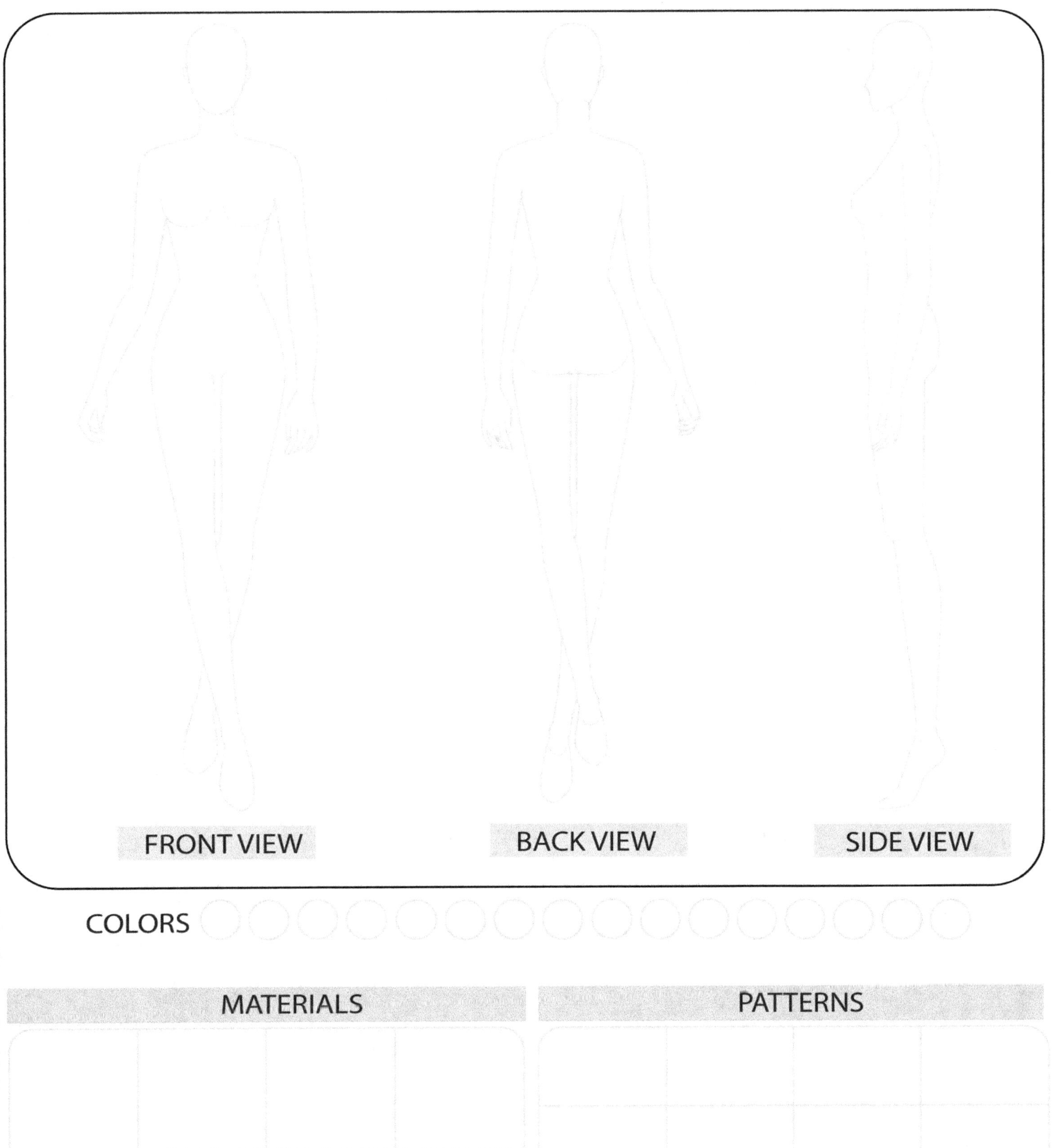

FRONT VIEW
BACK VIEW
SIDE VIEW
COLORS
MATERIALS
PATTERNS
ACCESSORIES

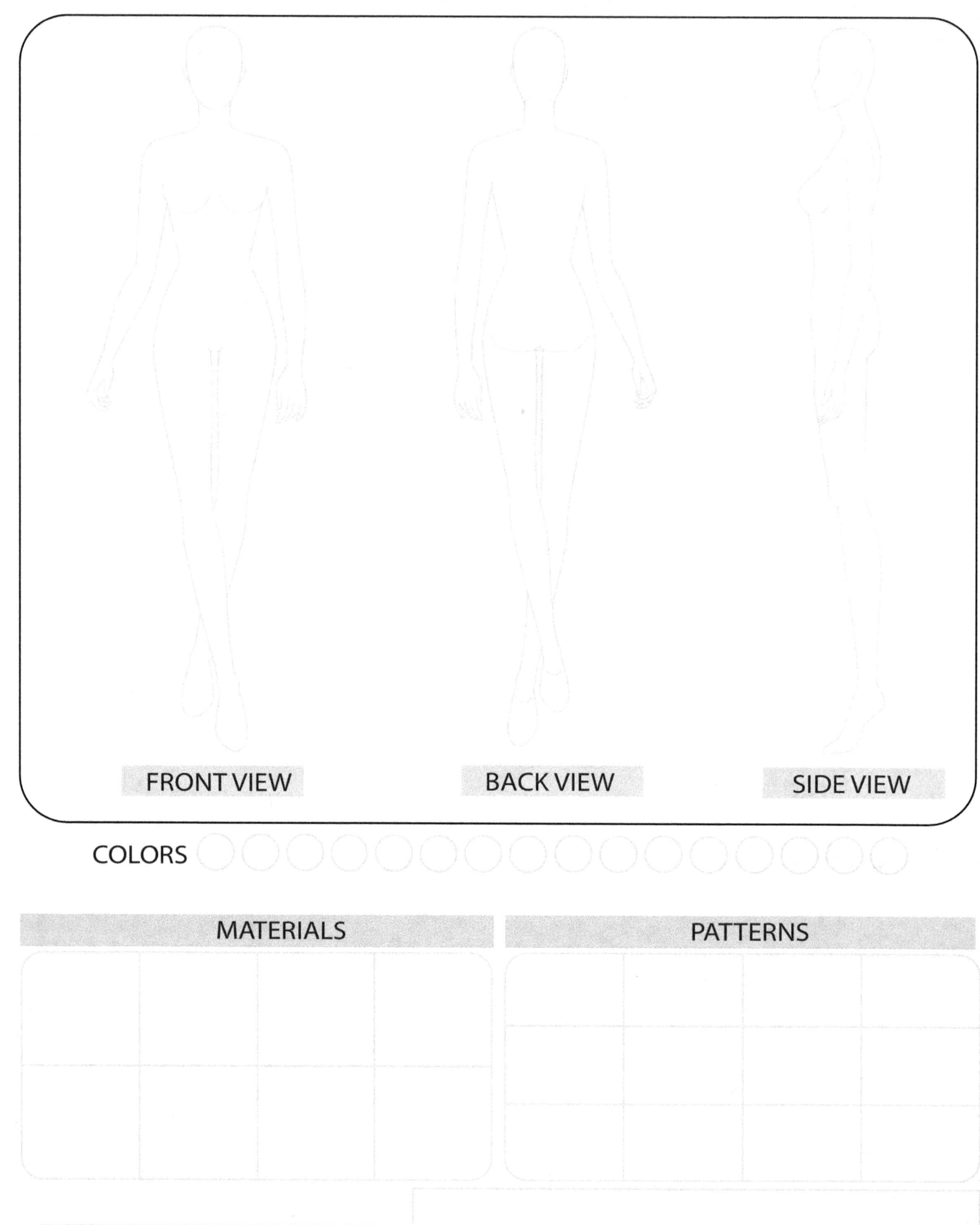

FRONT VIEW
BACK VIEW
SIDE VIEW
COLORS
MATERIALS
PATTERNS
ACCESSORIES

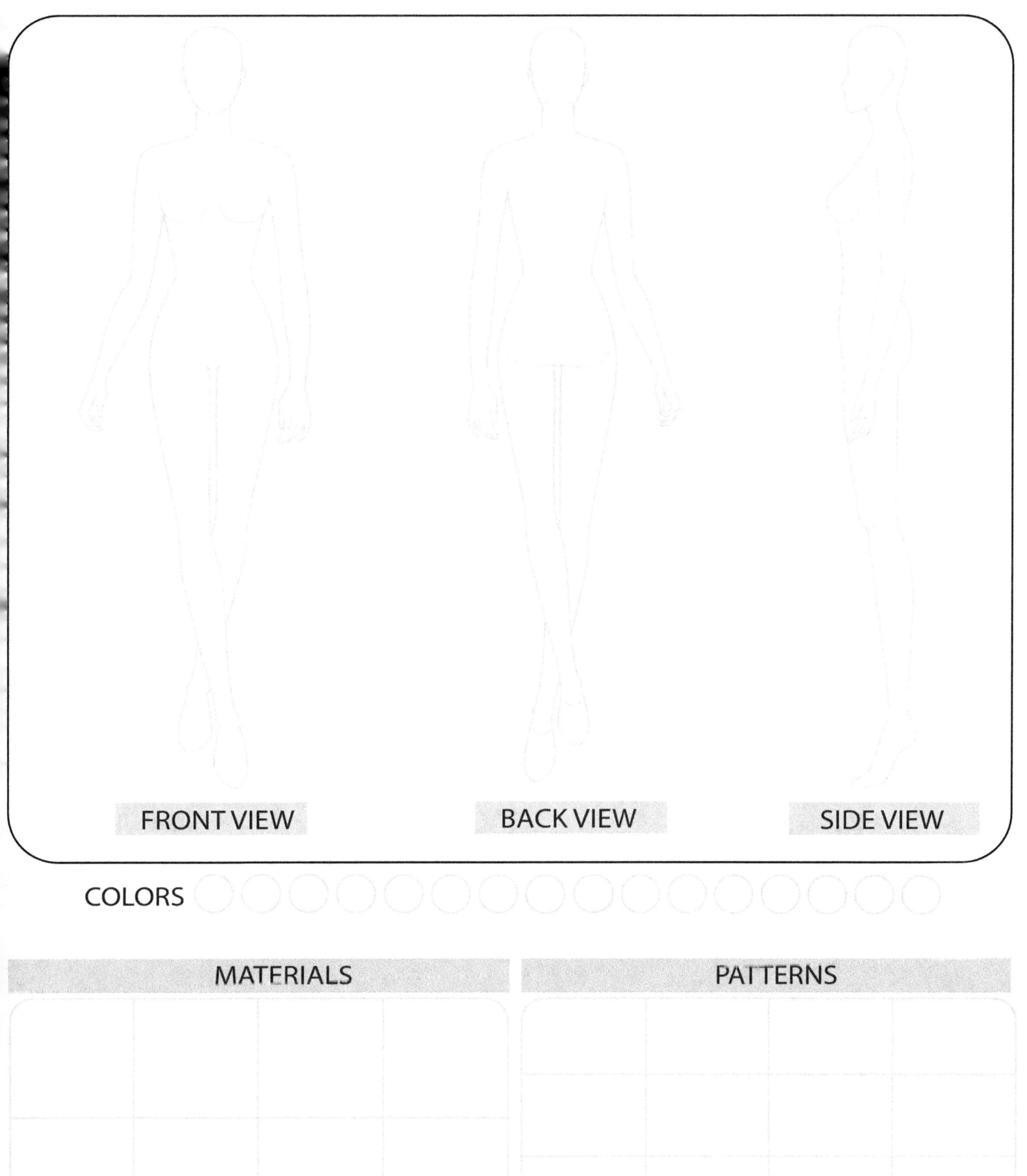

FRONT VIEW
BACK VIEW
SIDE VIEW
COLORS
MATERIALS
PATTERNS
ACCESSORIES

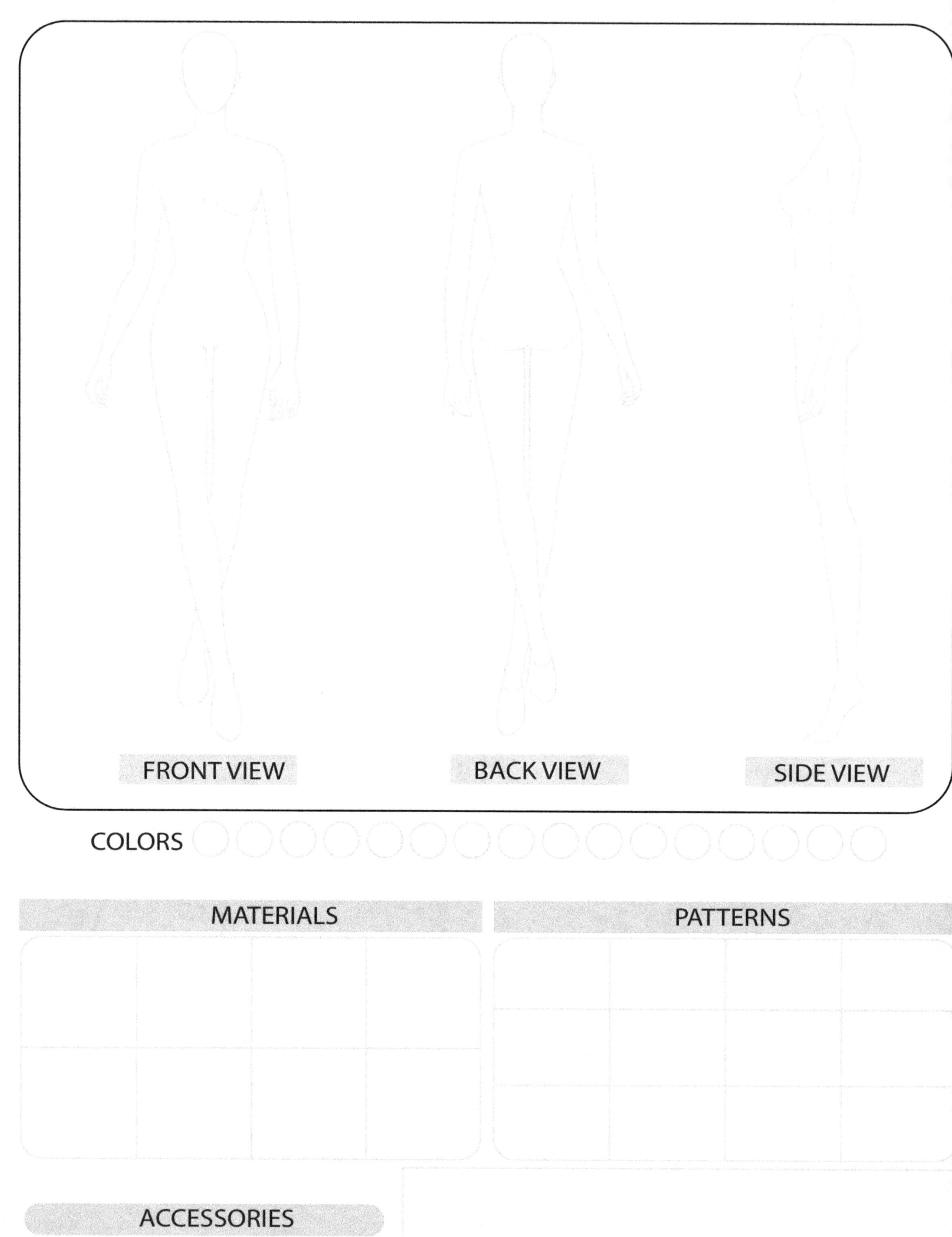

FRONT VIEW

BACK VIEW

SIDE VIEW

COLORS

MATERIALS

PATTERNS

ACCESSORIES

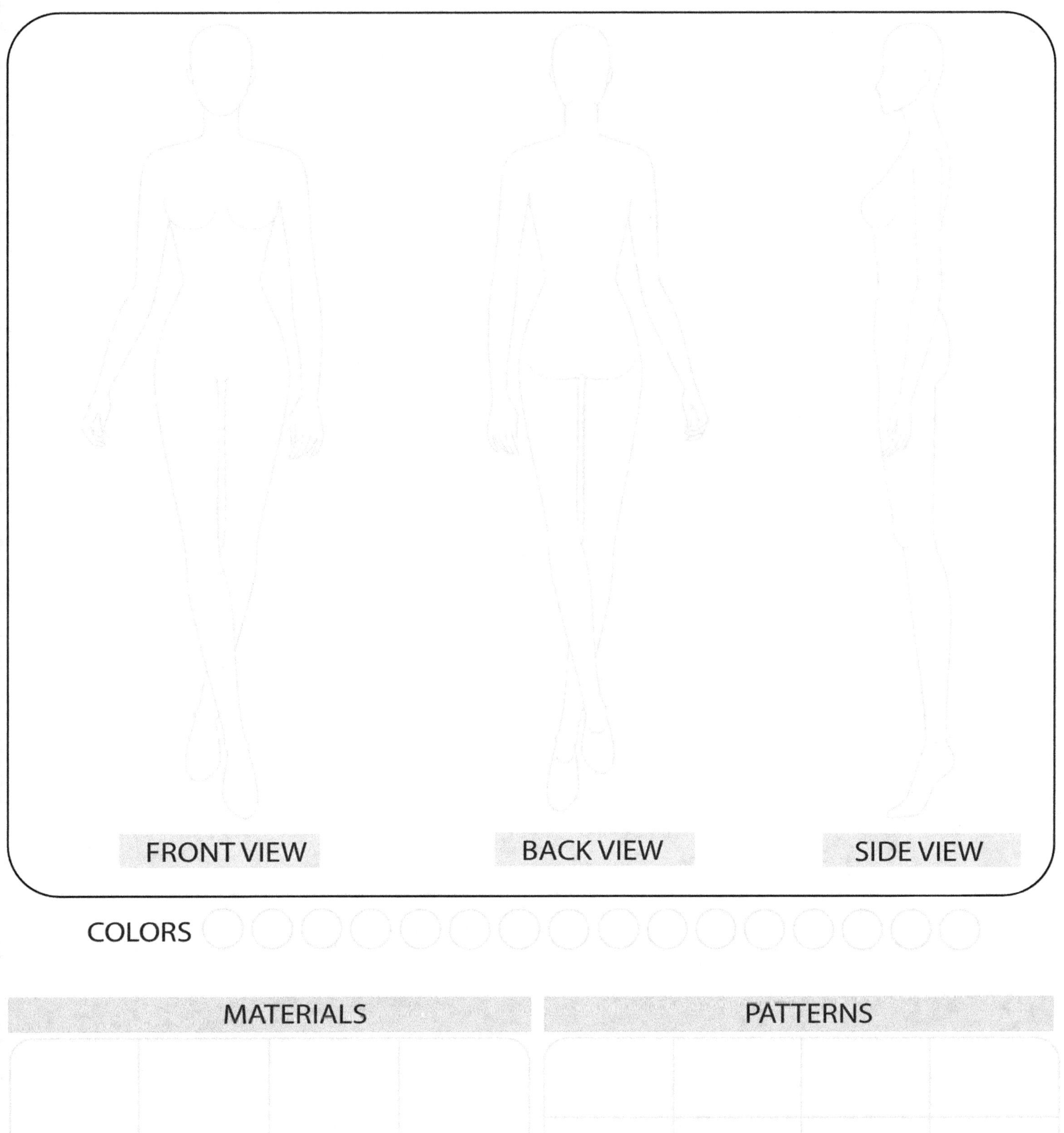

FRONT VIEW
BACK VIEW
SIDE VIEW
COLORS
MATERIALS
PATTERNS
ACCESSORIES

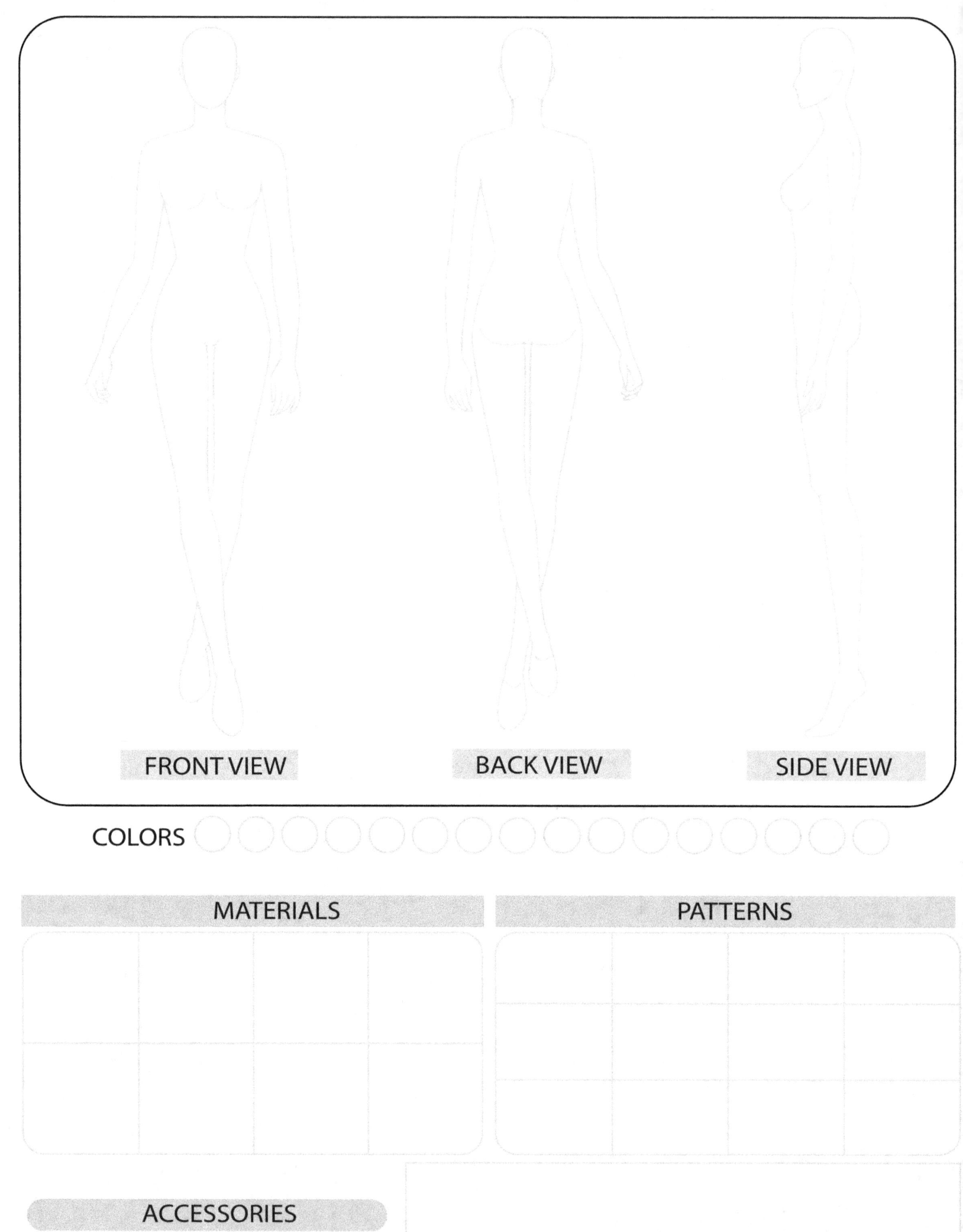

FRONT VIEW
BACK VIEW
SIDE VIEW
COLORS
MATERIALS
PATTERNS
ACCESSORIES

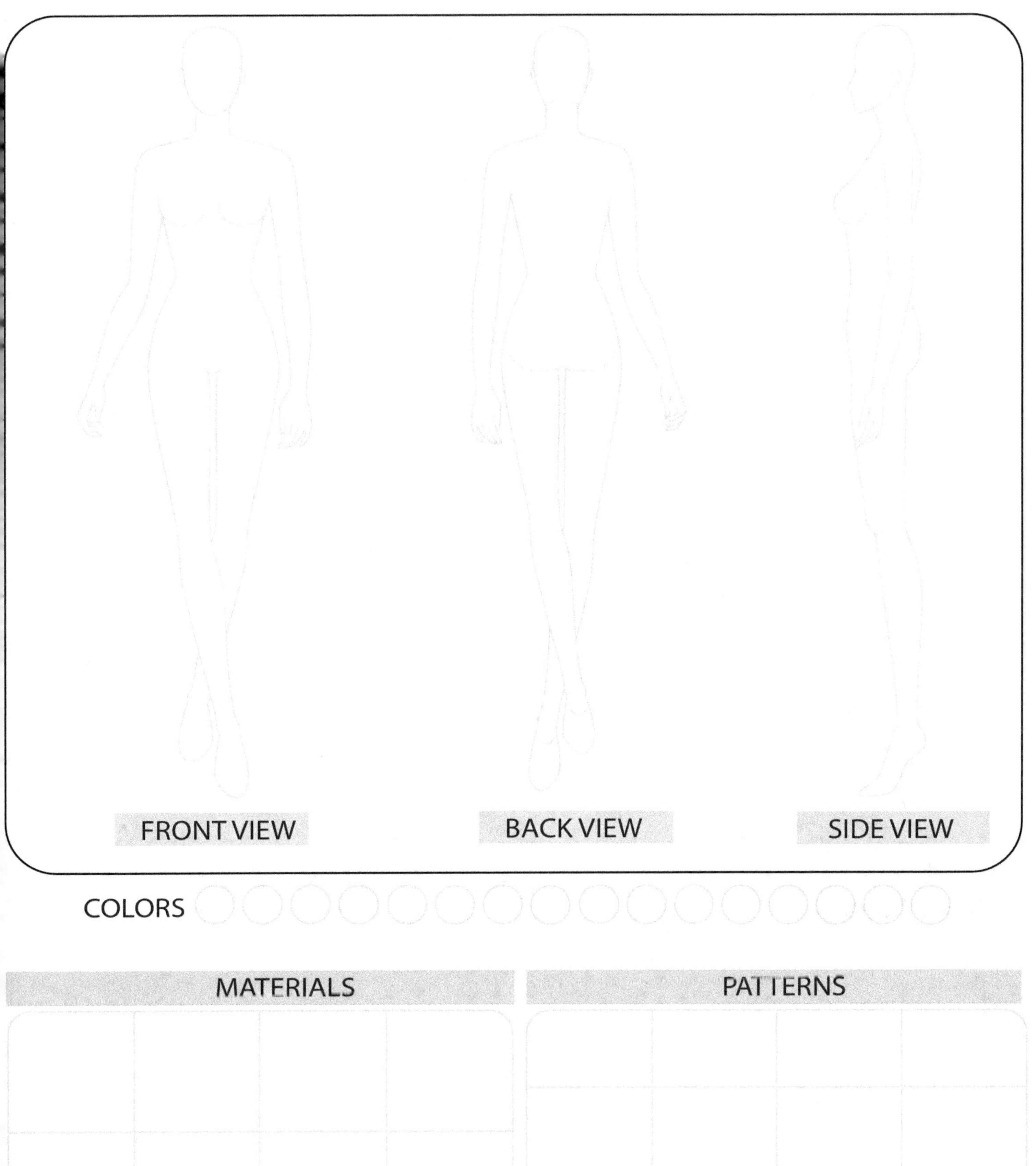

FRONT VIEW
BACK VIEW
SIDE VIEW
COLORS
MATERIALS
PATTERNS
ACCESSORIES

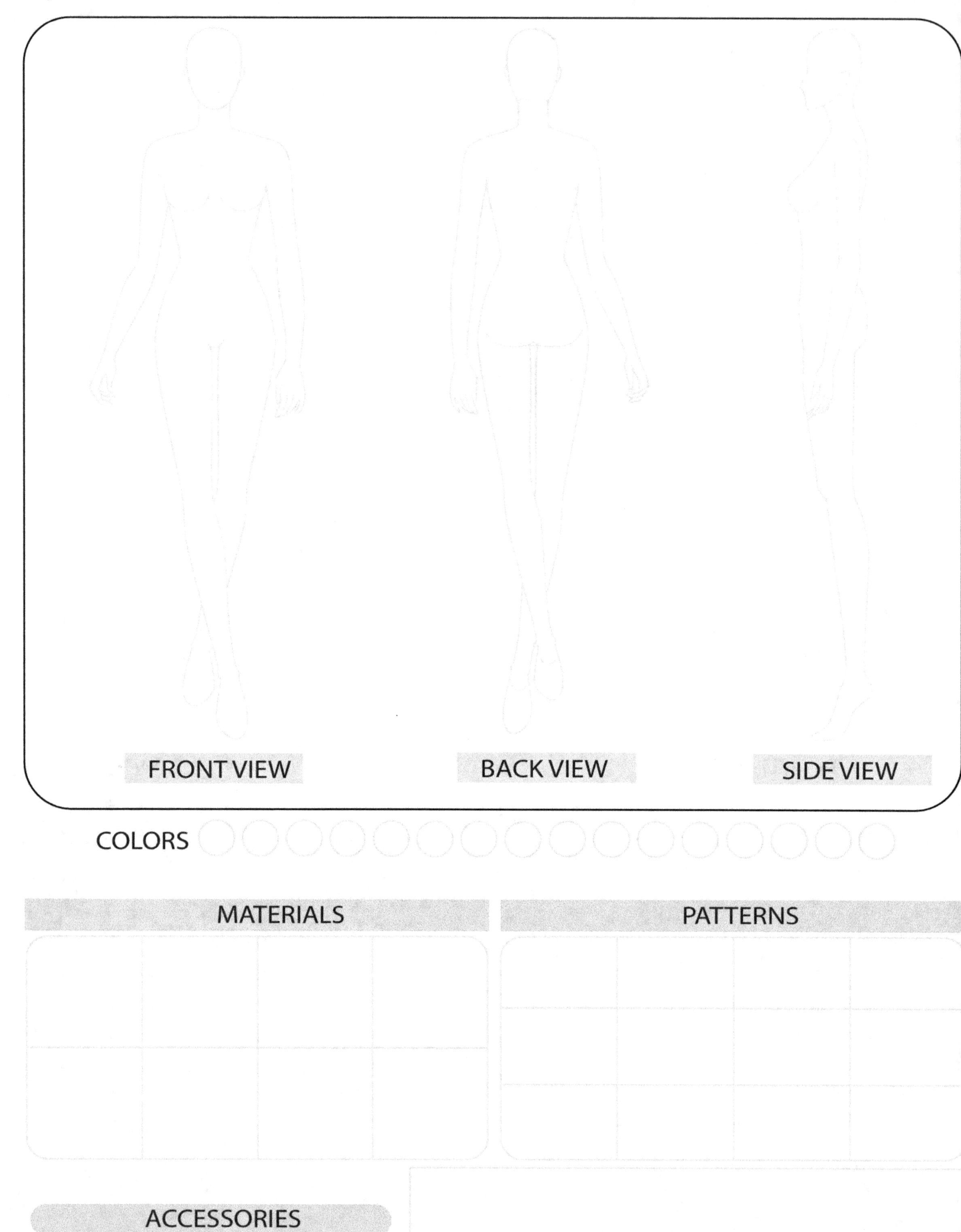

FRONT VIEW
BACK VIEW
SIDE VIEW
COLORS
MATERIALS
PATTERNS
ACCESSORIES

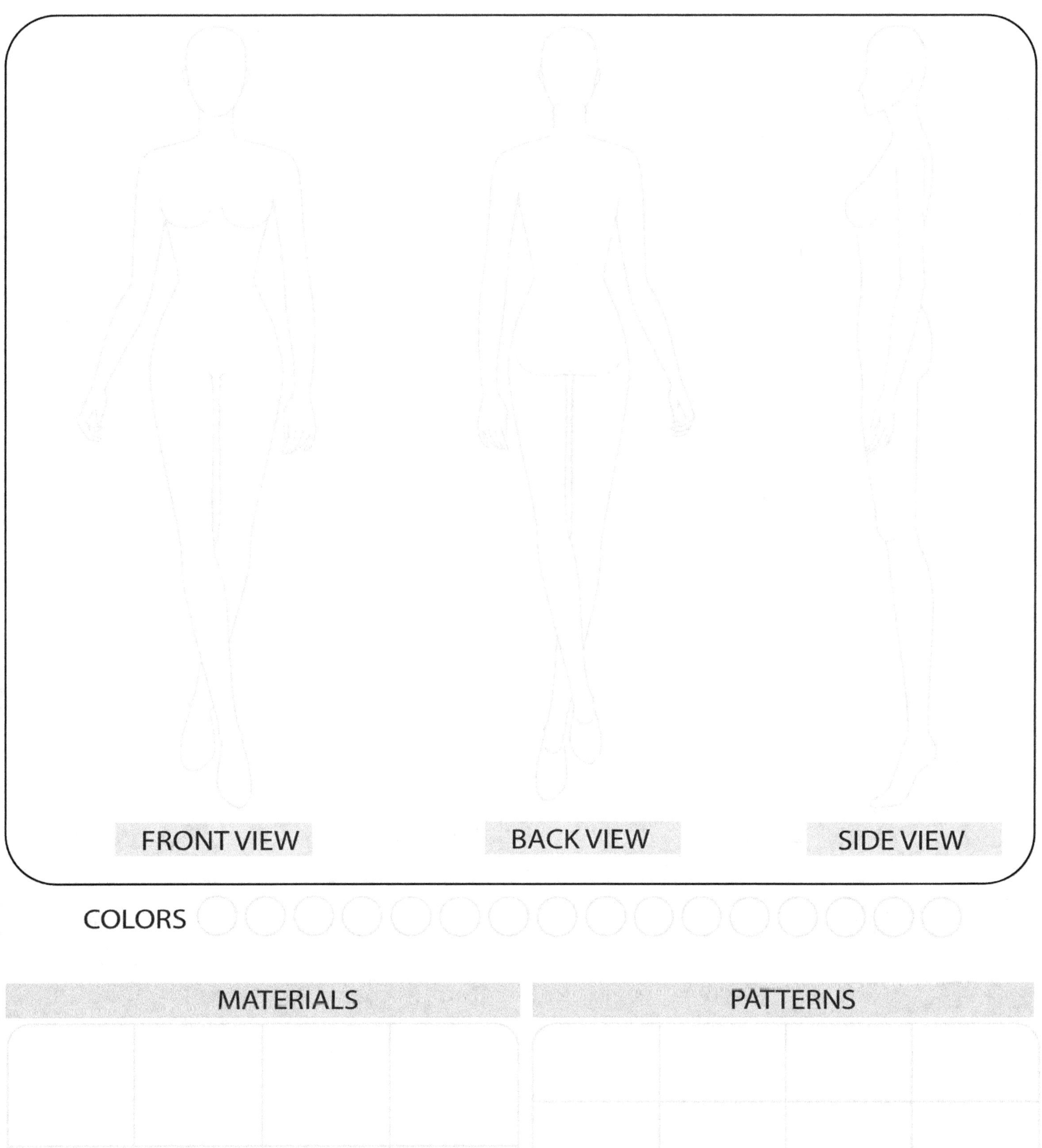

COLORS

MATERIALS

PATTERNS

ACCESSORIES

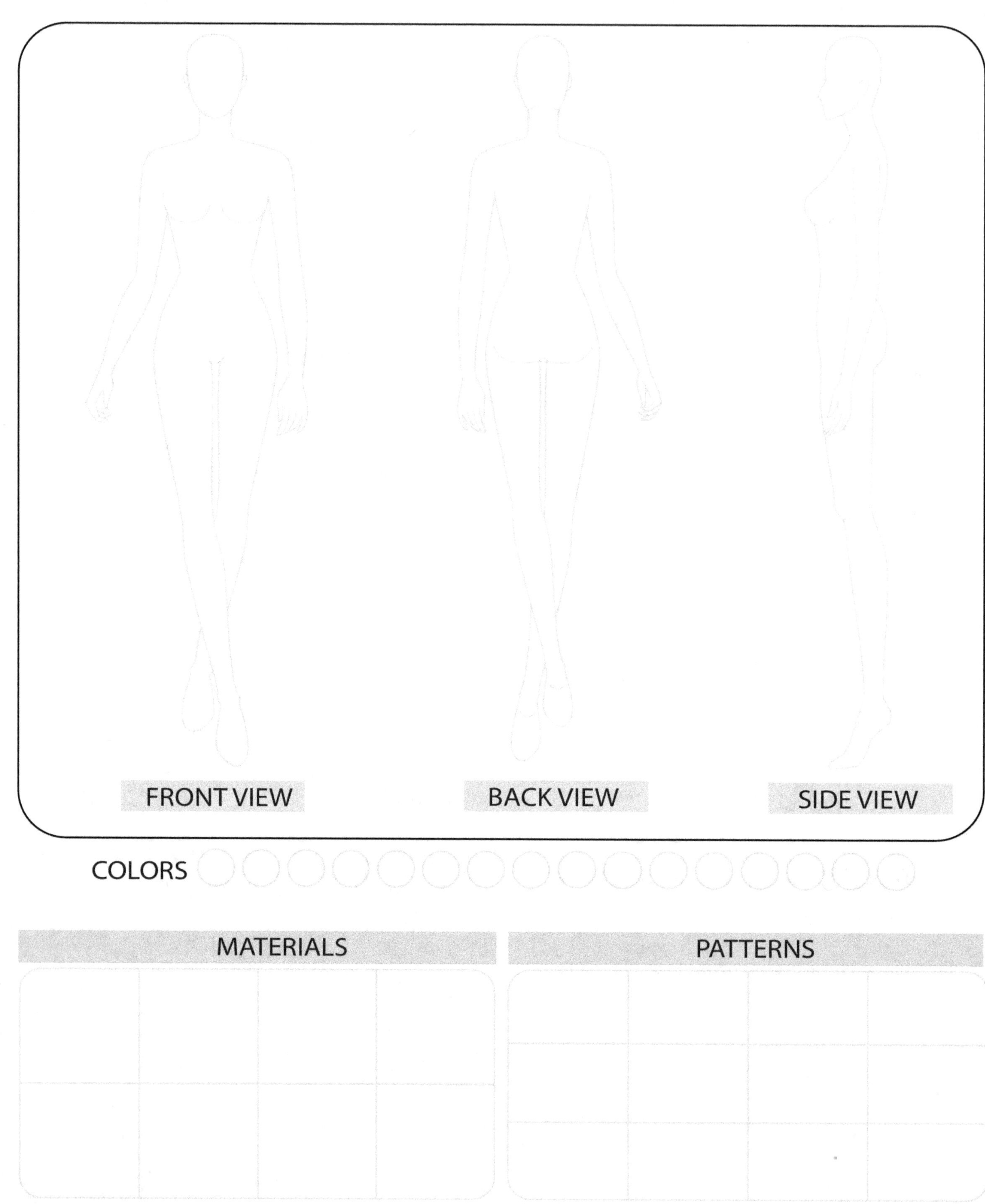

FRONT VIEW

BACK VIEW

SIDE VIEW

COLORS

MATERIALS

PATTERNS

ACCESSORIES

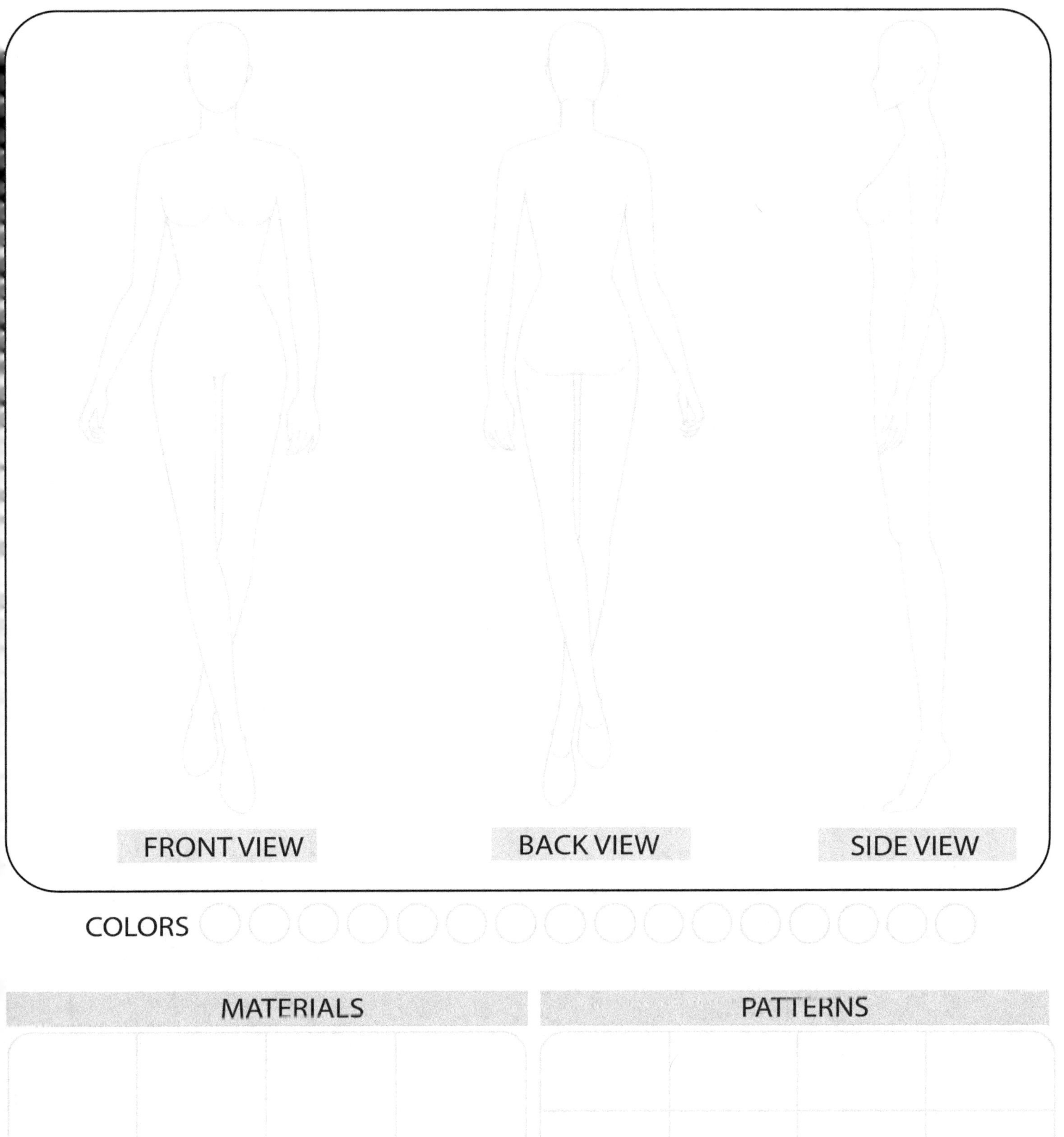

COLORS

MATERIALS

PATTERNS

ACCESSORIES

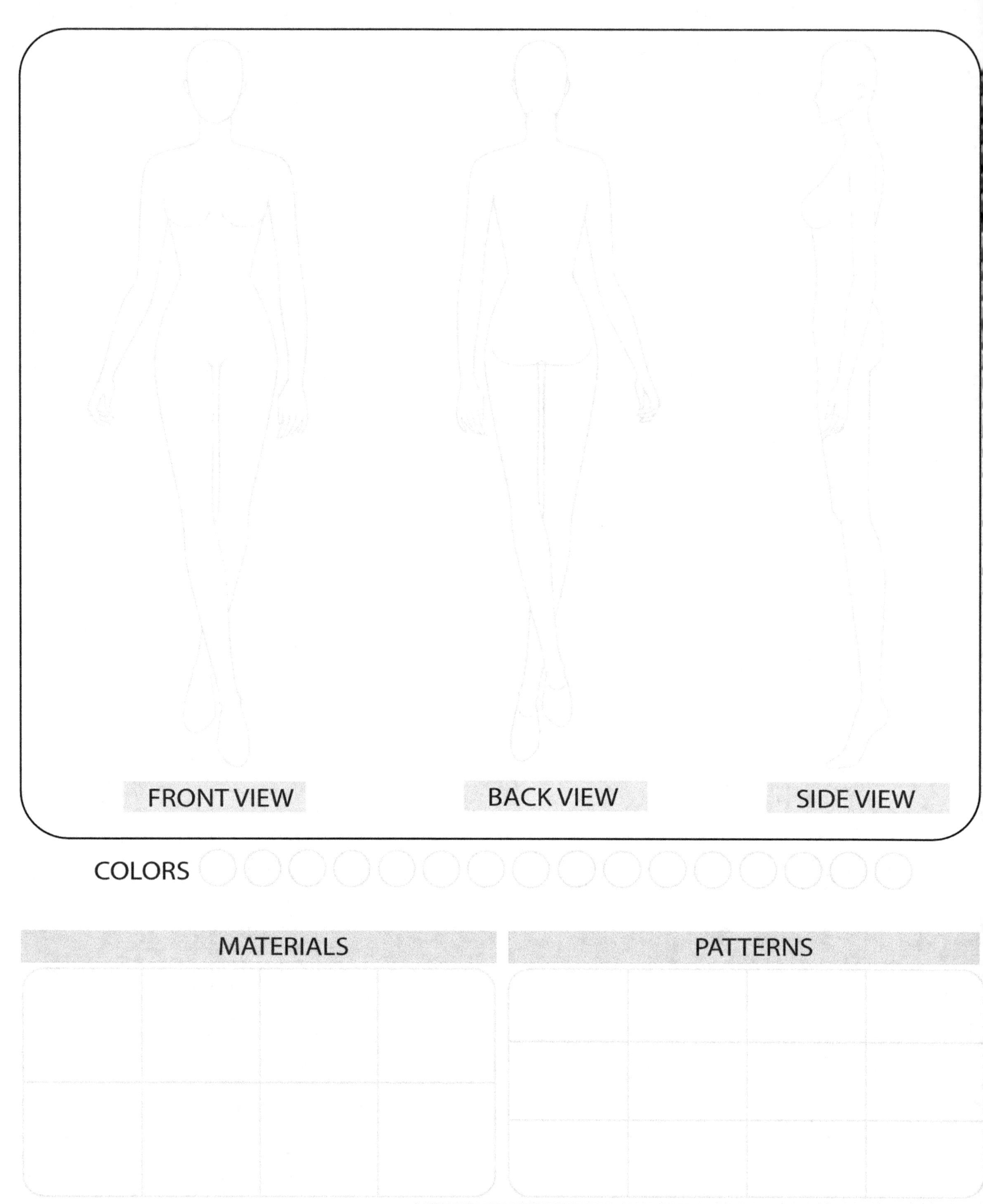

FRONT VIEW
BACK VIEW
SIDE VIEW
COLORS
MATERIALS
PATTERNS
ACCESSORIES

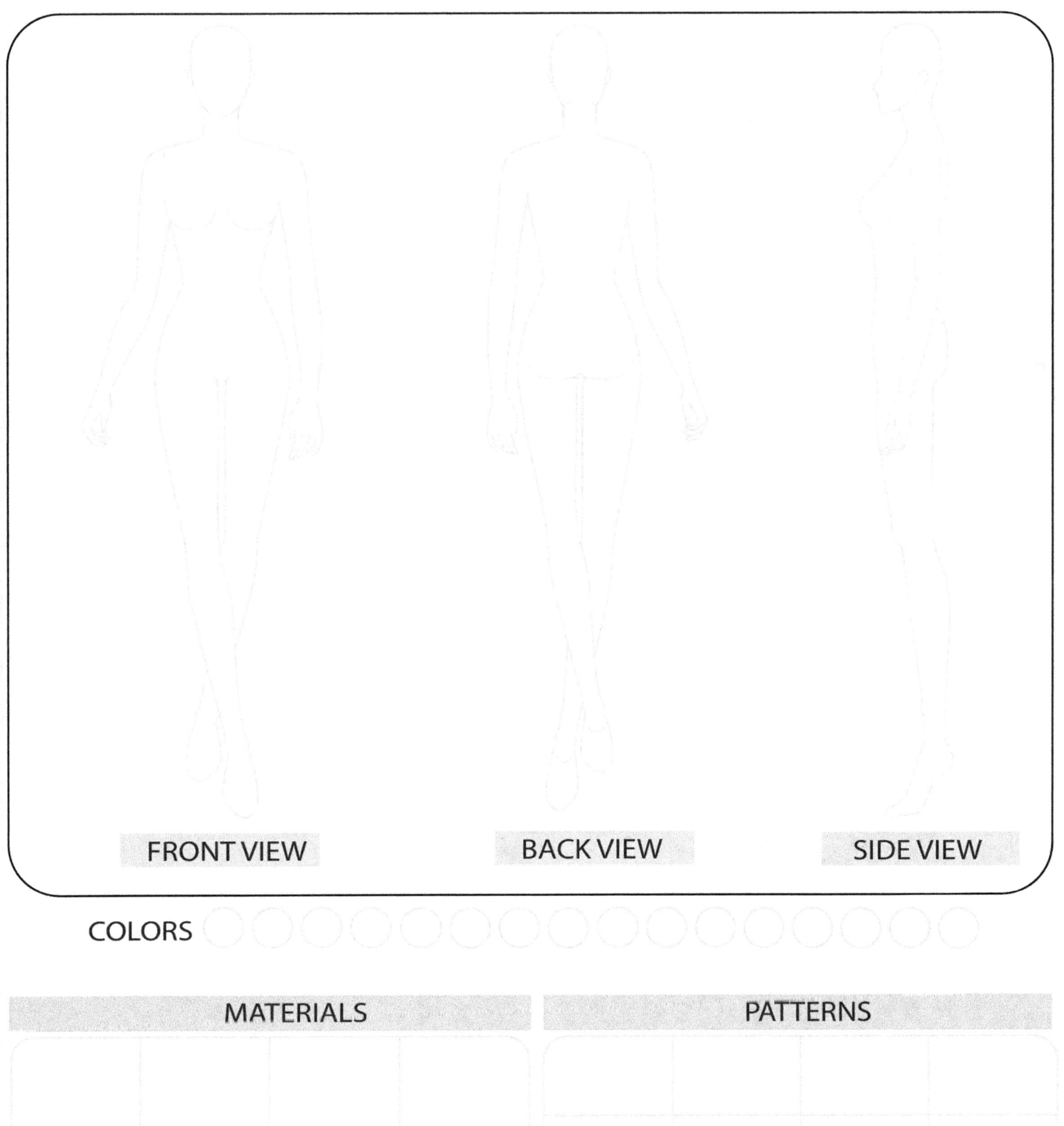

COLORS

MATERIALS

PATTERNS

ACCESSORIES

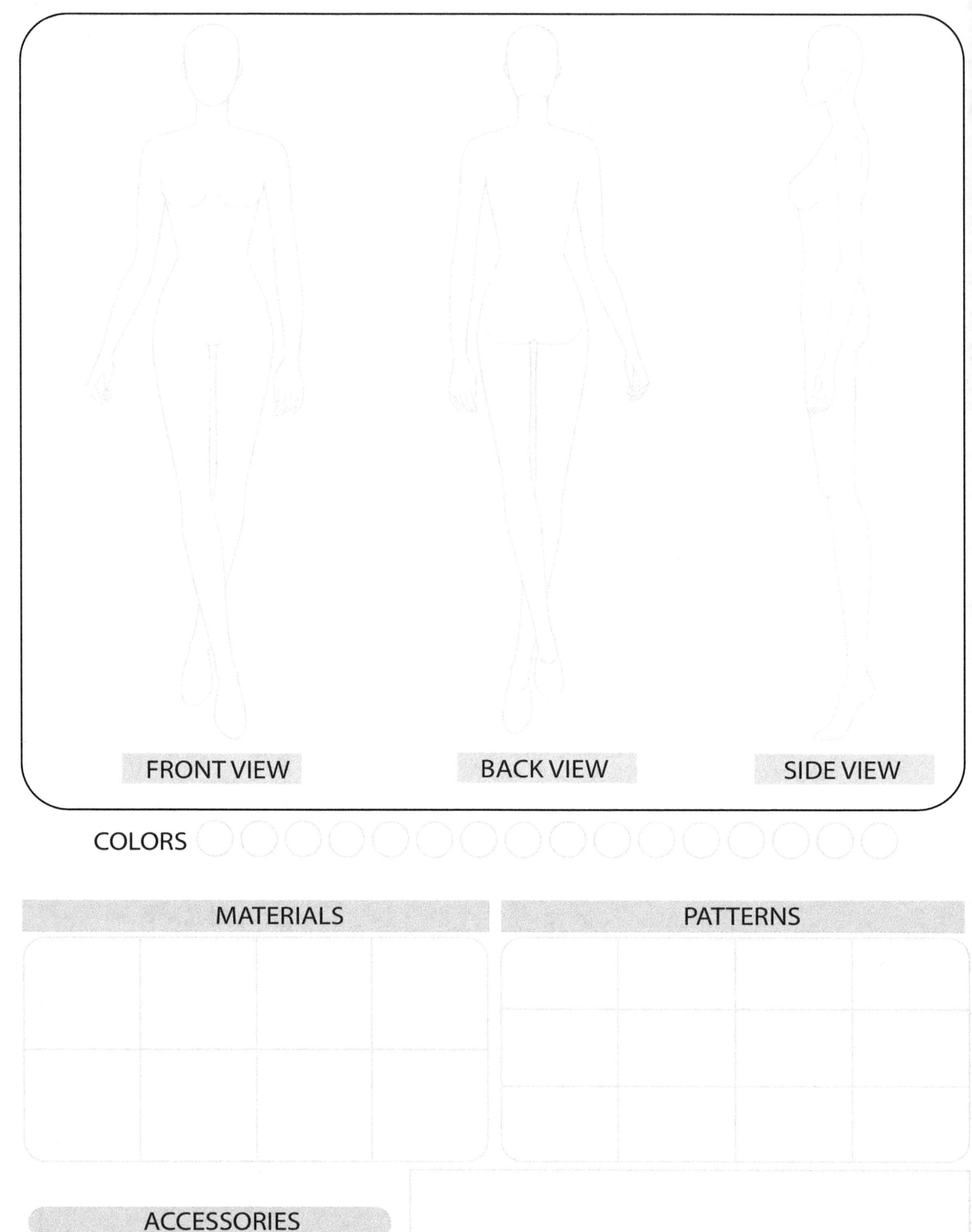

FRONT VIEW
BACK VIEW
SIDE VIEW
COLORS
MATERIALS
PATTERNS
ACCESSORIES

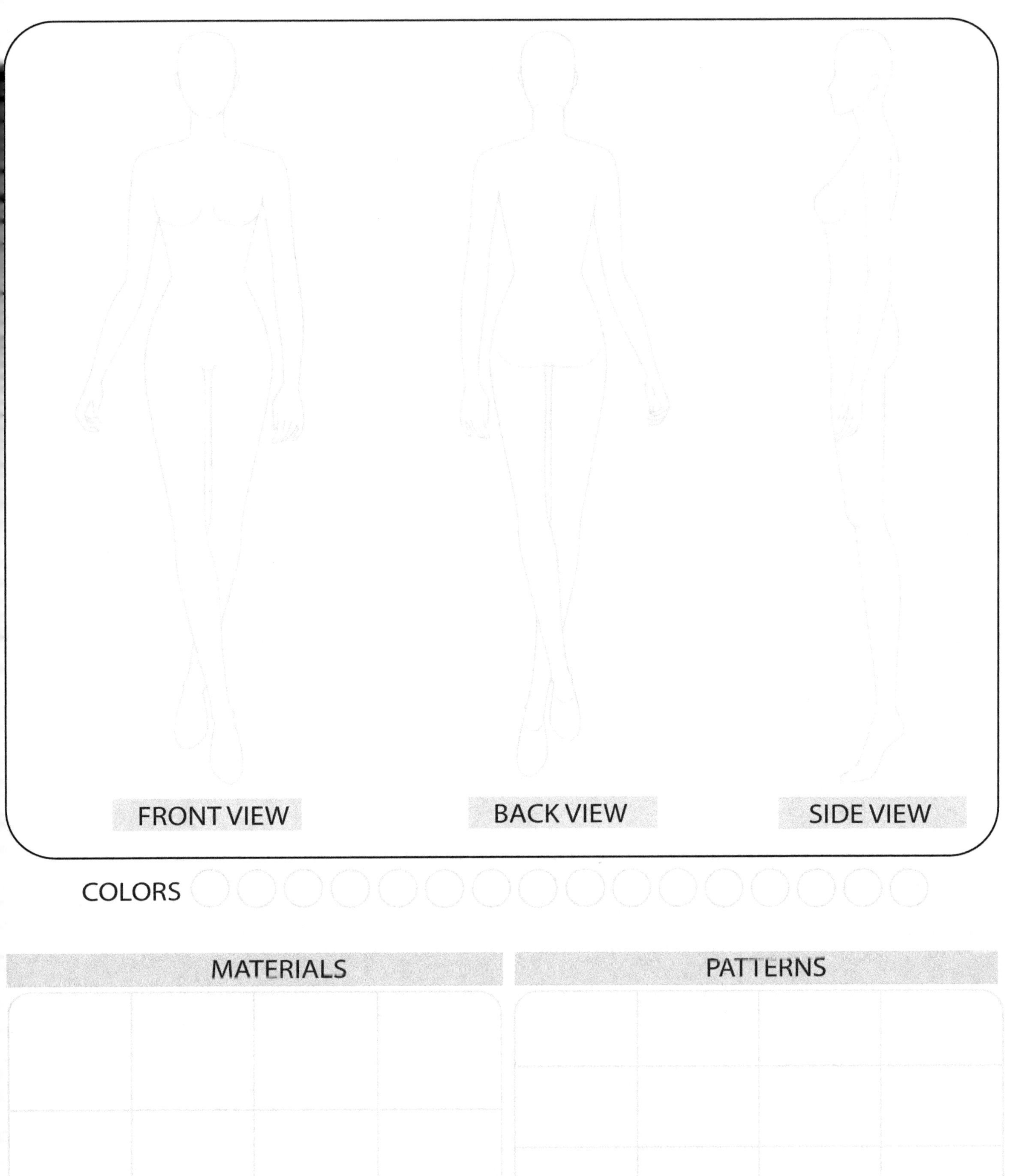

FRONT VIEW

BACK VIEW

SIDE VIEW

COLORS

MATERIALS

PATTERNS

ACCESSORIES

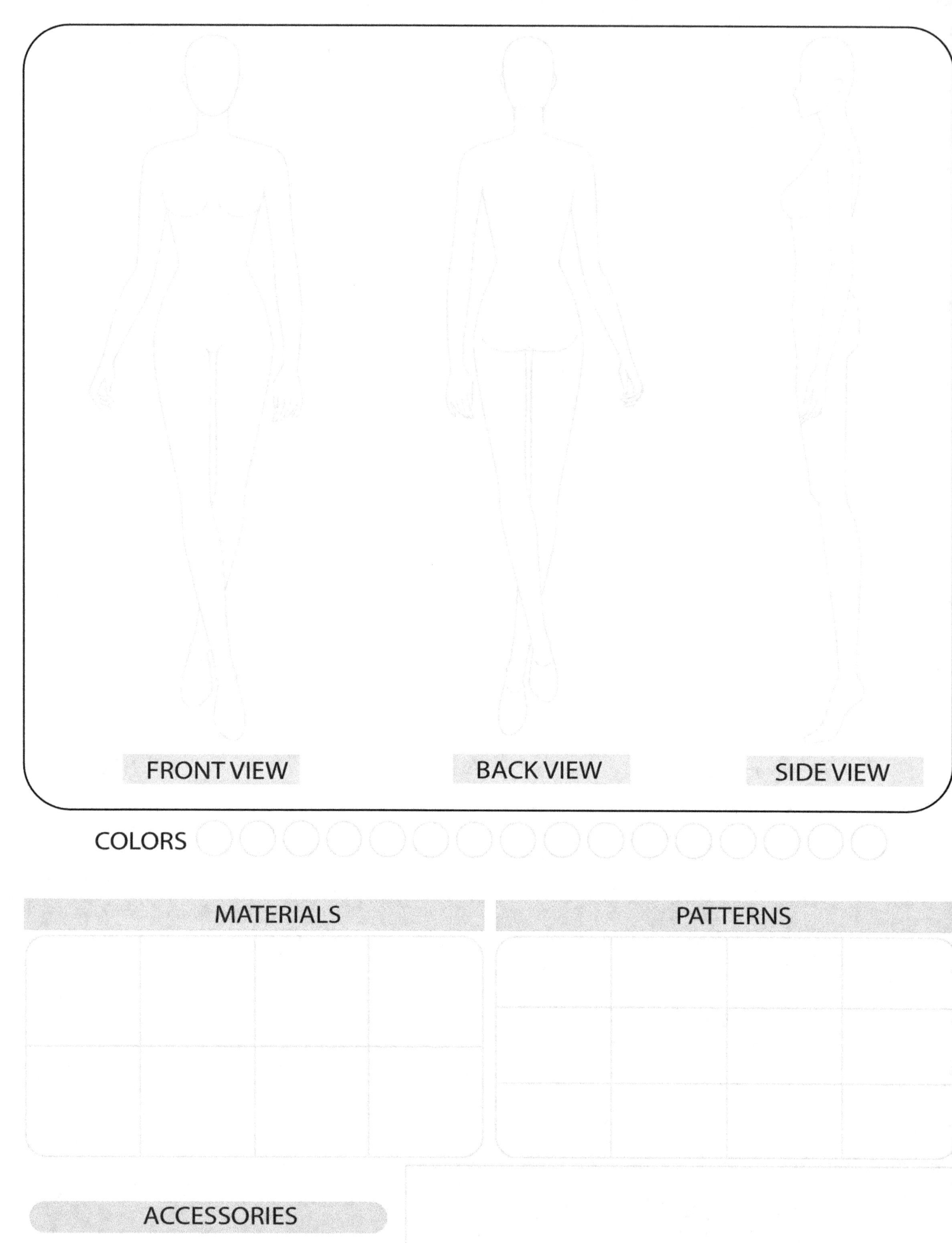

FRONT VIEW
BACK VIEW
SIDE VIEW
COLORS
MATERIALS
PATTERNS
ACCESSORIES

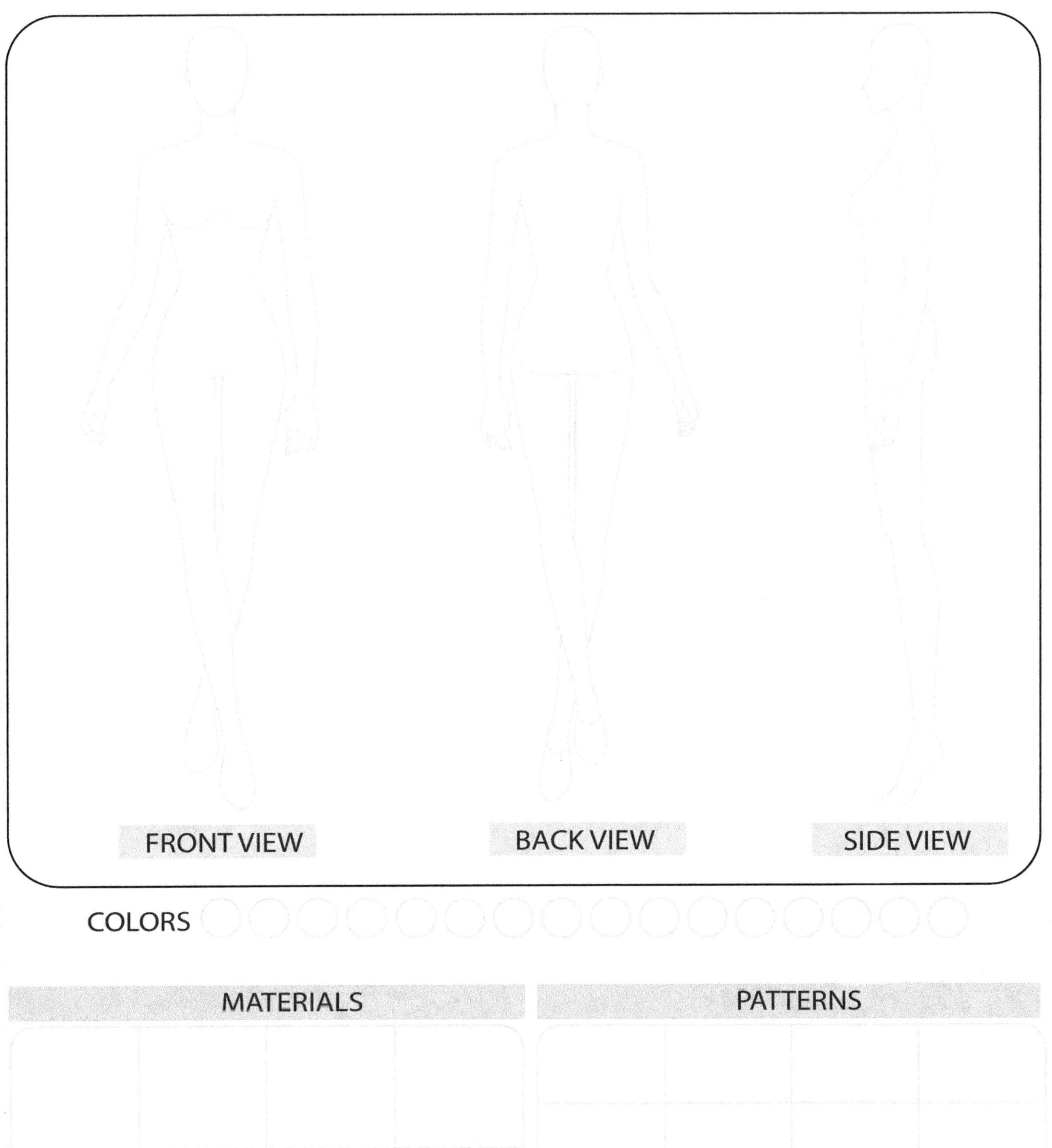

FRONT VIEW
BACK VIEW
SIDE VIEW
COLORS
MATERIALS
PATTERNS
ACCESSORIES

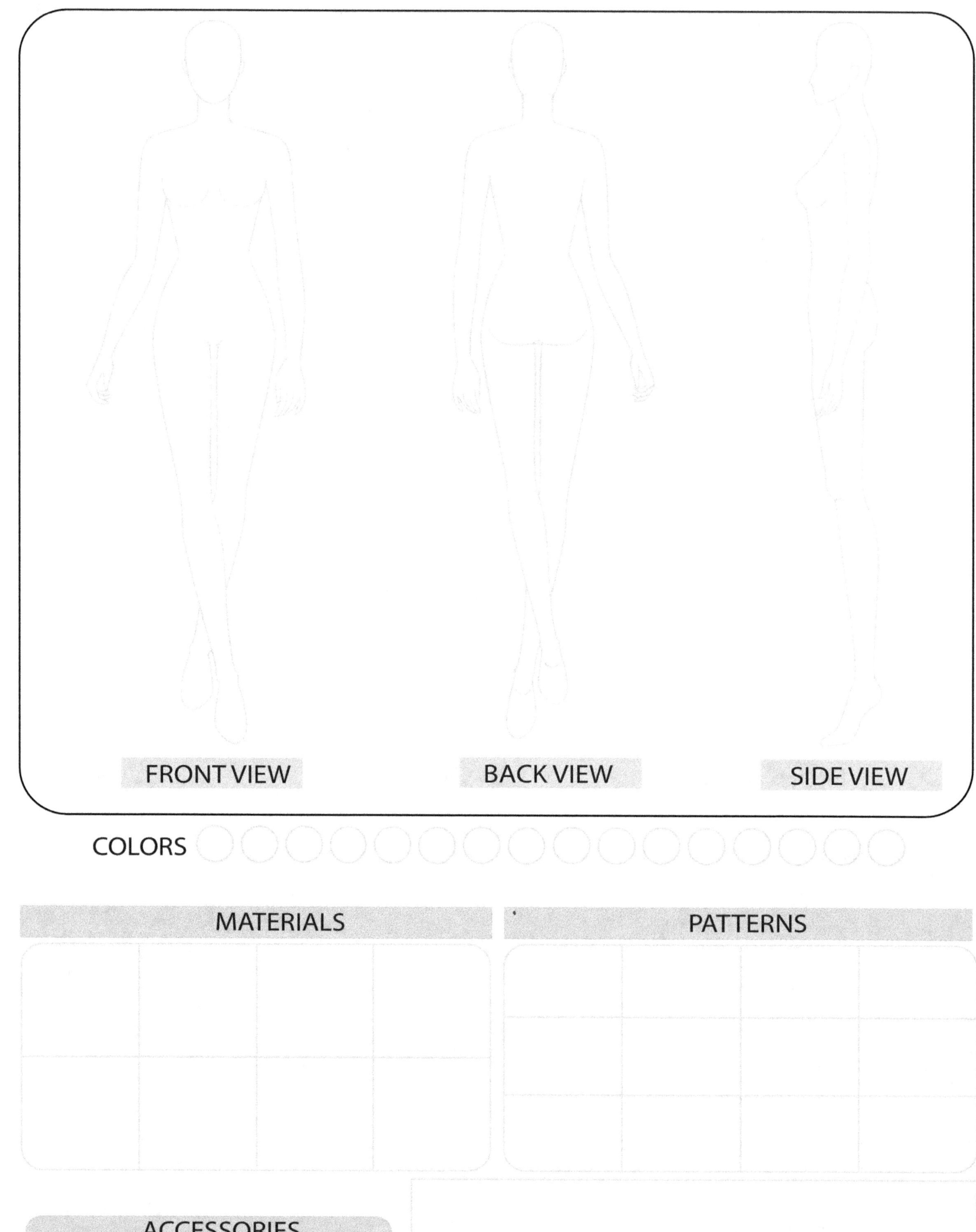

FRONT VIEW
BACK VIEW
SIDE VIEW
COLORS
MATERIALS
PATTERNS
ACCESSORIES

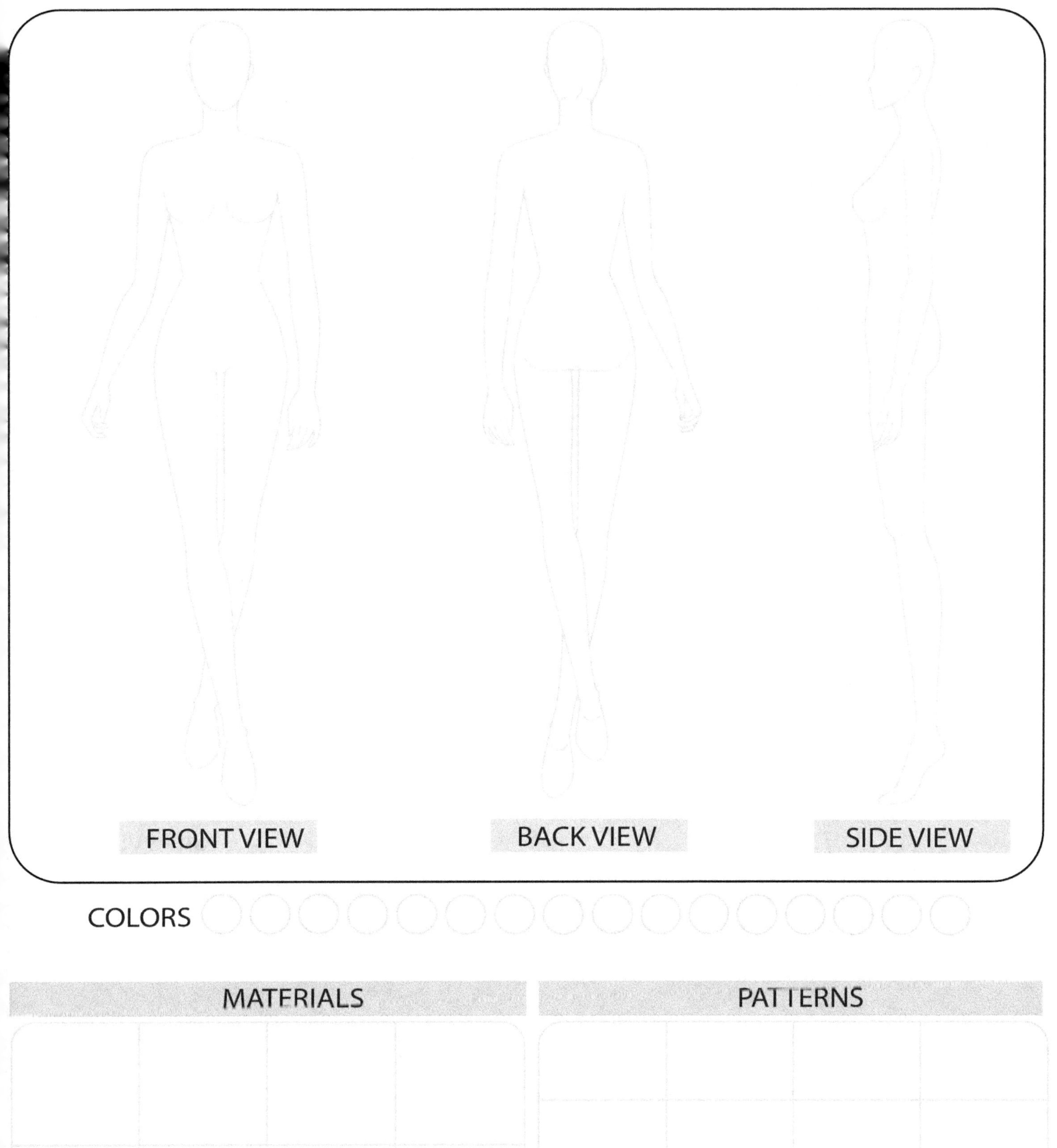

COLORS ○ ○ ○ ○ ○ ○ ○ ○ ○ ○ ○ ○ ○ ○ ○ ○

MATERIALS

PATTERNS

ACCESSORIES

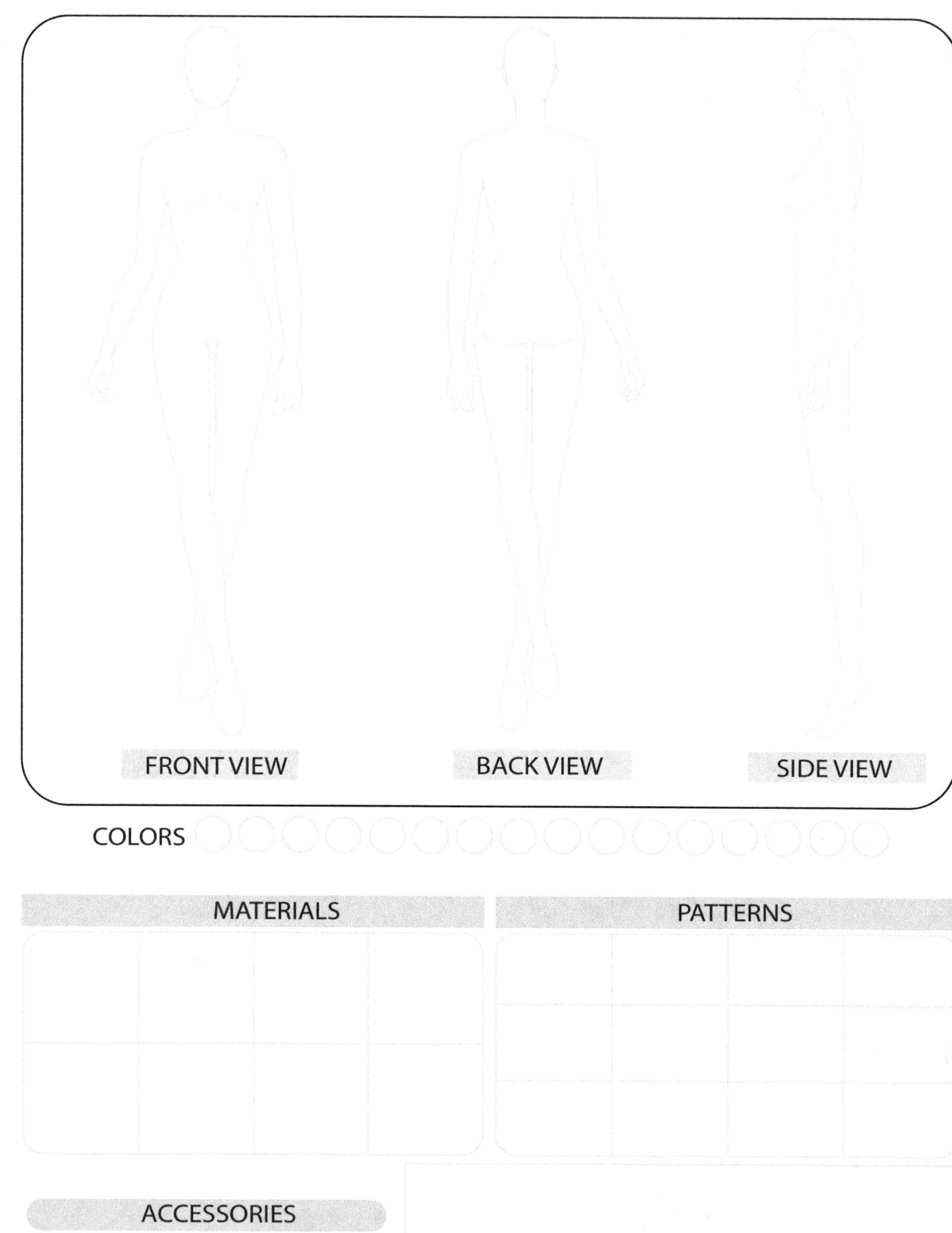

FRONT VIEW
BACK VIEW
SIDE VIEW
COLORS
MATERIALS
PATTERNS
ACCESSORIES

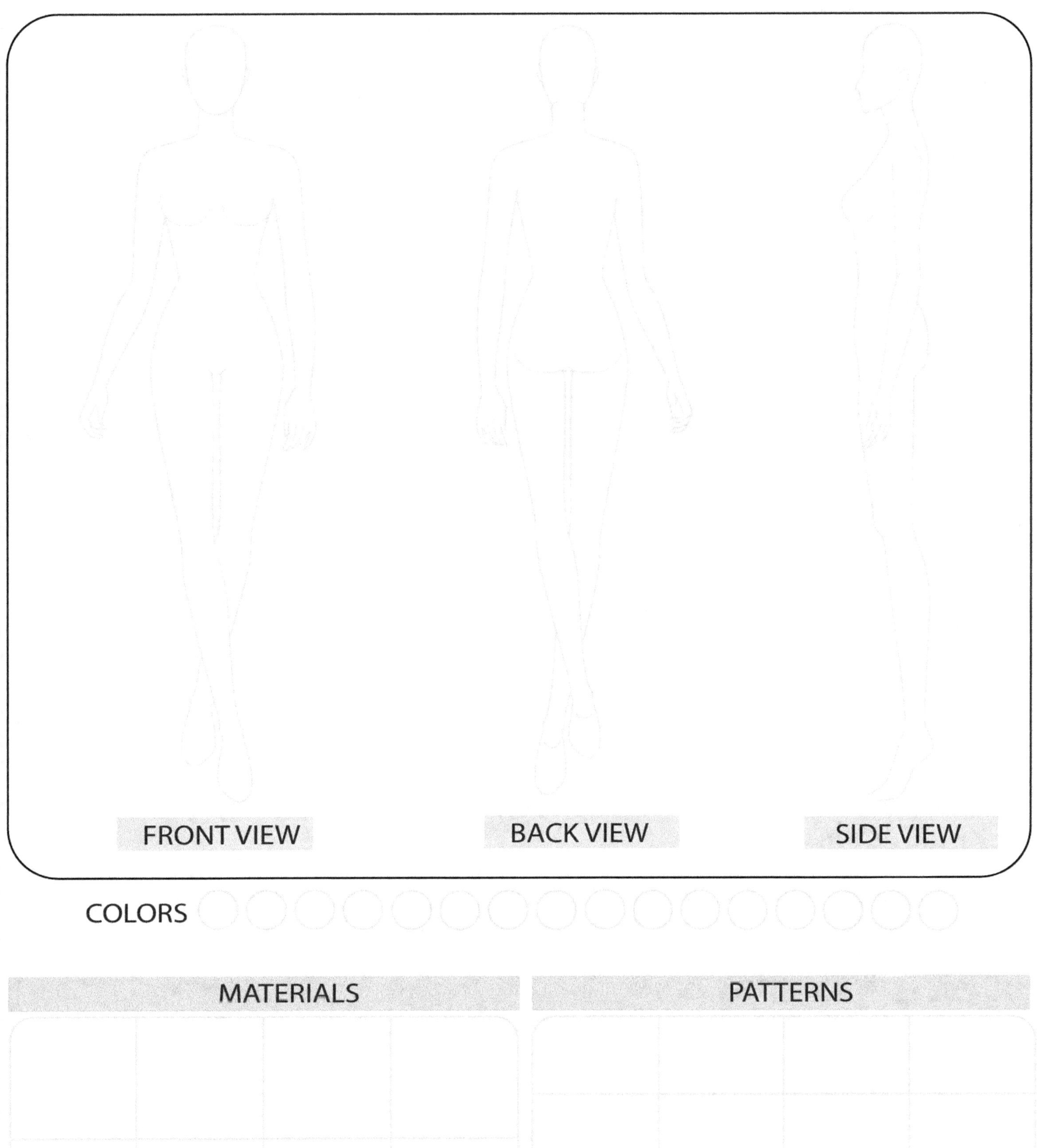

FRONT VIEW
BACK VIEW
SIDE VIEW
COLORS
MATERIALS
PATTERNS
ACCESSORIES

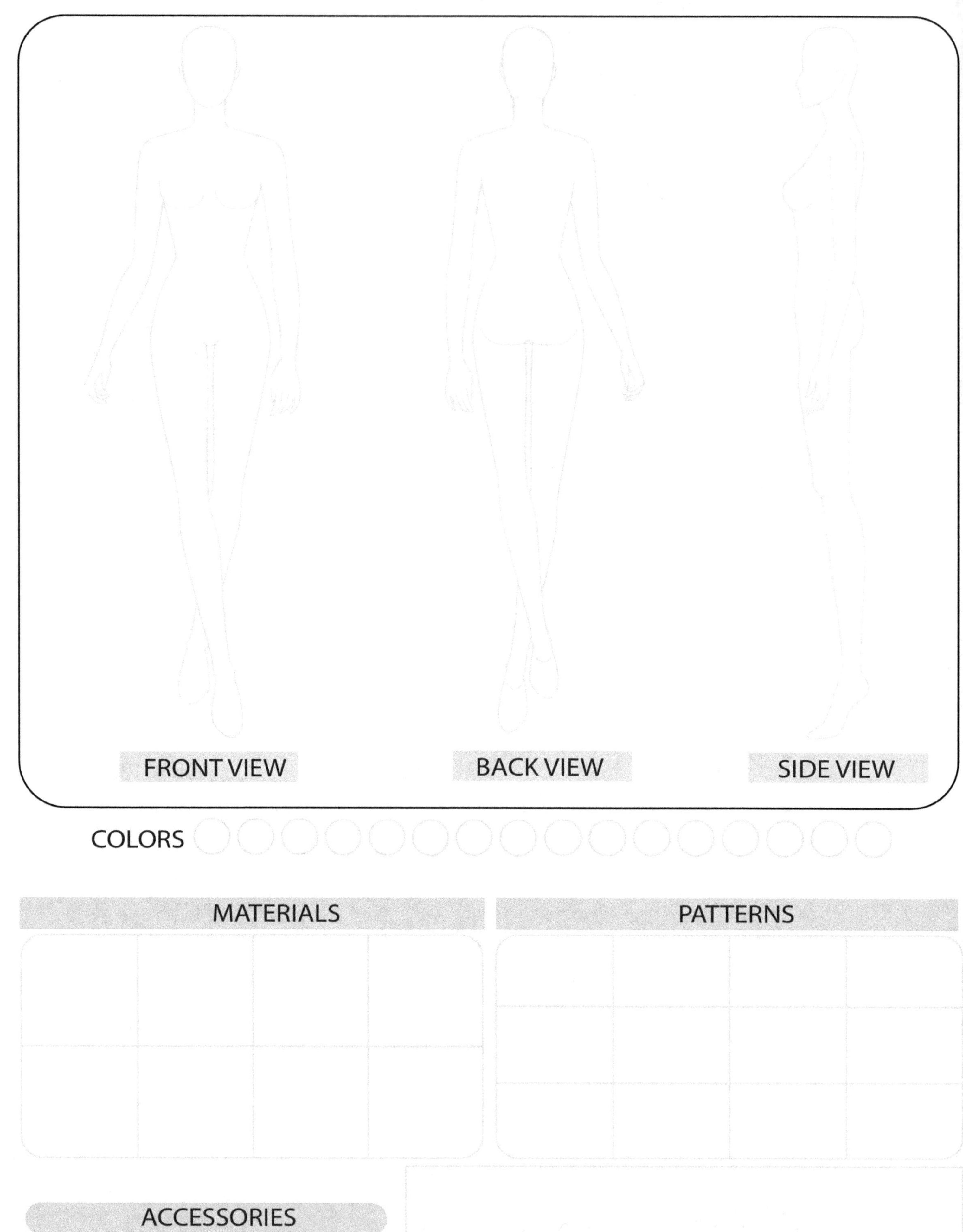

FRONT VIEW
BACK VIEW
SIDE VIEW
COLORS
MATERIALS
PATTERNS
ACCESSORIES

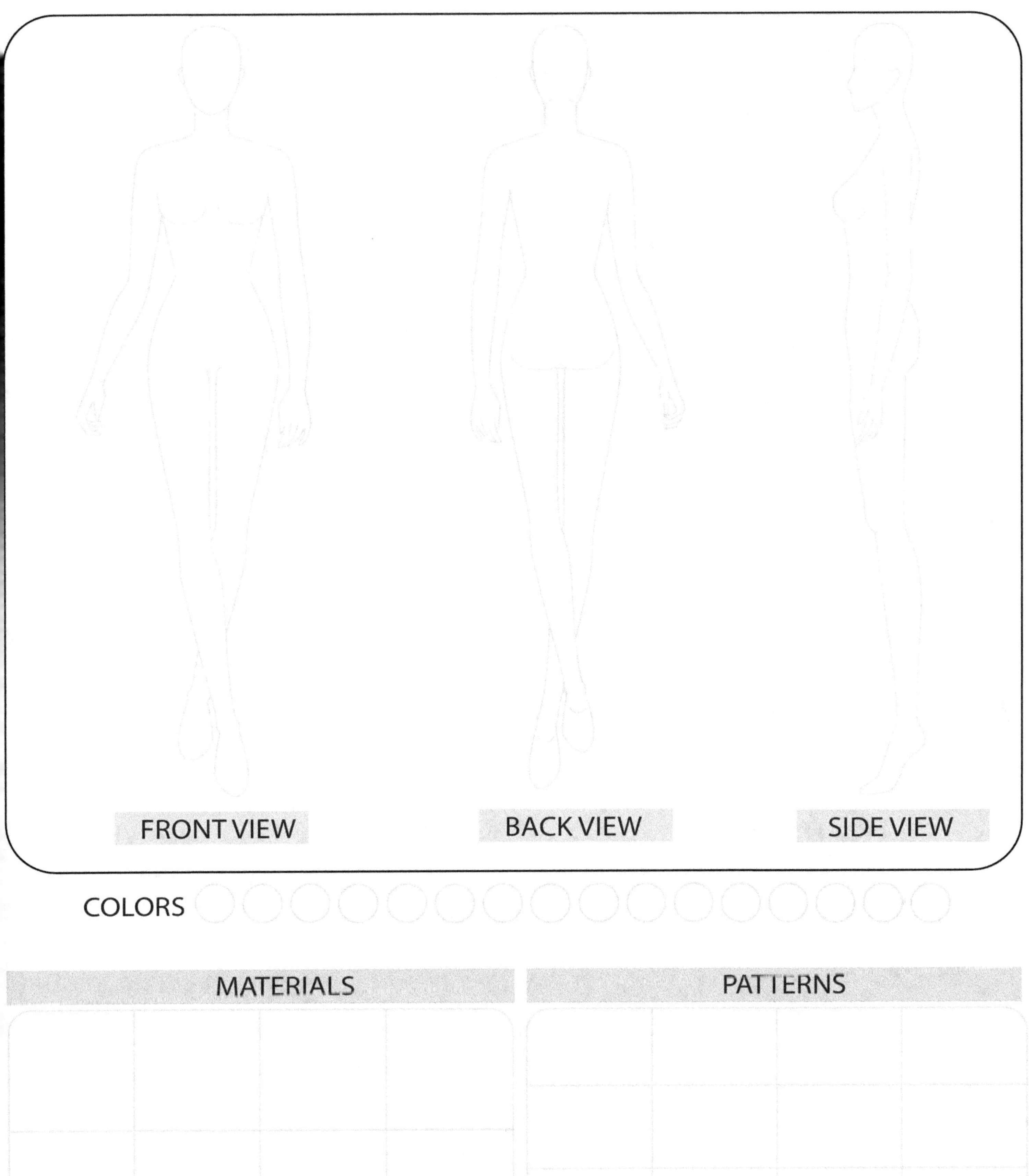

COLORS

MATERIALS

PATTERNS

ACCESSORIES

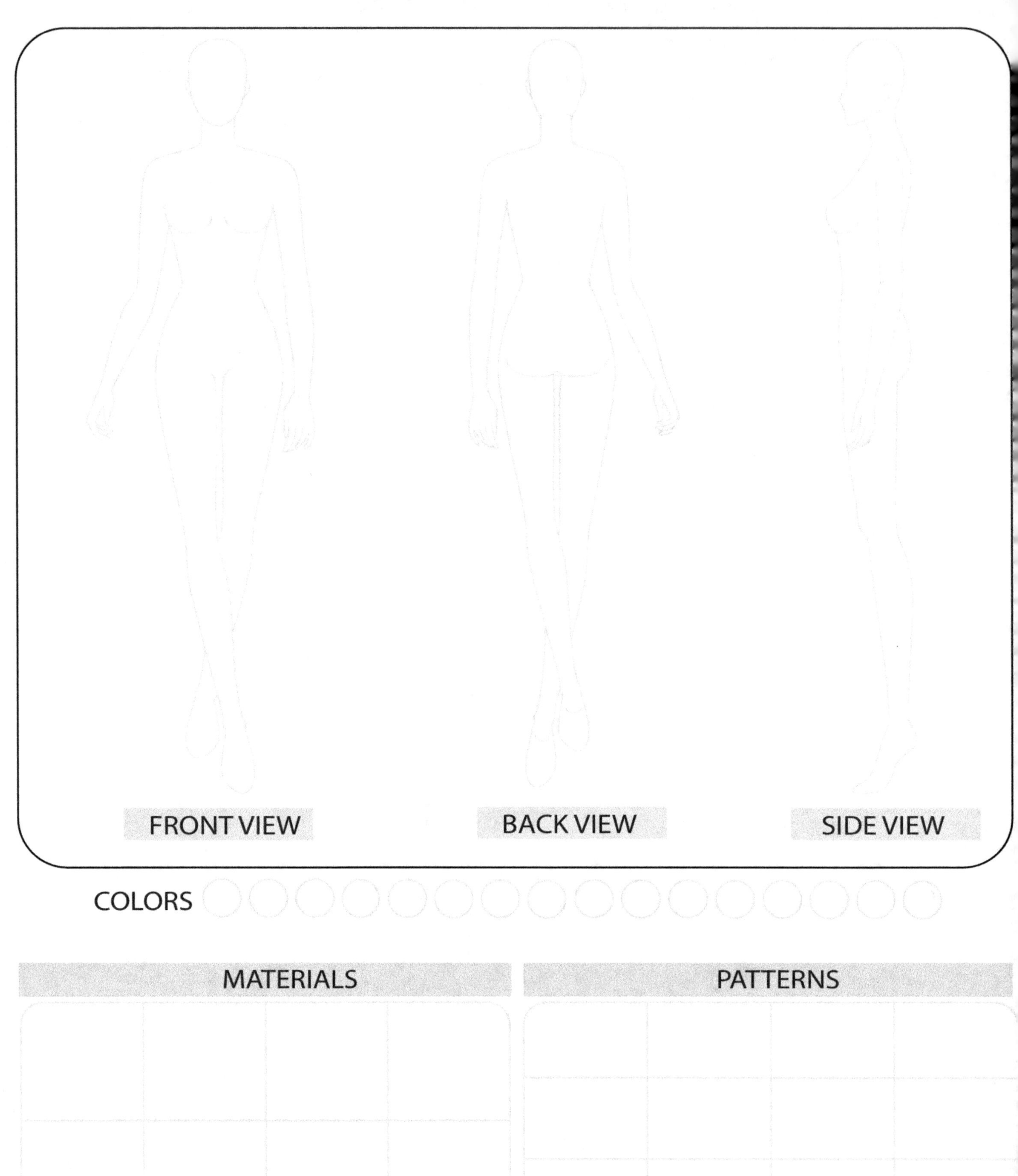

COLORS

MATERIALS

PATTERNS

ACCESSORIES

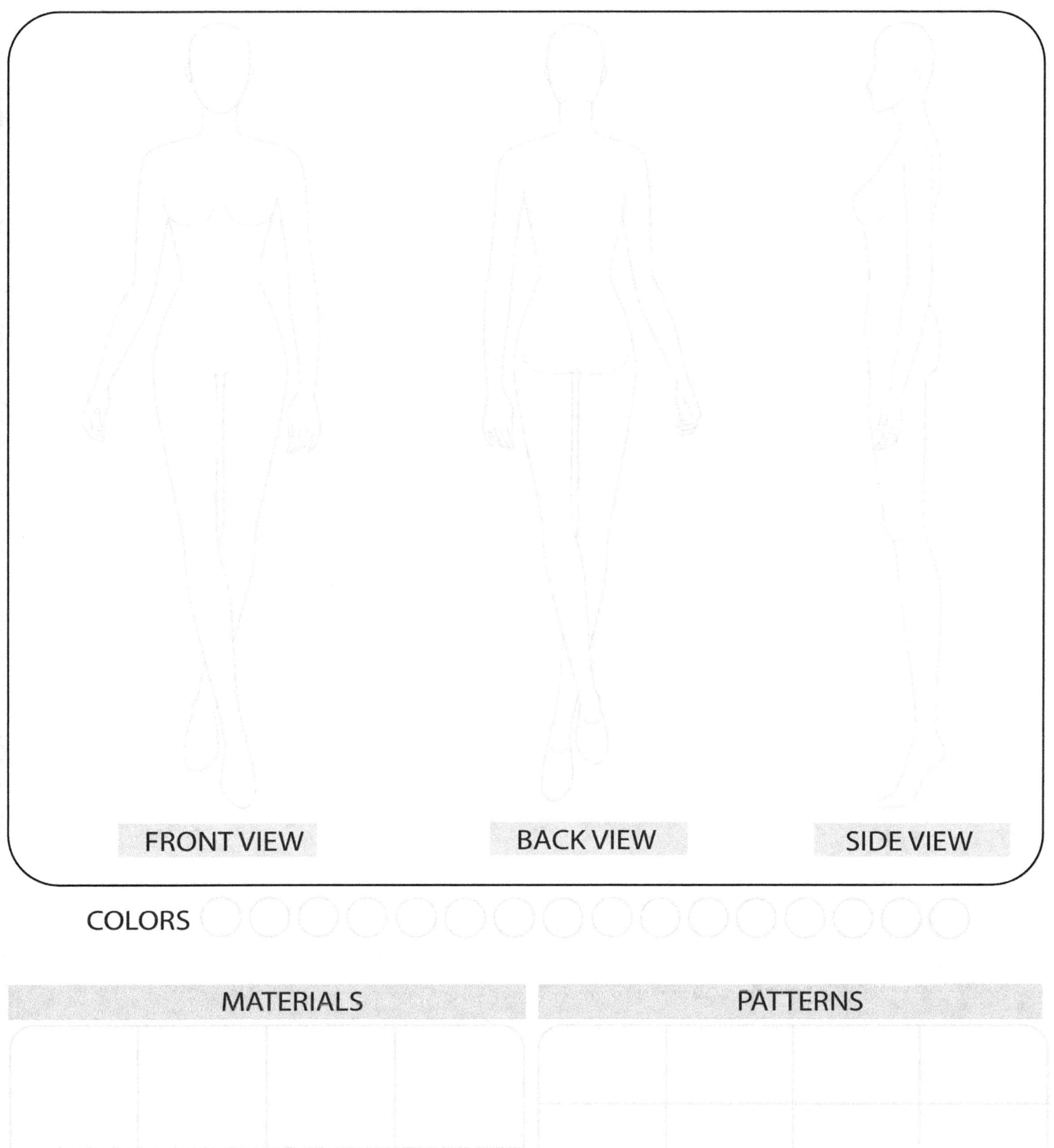

COLORS

MATERIALS

PATTERNS

ACCESSORIES

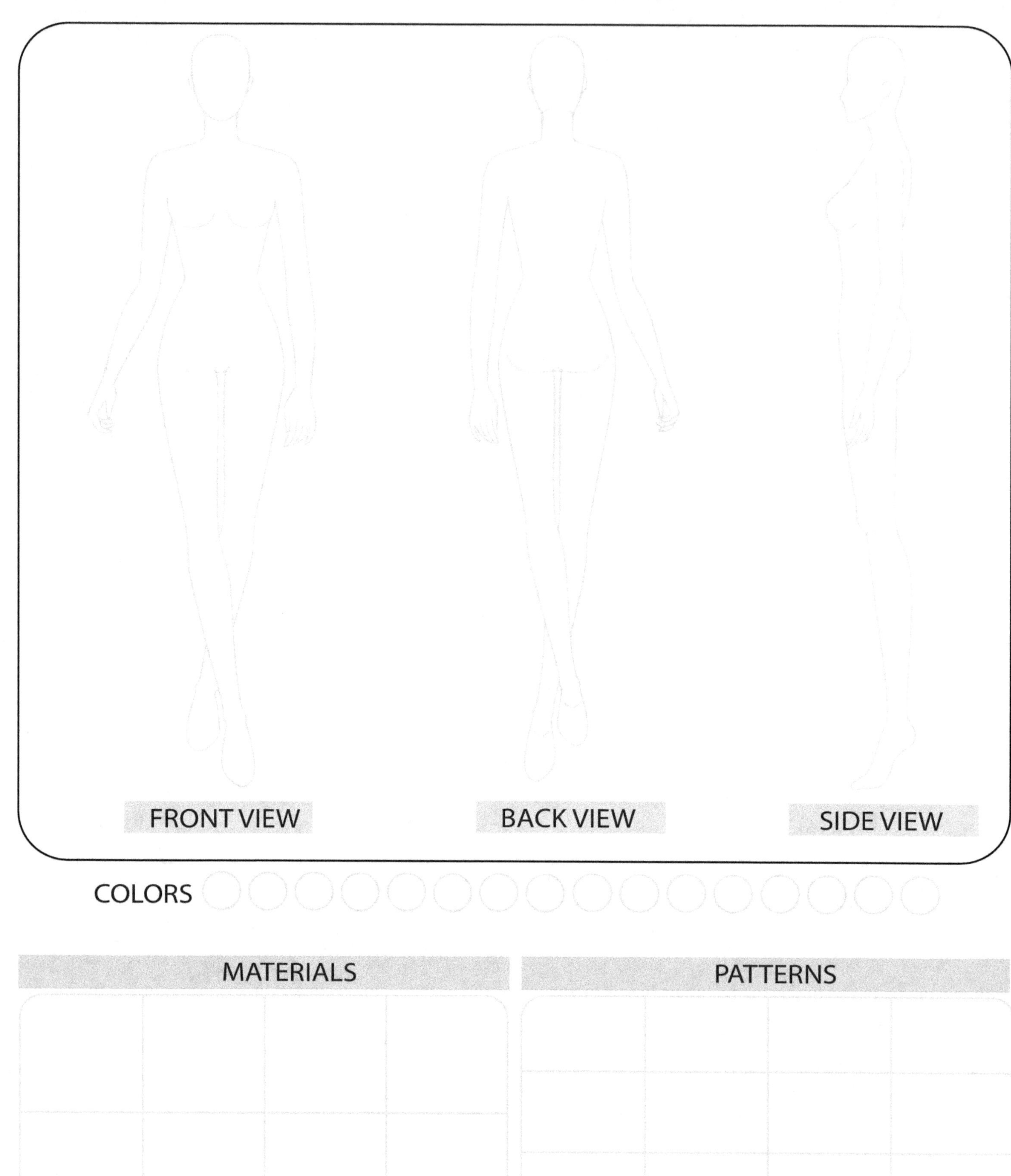

FRONT VIEW
BACK VIEW
SIDE VIEW
COLORS
MATERIALS
PATTERNS
ACCESSORIES

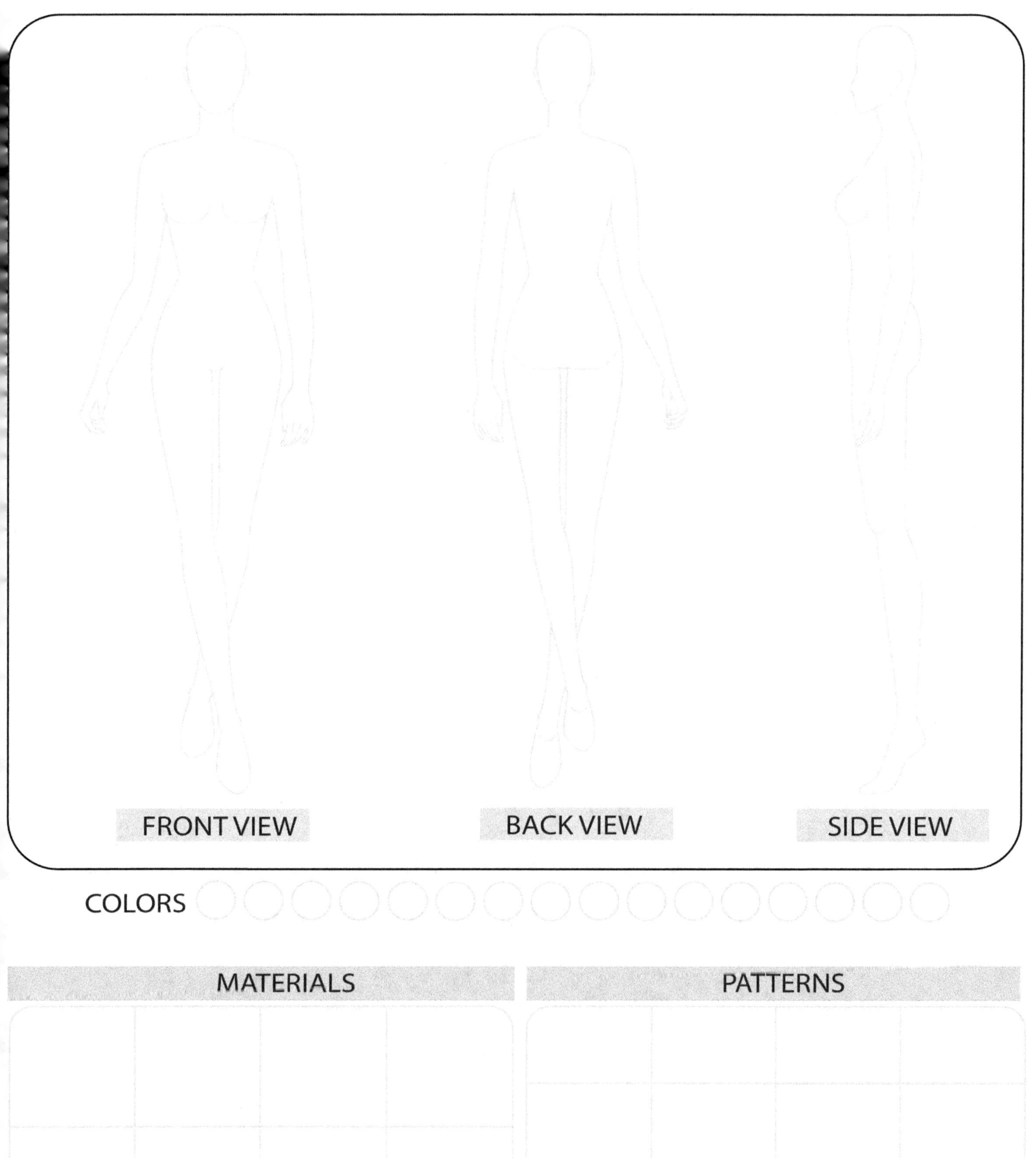

COLORS

MATERIALS

PATTERNS

ACCESSORIES

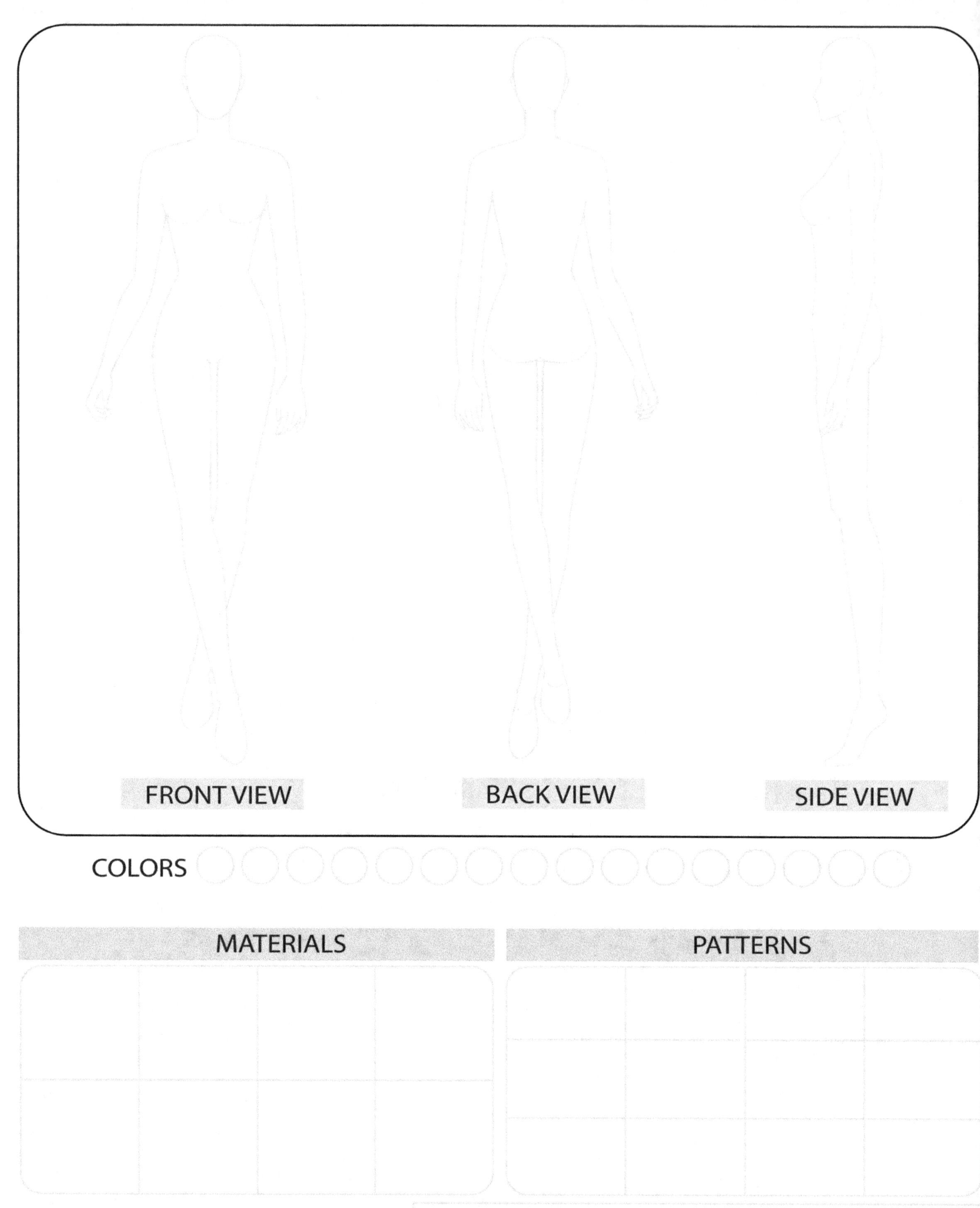

FRONT VIEW

BACK VIEW

SIDE VIEW

COLORS

MATERIALS

PATTERNS

ACCESSORIES

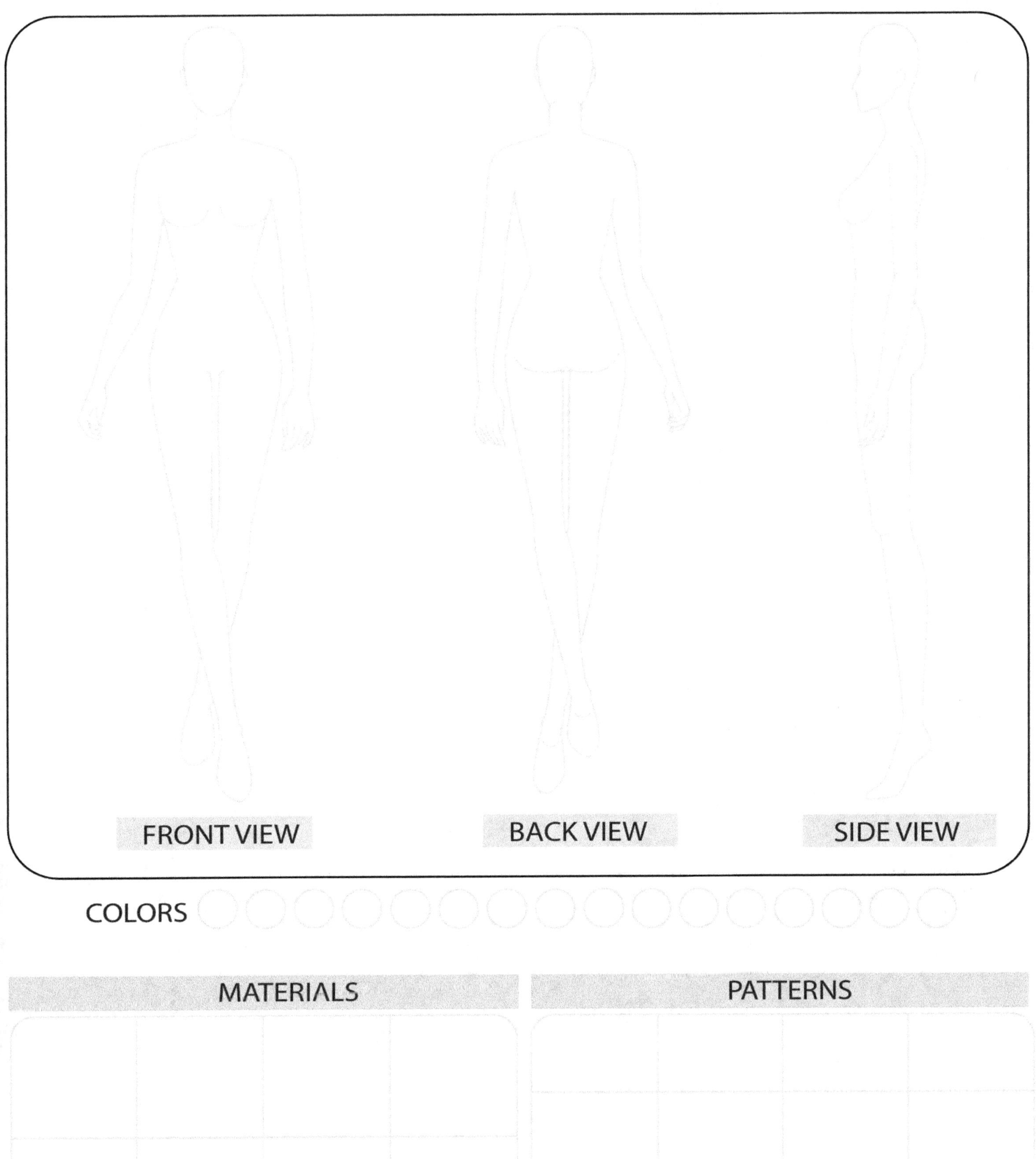

FRONT VIEW
BACK VIEW
SIDE VIEW
COLORS
MATERIALS
PATTERNS
ACCESSORIES

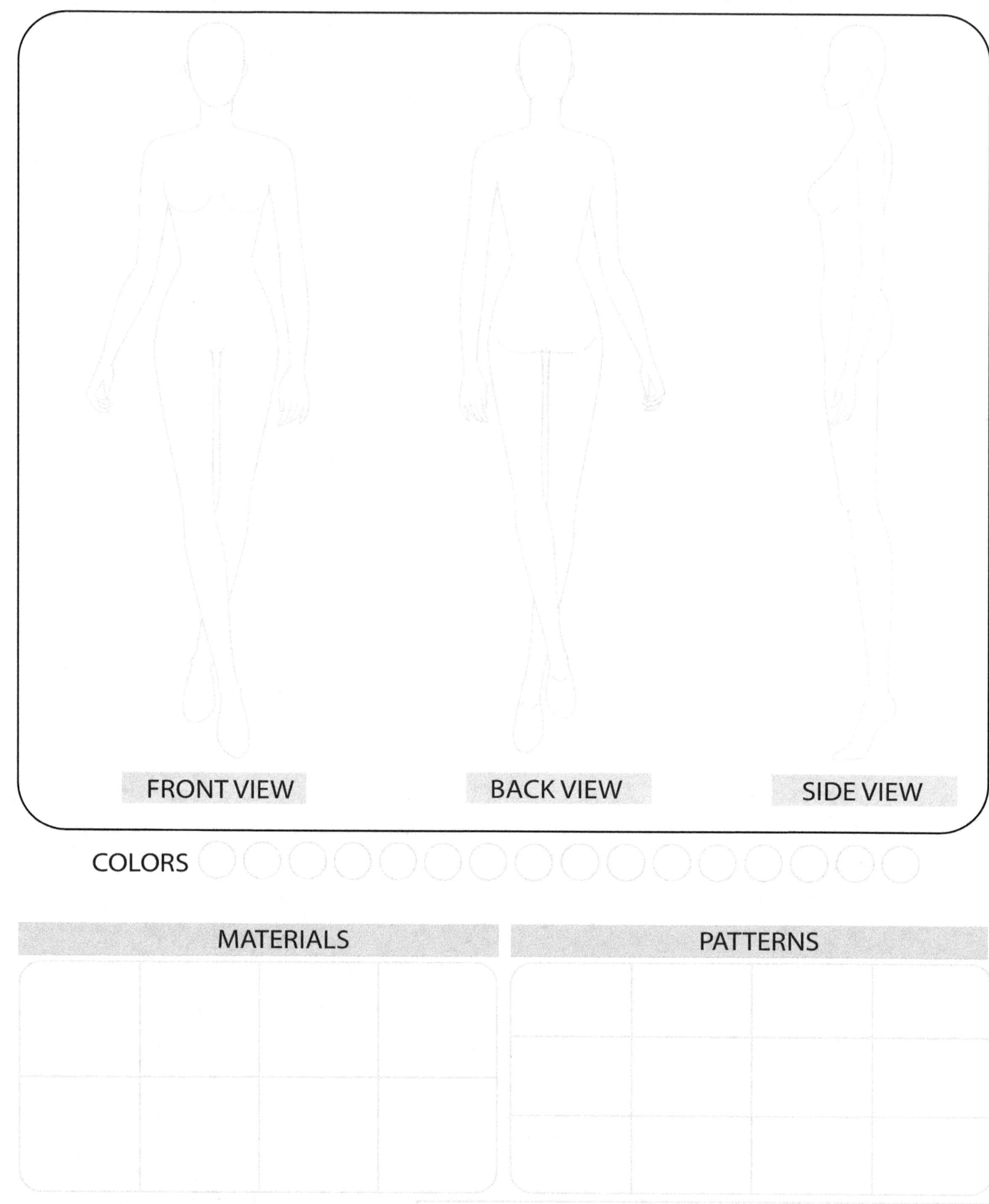

FRONT VIEW

BACK VIEW

SIDE VIEW

COLORS

MATERIALS

PATTERNS

ACCESSORIES

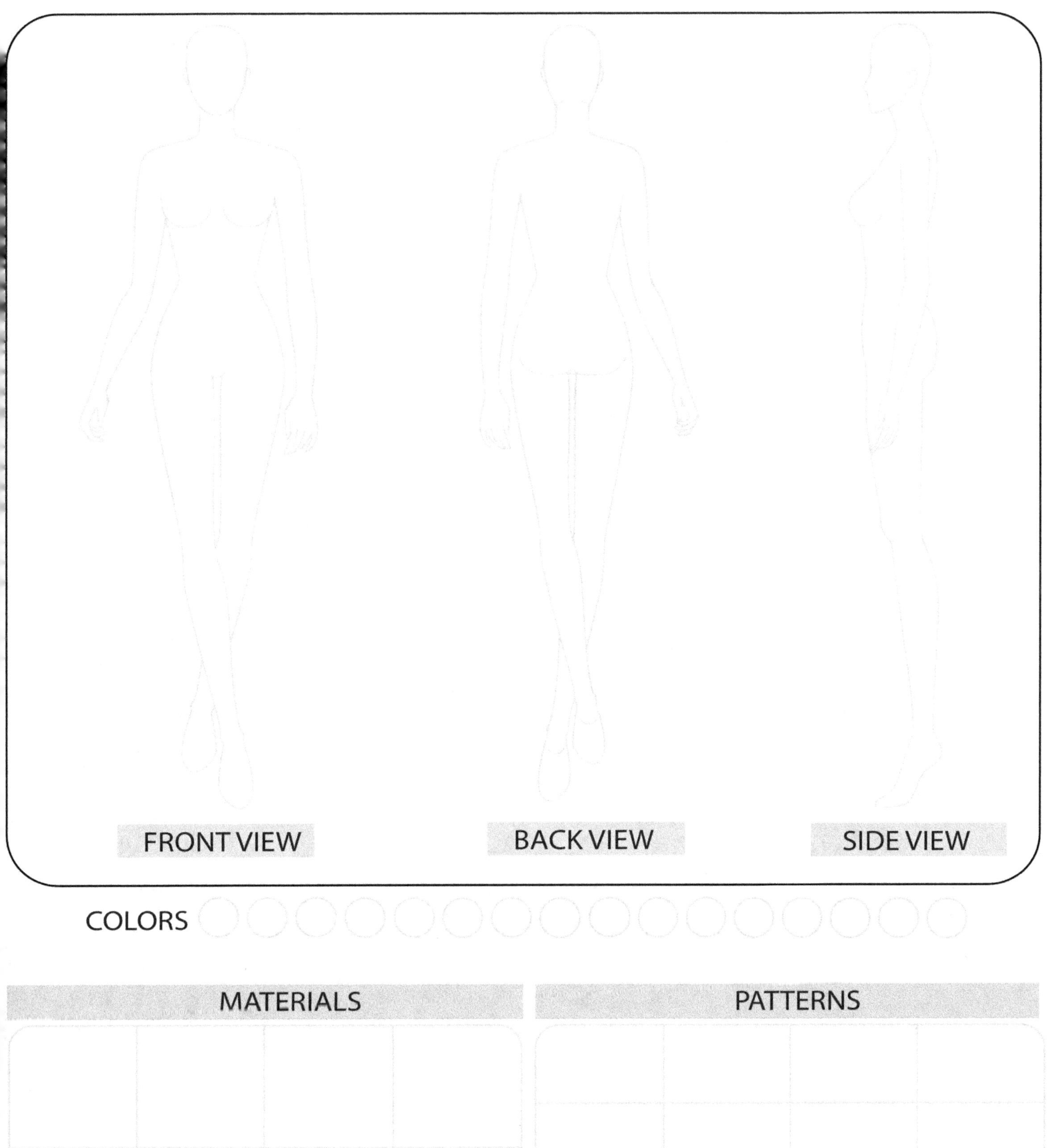

FRONT VIEW

BACK VIEW

SIDE VIEW

COLORS

MATERIALS

PATTERNS

ACCESSORIES

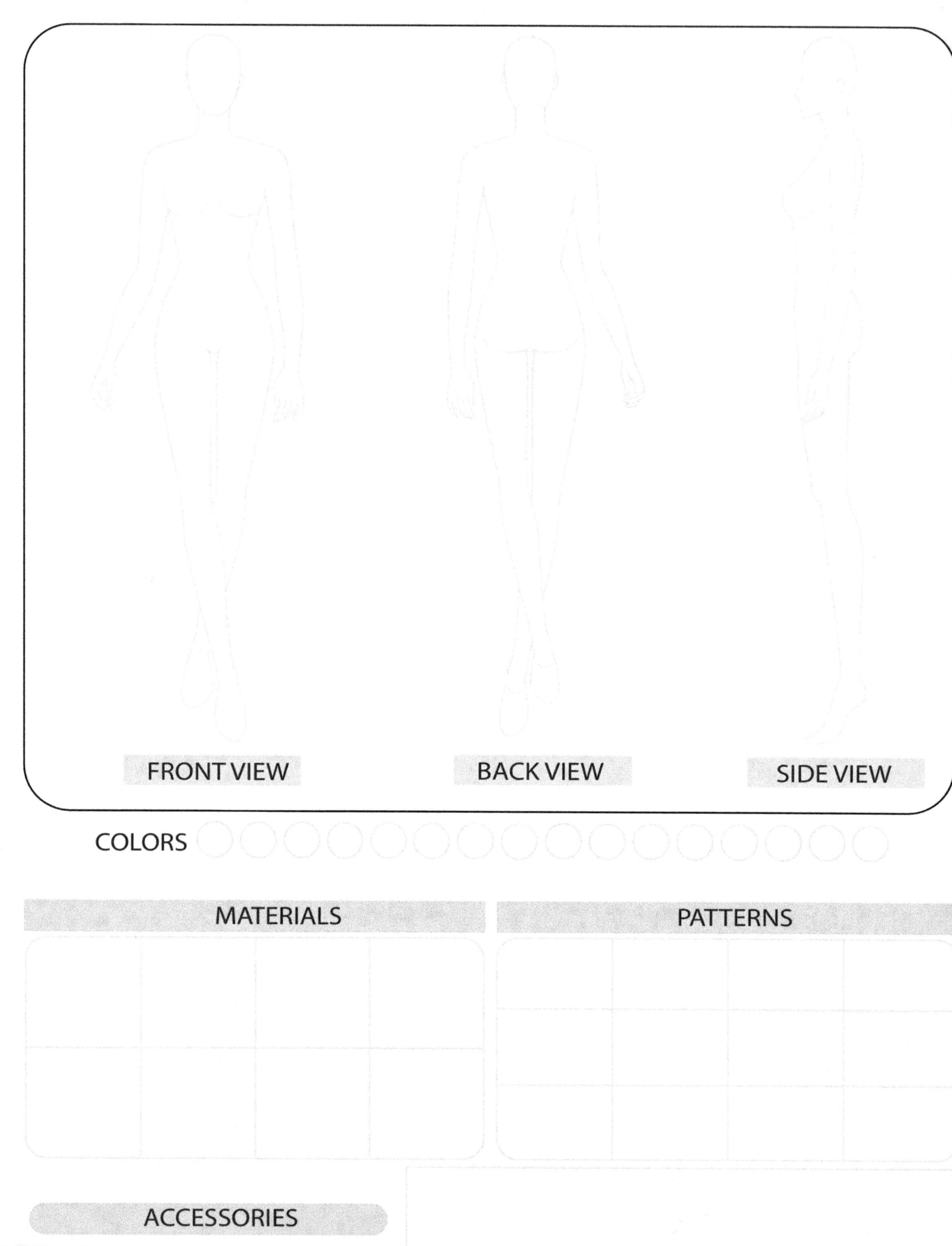

FRONT VIEW
BACK VIEW
SIDE VIEW
COLORS
MATERIALS
PATTERNS
ACCESSORIES

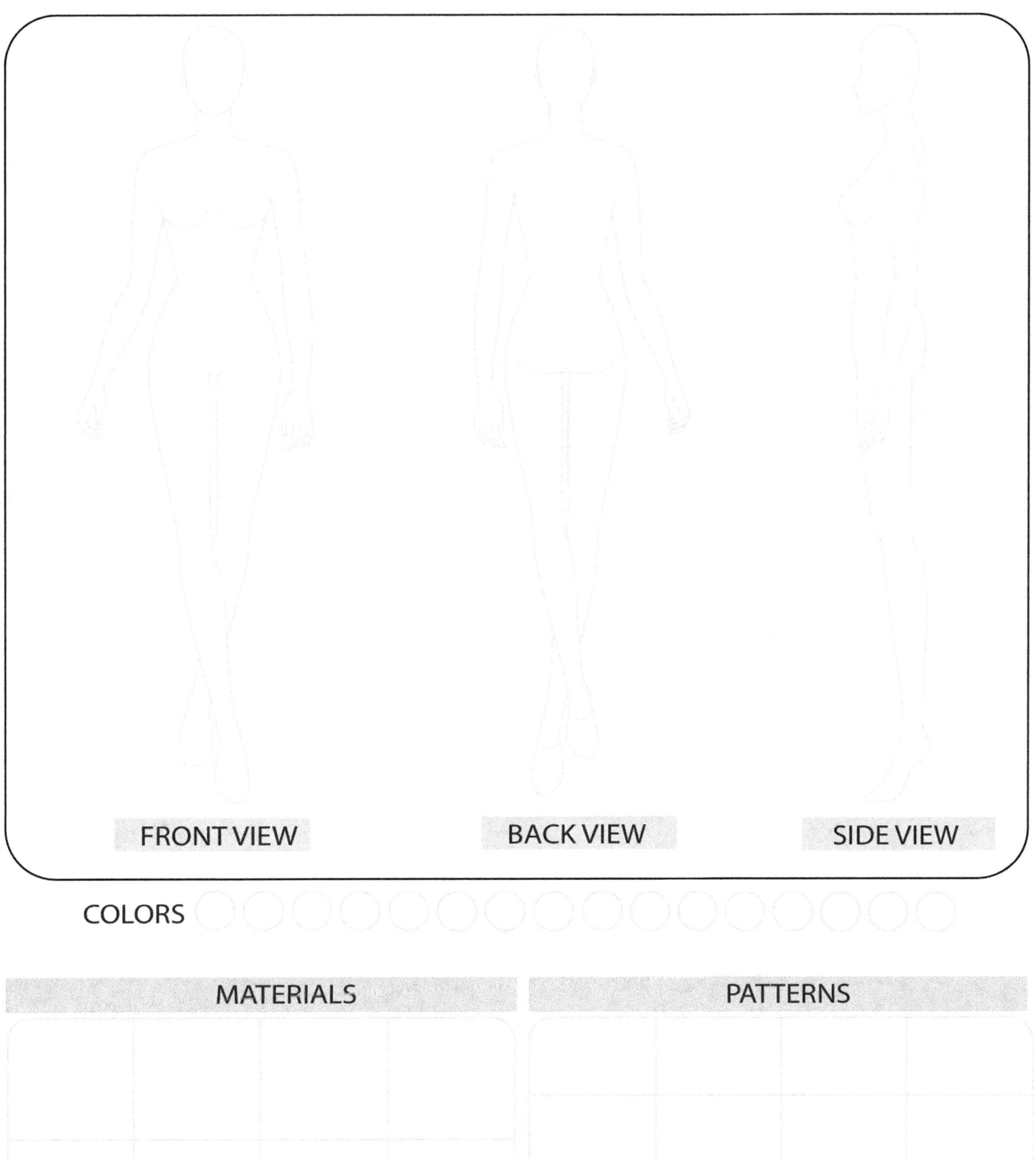

COLORS

MATERIALS

PATTERNS

ACCESSORIES

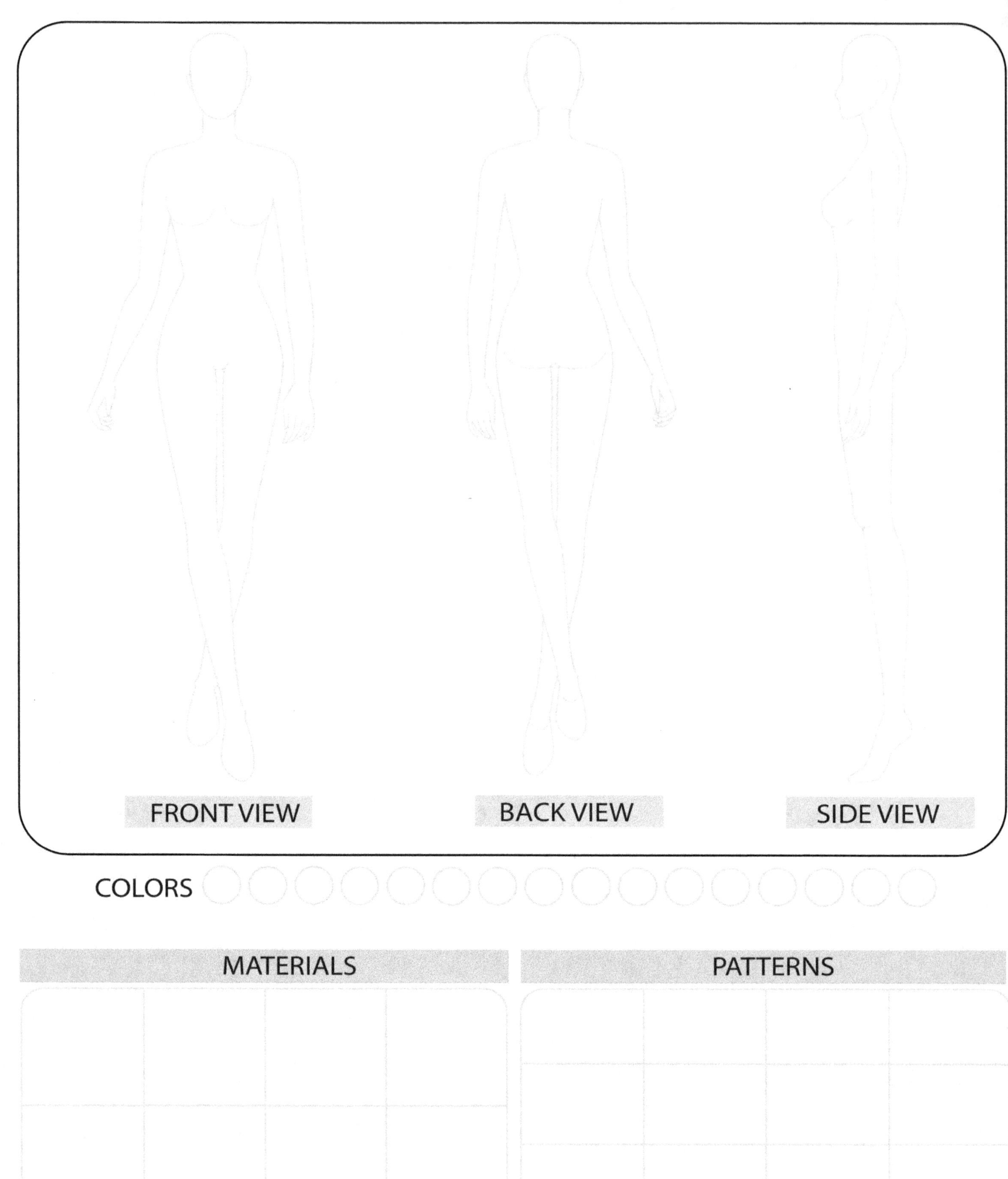

FRONT VIEW

BACK VIEW

SIDE VIEW

COLORS

MATERIALS

PATTERNS

ACCESSORIES

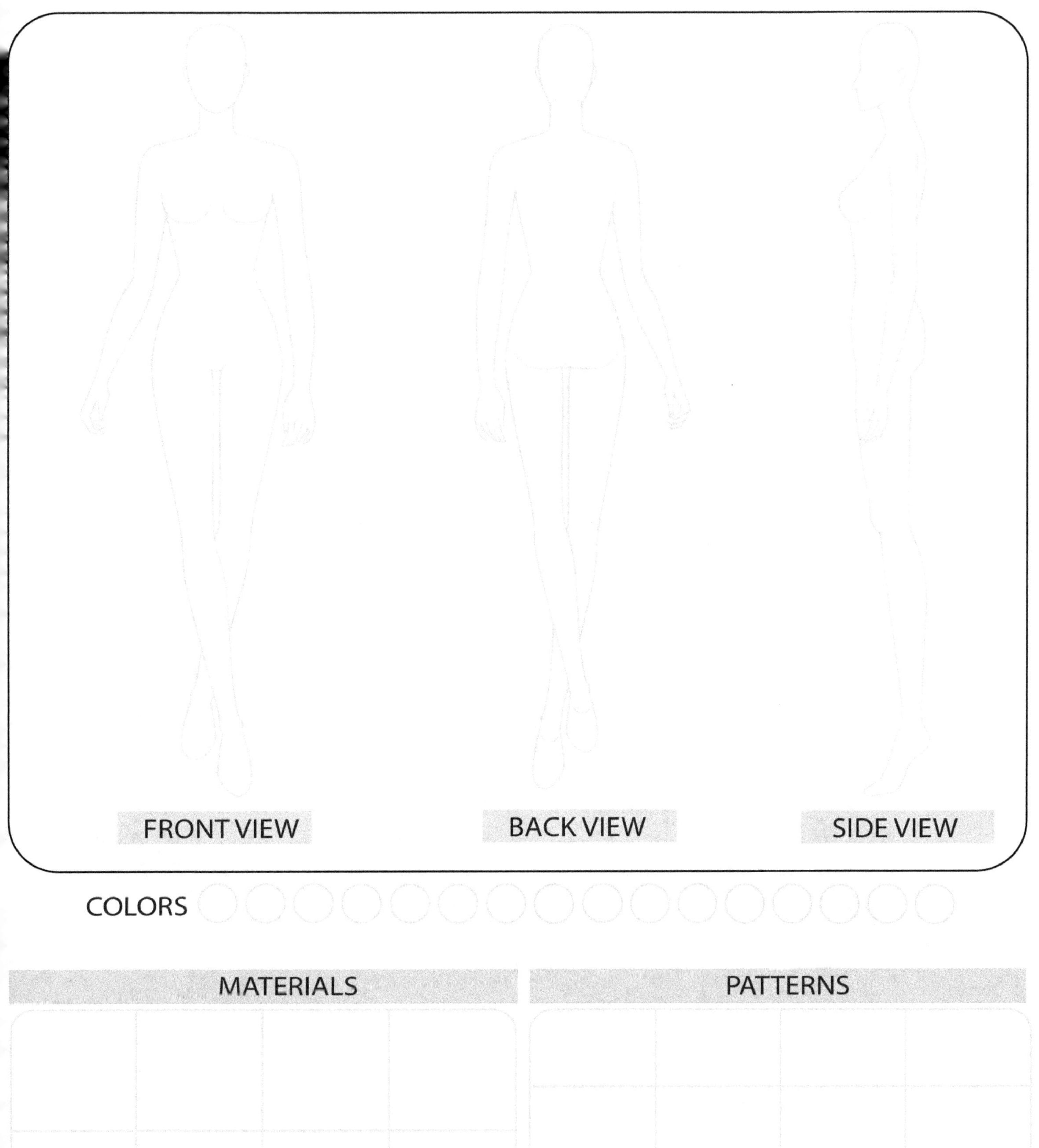

COLORS ○ ○ ○ ○ ○ ○ ○ ○ ○ ○ ○ ○ ○ ○ ○

MATERIALS

PATTERNS

ACCESSORIES

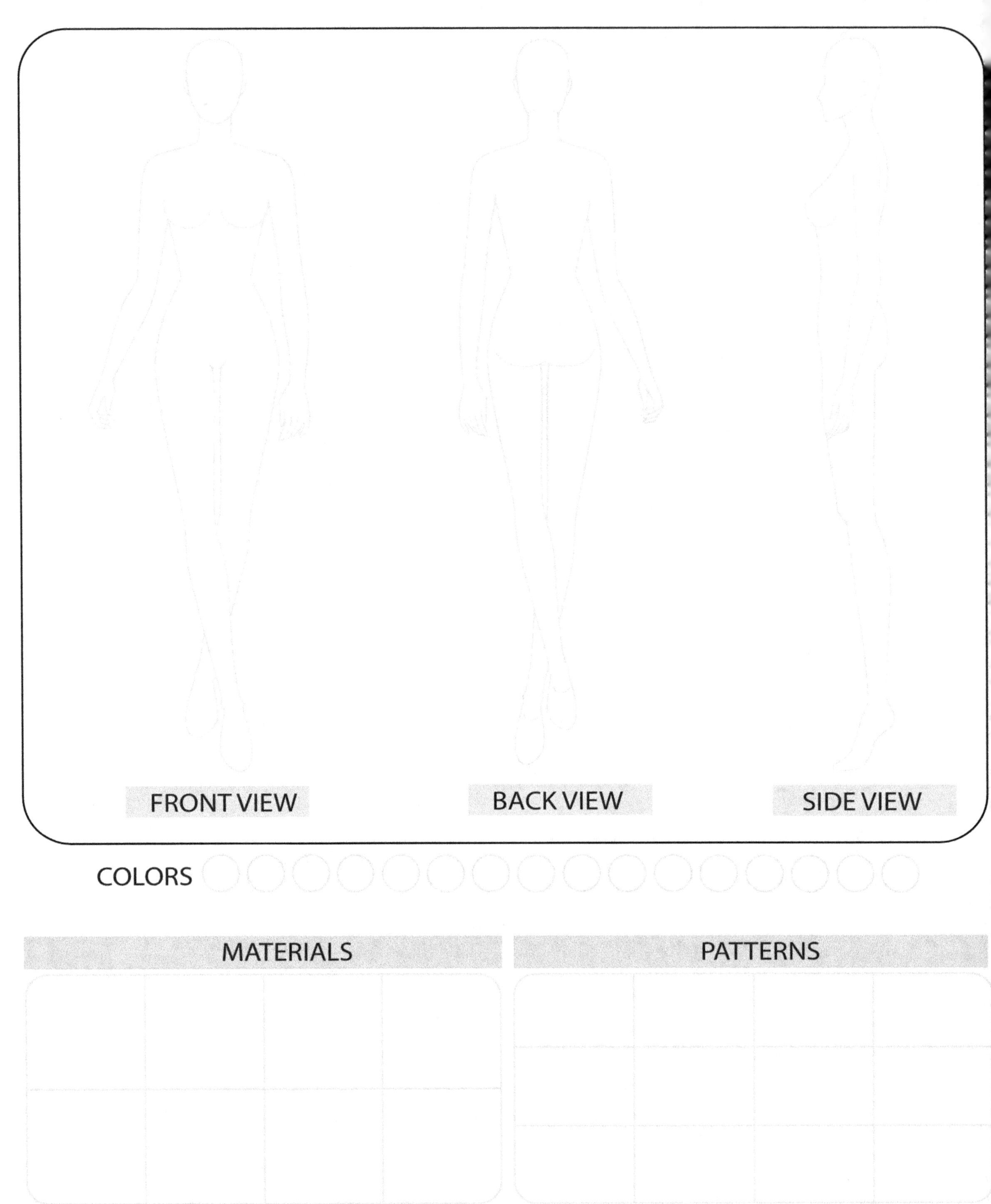

FRONT VIEW
BACK VIEW
SIDE VIEW
COLORS
MATERIALS
PATTERNS
ACCESSORIES

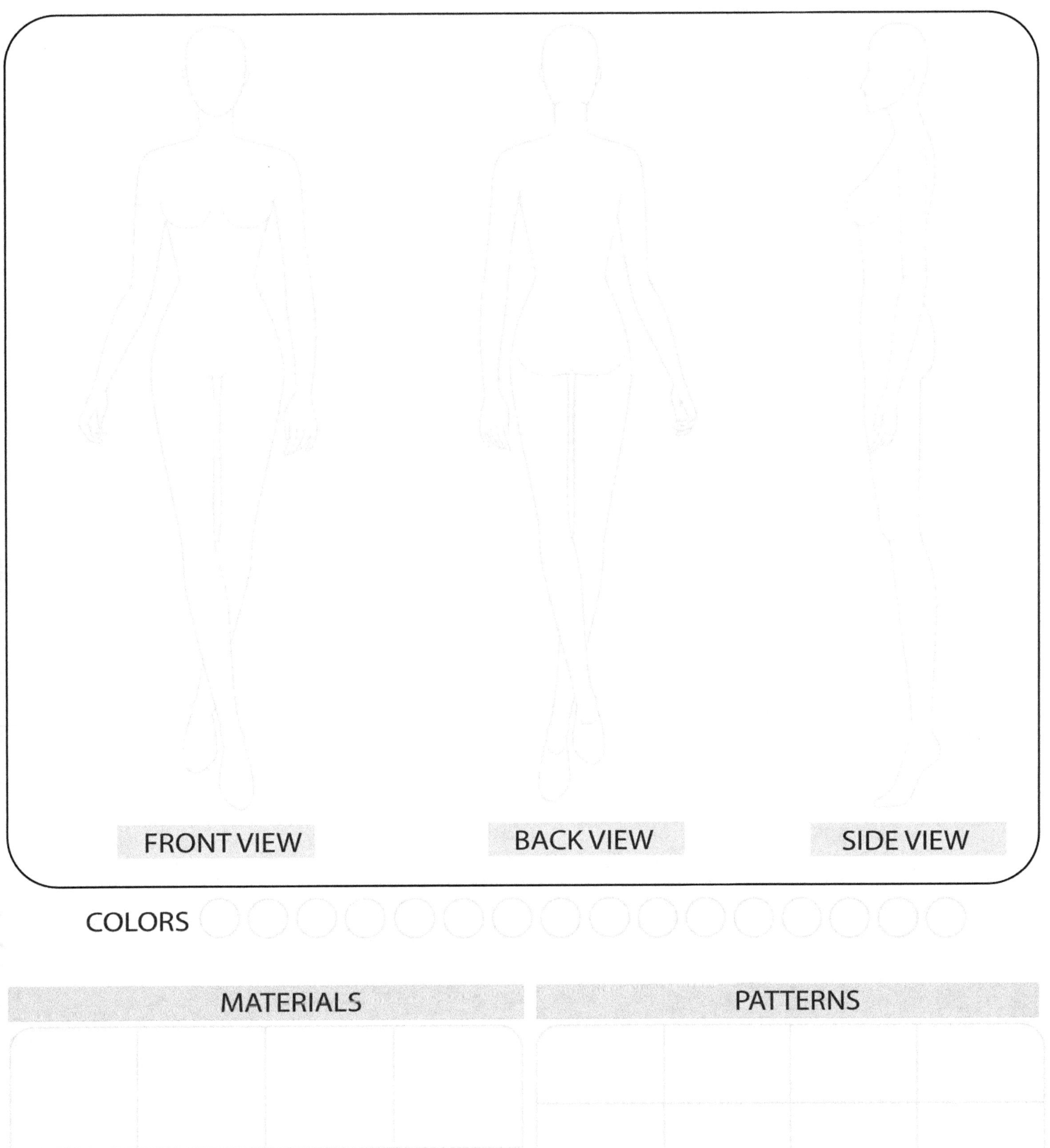

COLORS

MATERIALS

PATTERNS

ACCESSORIES

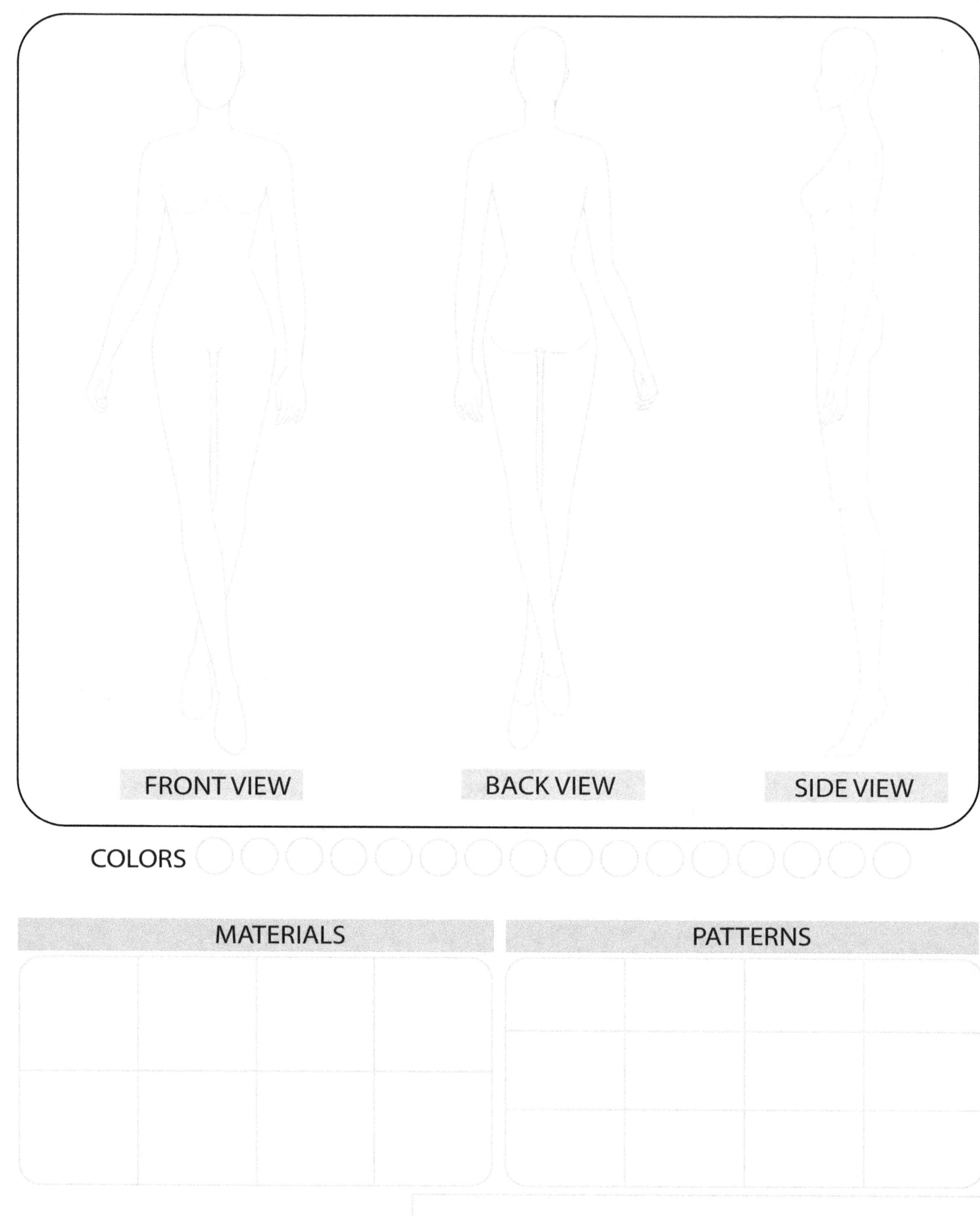

FRONT VIEW
BACK VIEW
SIDE VIEW
COLORS
MATERIALS
PATTERNS
ACCESSORIES

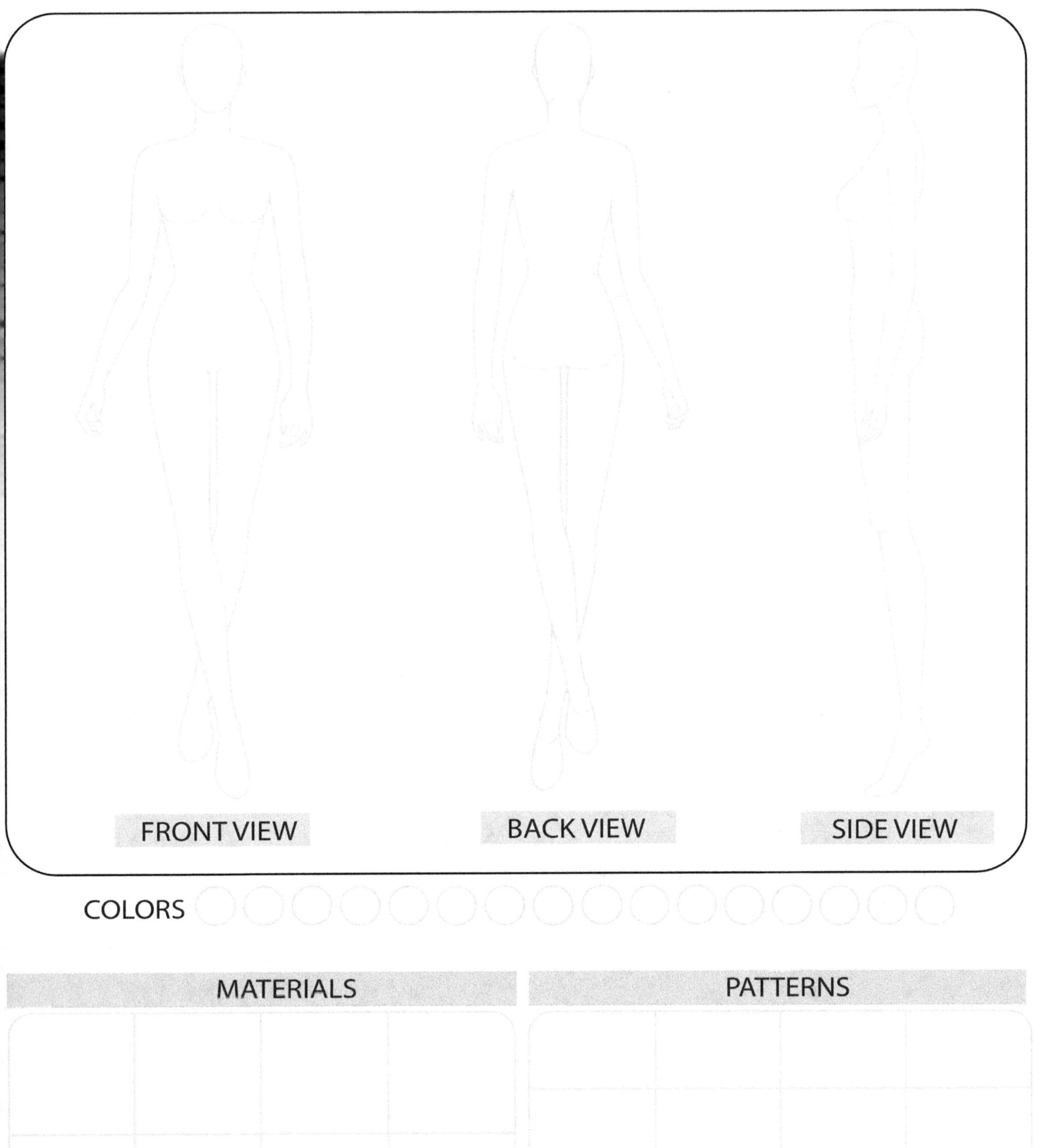

FRONT VIEW

BACK VIEW

SIDE VIEW

COLORS

MATERIALS

PATTERNS

ACCESSORIES

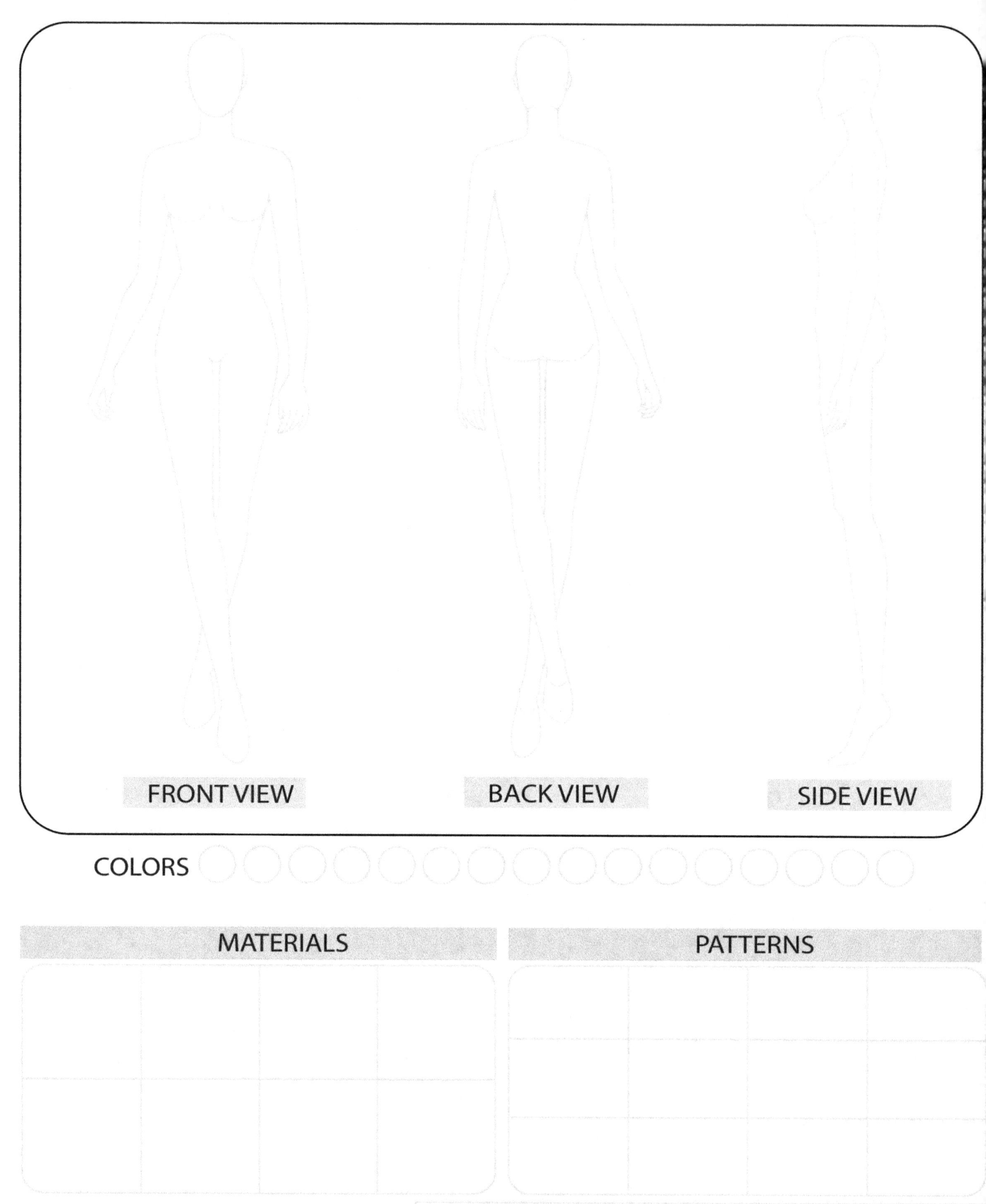

FRONT VIEW
BACK VIEW
SIDE VIEW
COLORS
MATERIALS
PATTERNS
ACCESSORIES

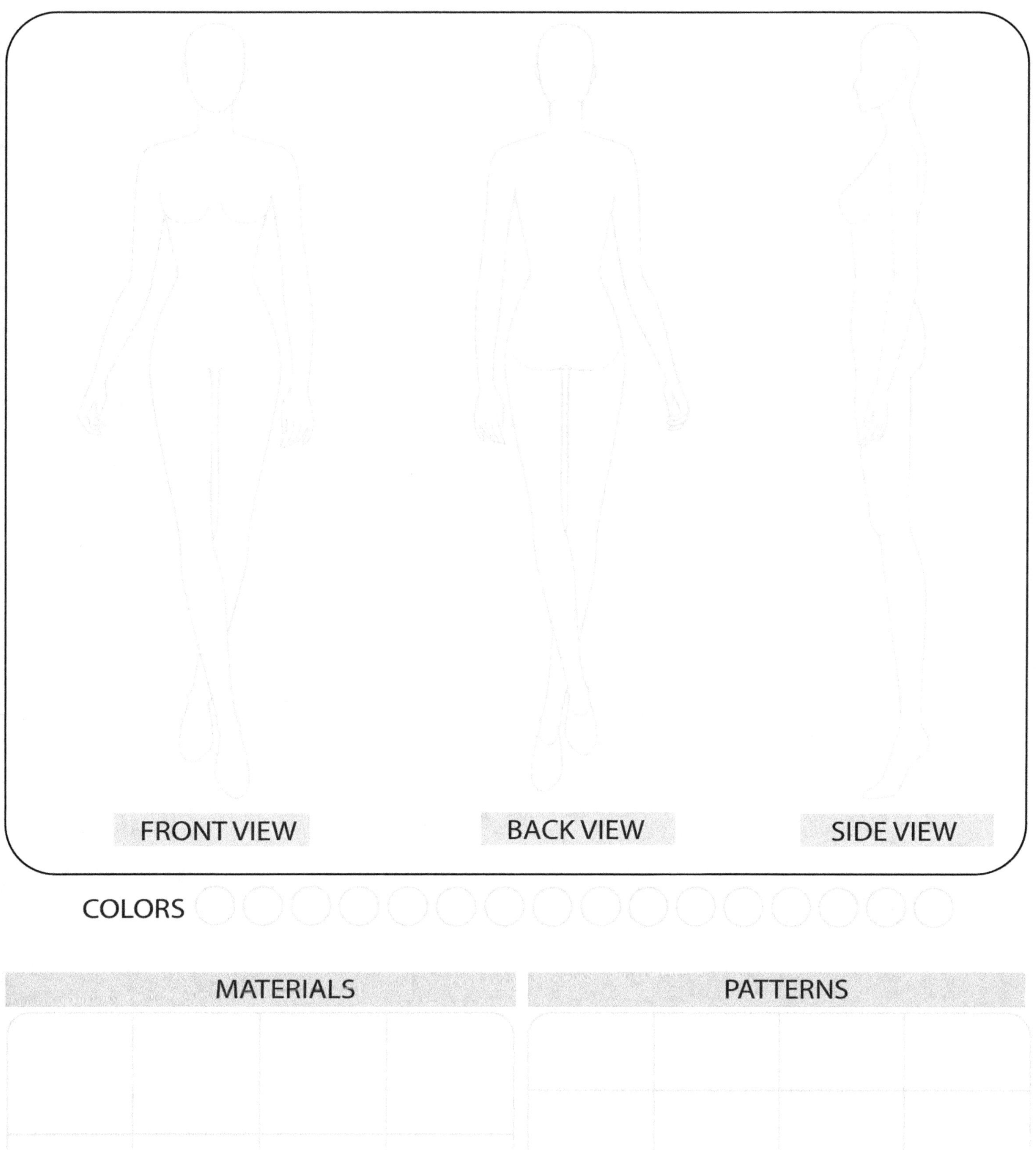

COLORS

MATERIALS

PATTERNS

ACCESSORIES

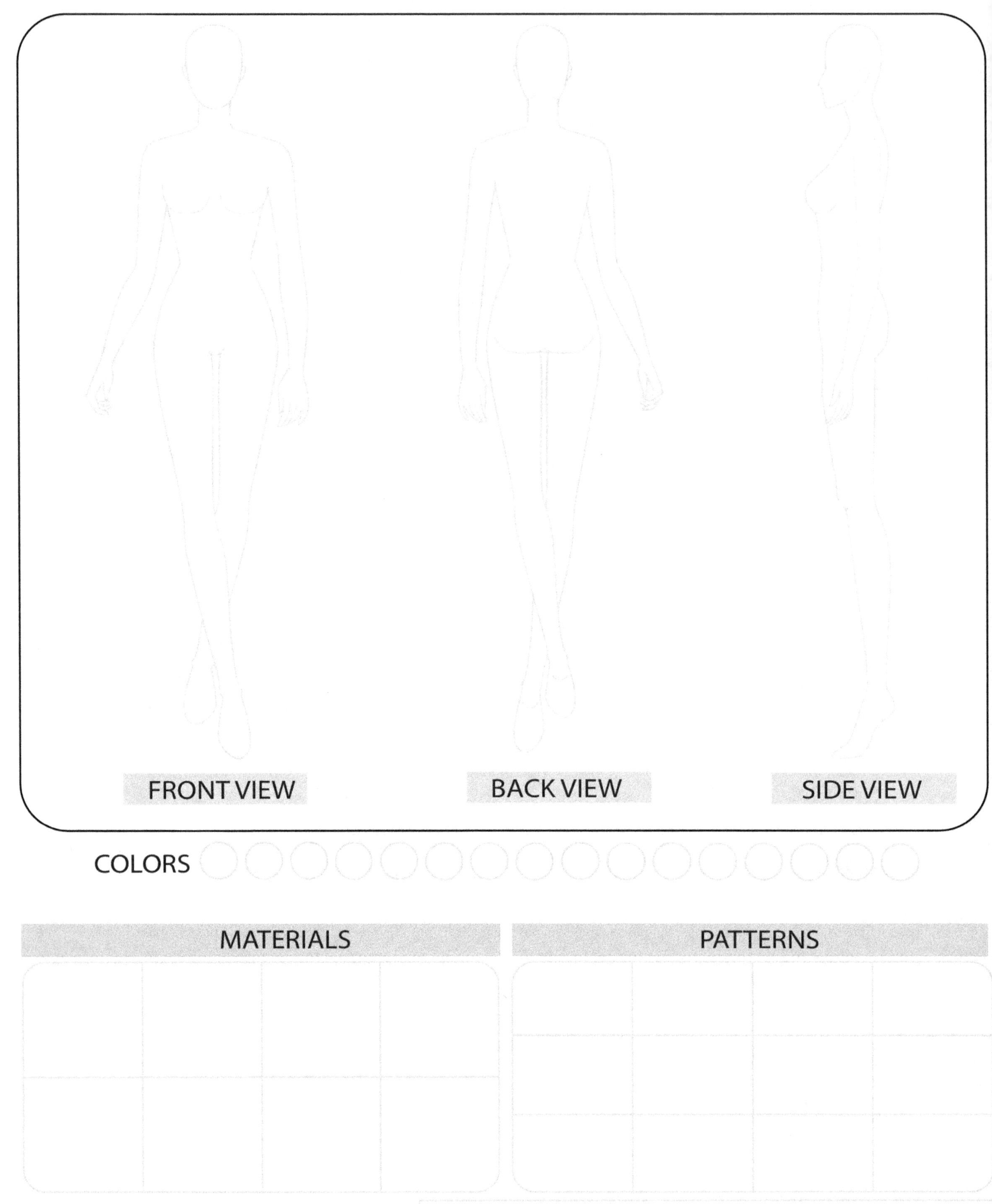

FRONT VIEW

BACK VIEW

SIDE VIEW

COLORS

MATERIALS

PATTERNS

ACCESSORIES

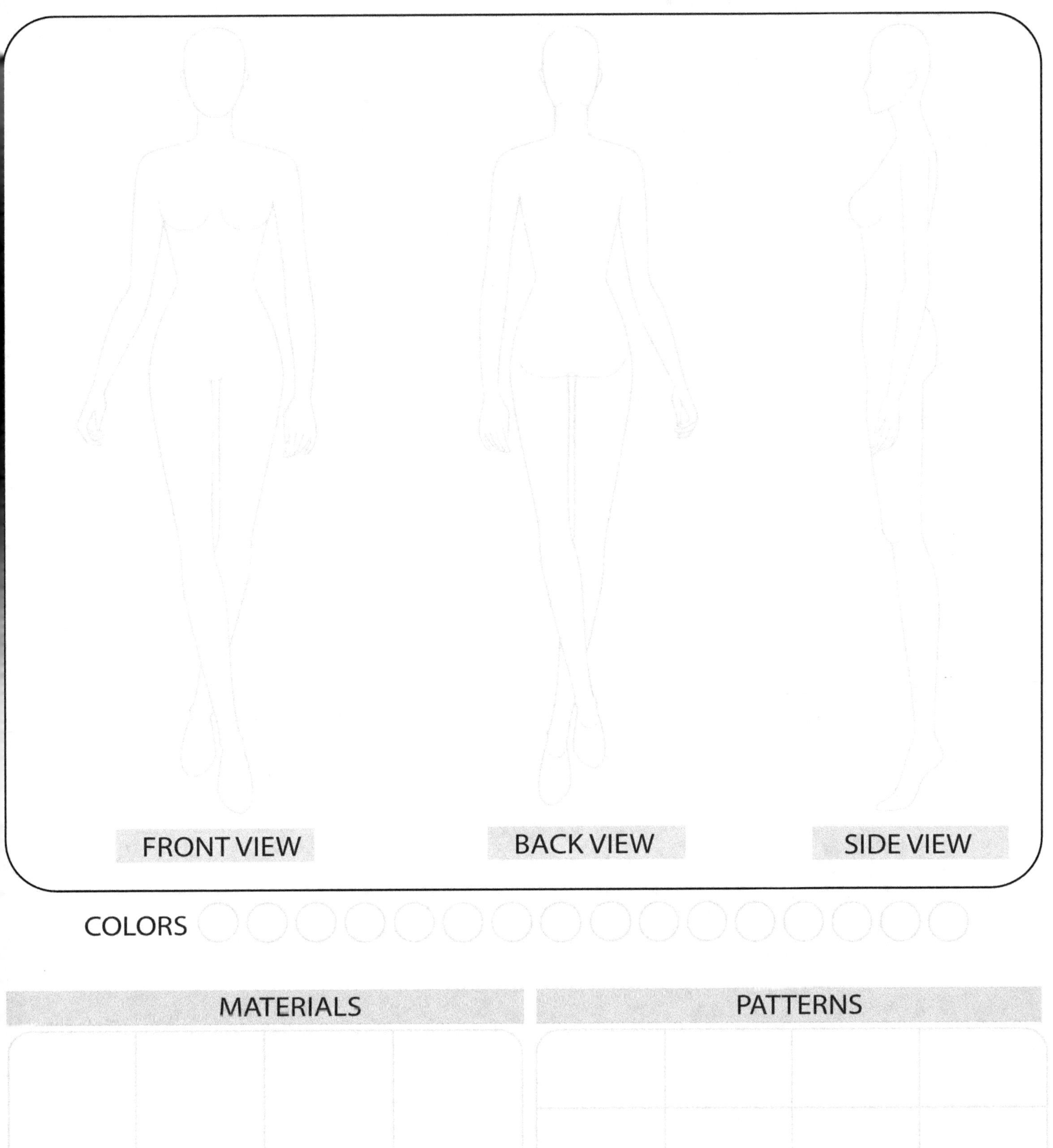

COLORS

MATERIALS

PATTERNS

ACCESSORIES

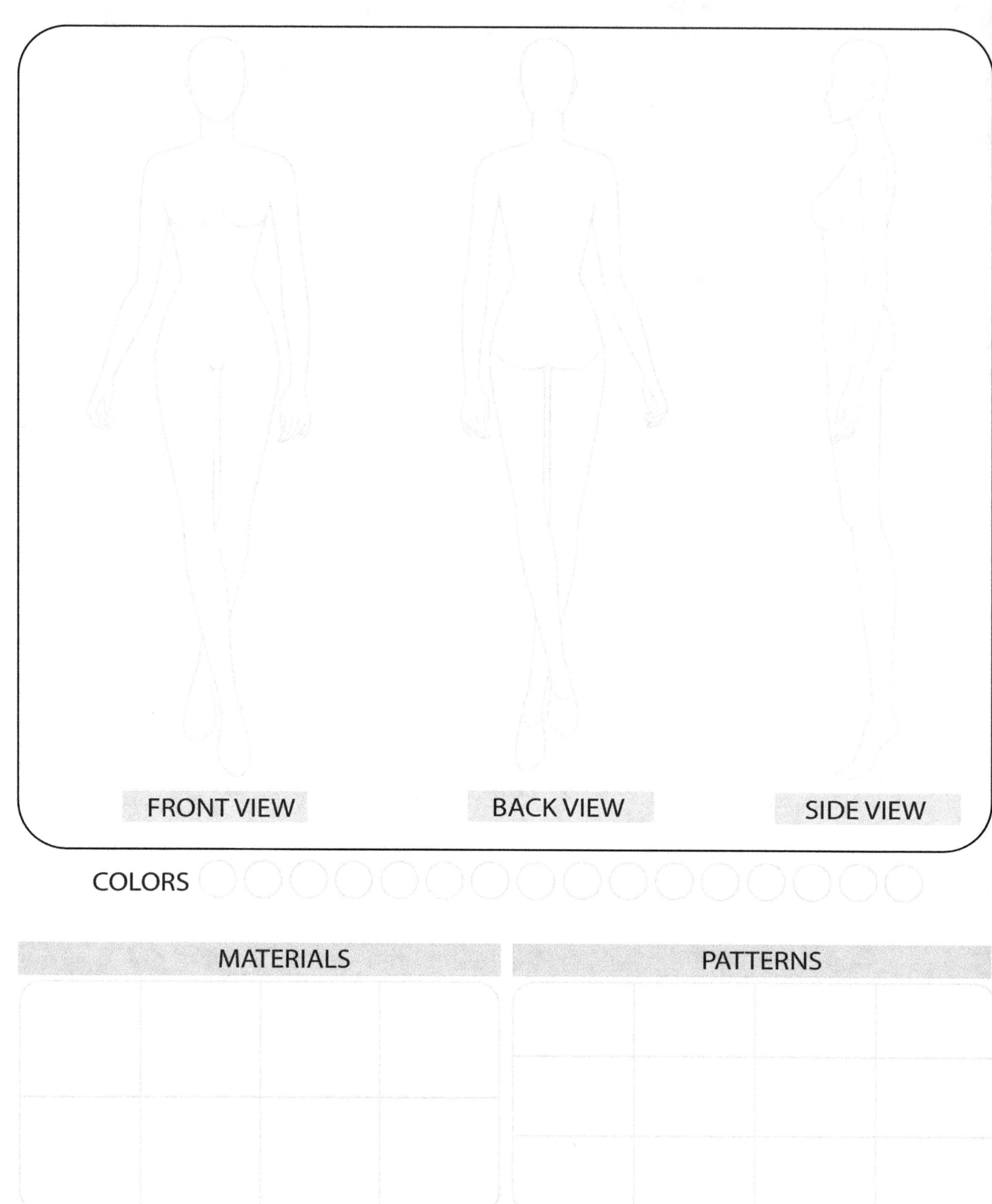

FRONT VIEW
BACK VIEW
SIDE VIEW
COLORS
MATERIALS
PATTERNS
ACCESSORIES

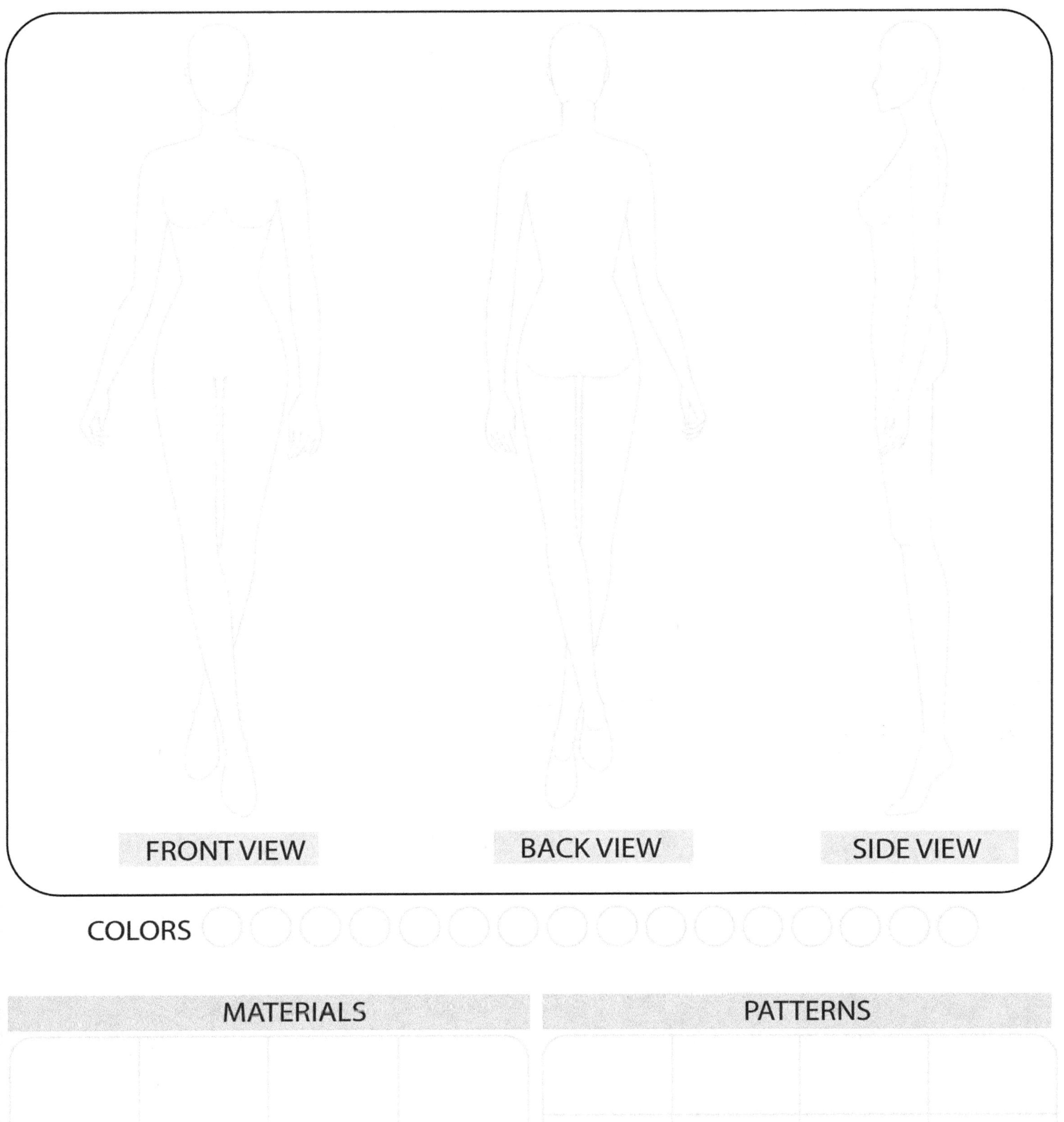

FRONT VIEW

BACK VIEW

SIDE VIEW

COLORS

MATERIALS

PATTERNS

ACCESSORIES

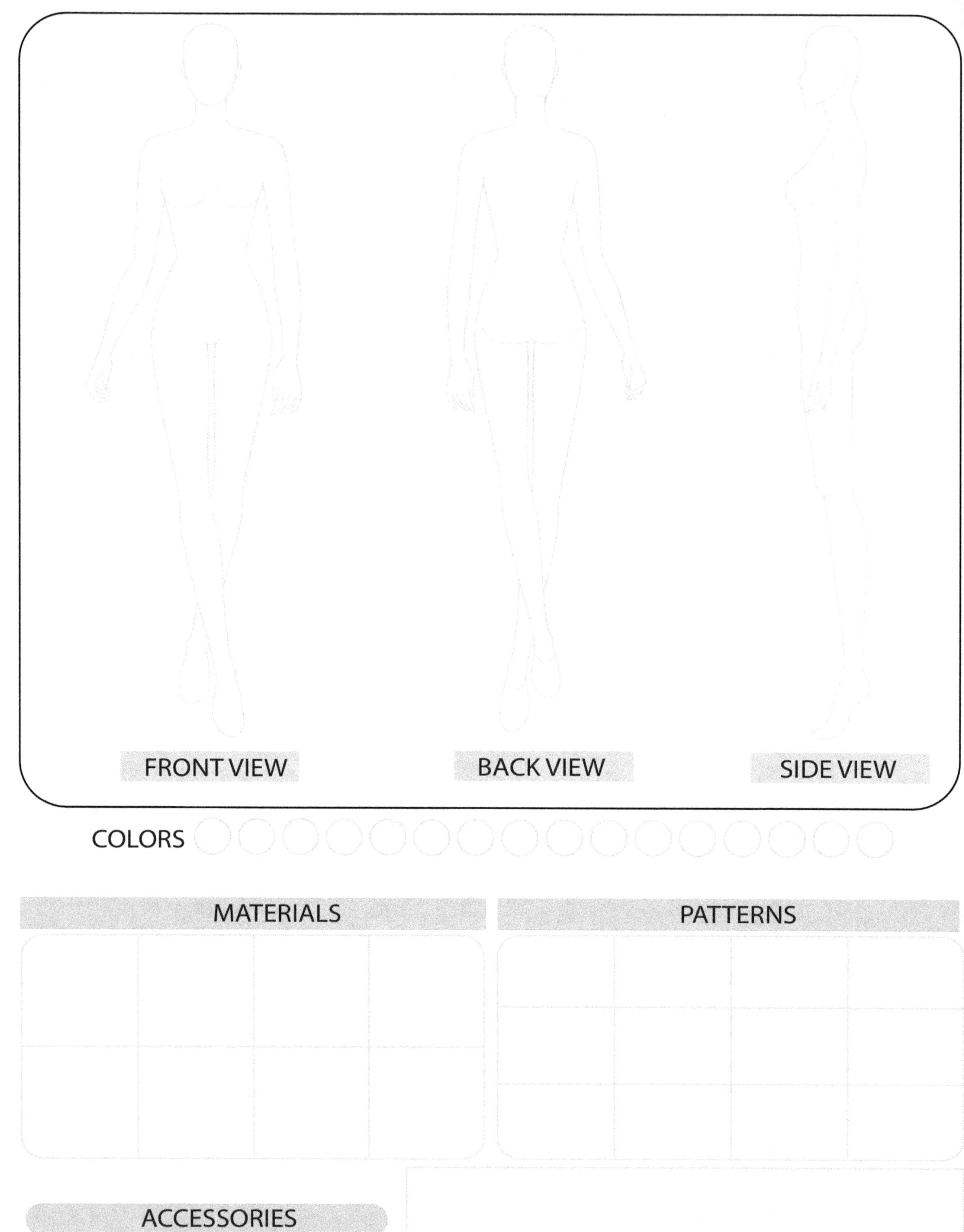

FRONT VIEW
BACK VIEW
SIDE VIEW
COLORS
MATERIALS
PATTERNS
ACCESSORIES

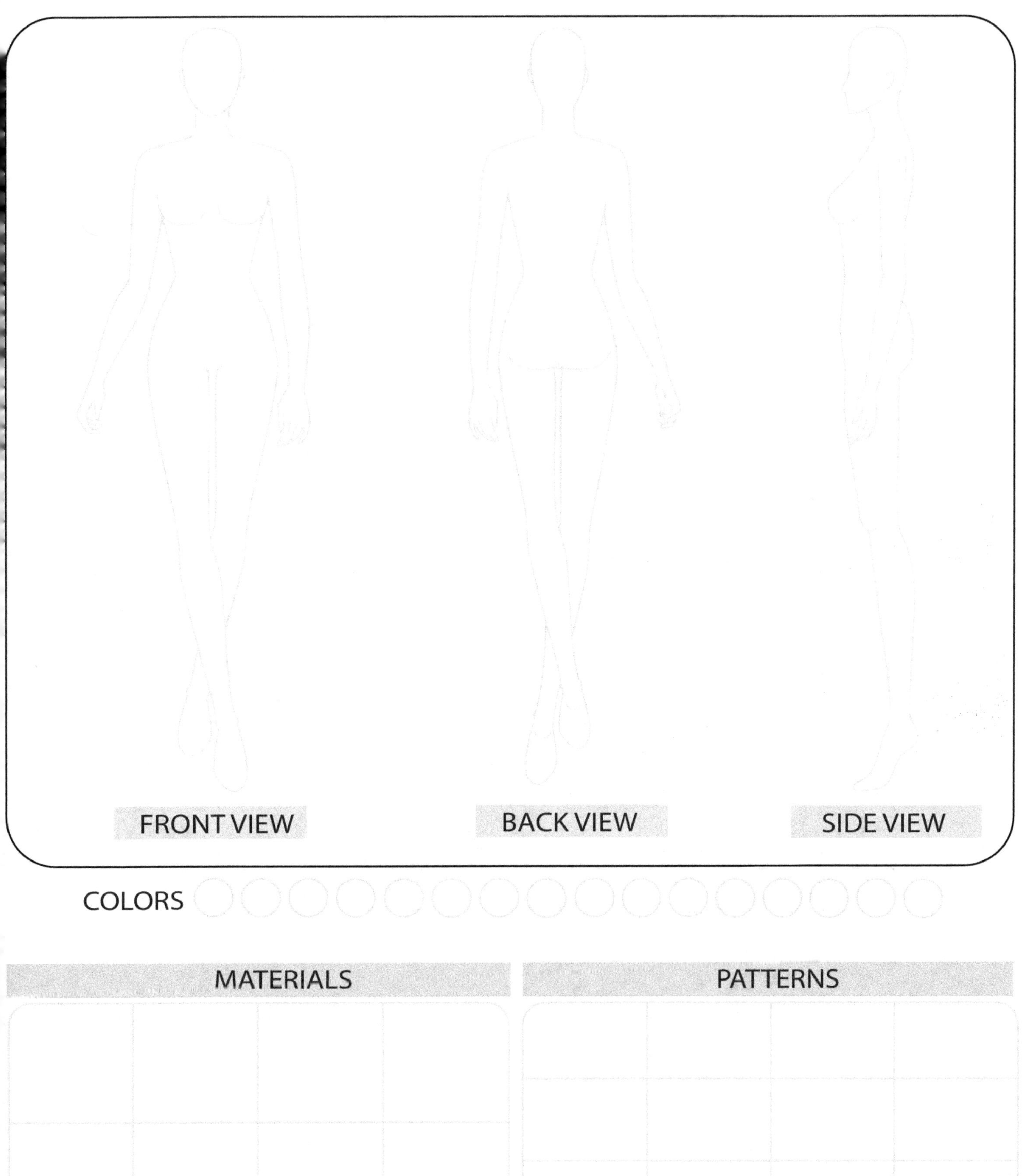

FRONT VIEW

BACK VIEW

SIDE VIEW

COLORS

MATERIALS

PATTERNS

ACCESSORIES

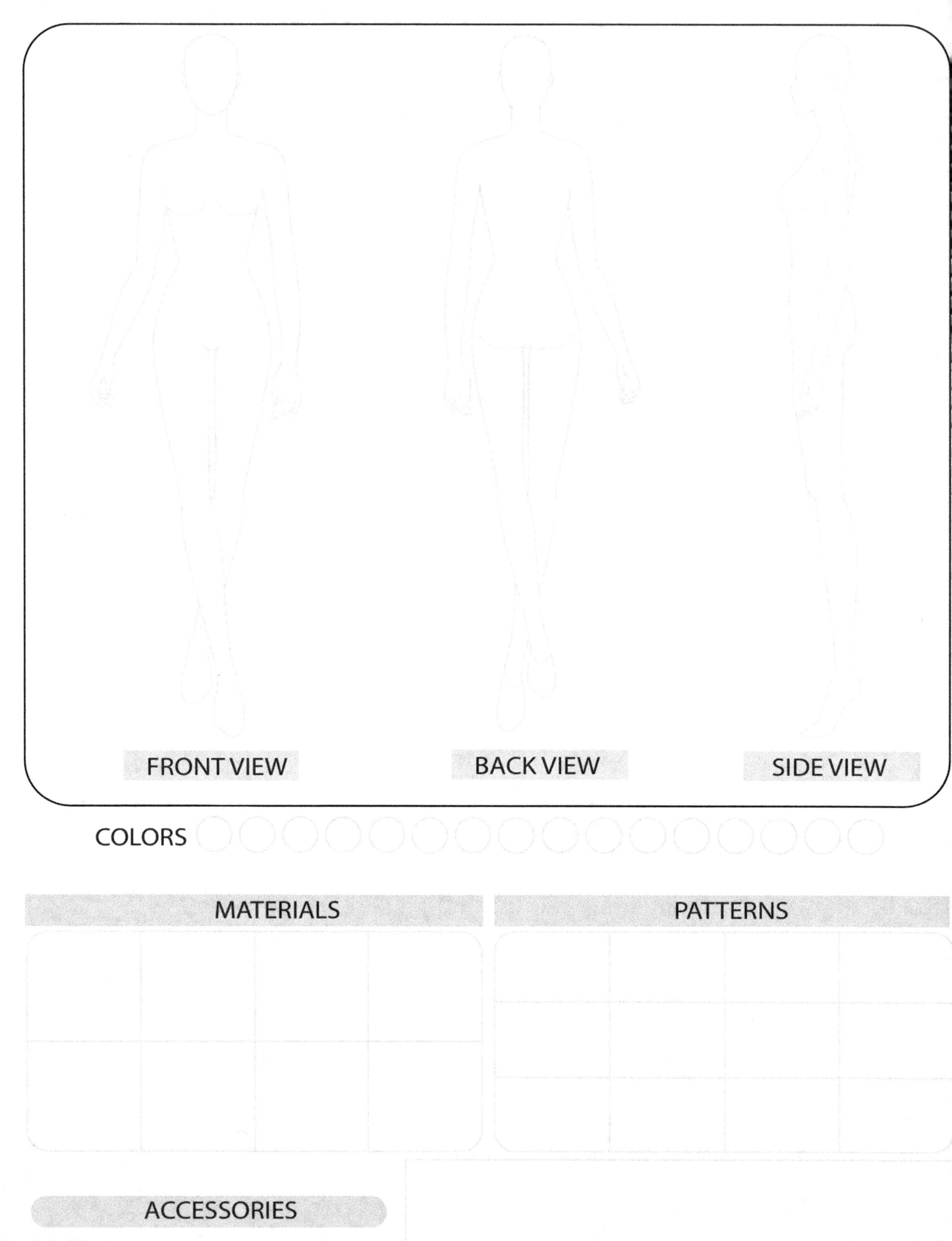

FRONT VIEW
BACK VIEW
SIDE VIEW
COLORS
MATERIALS
PATTERNS
ACCESSORIES

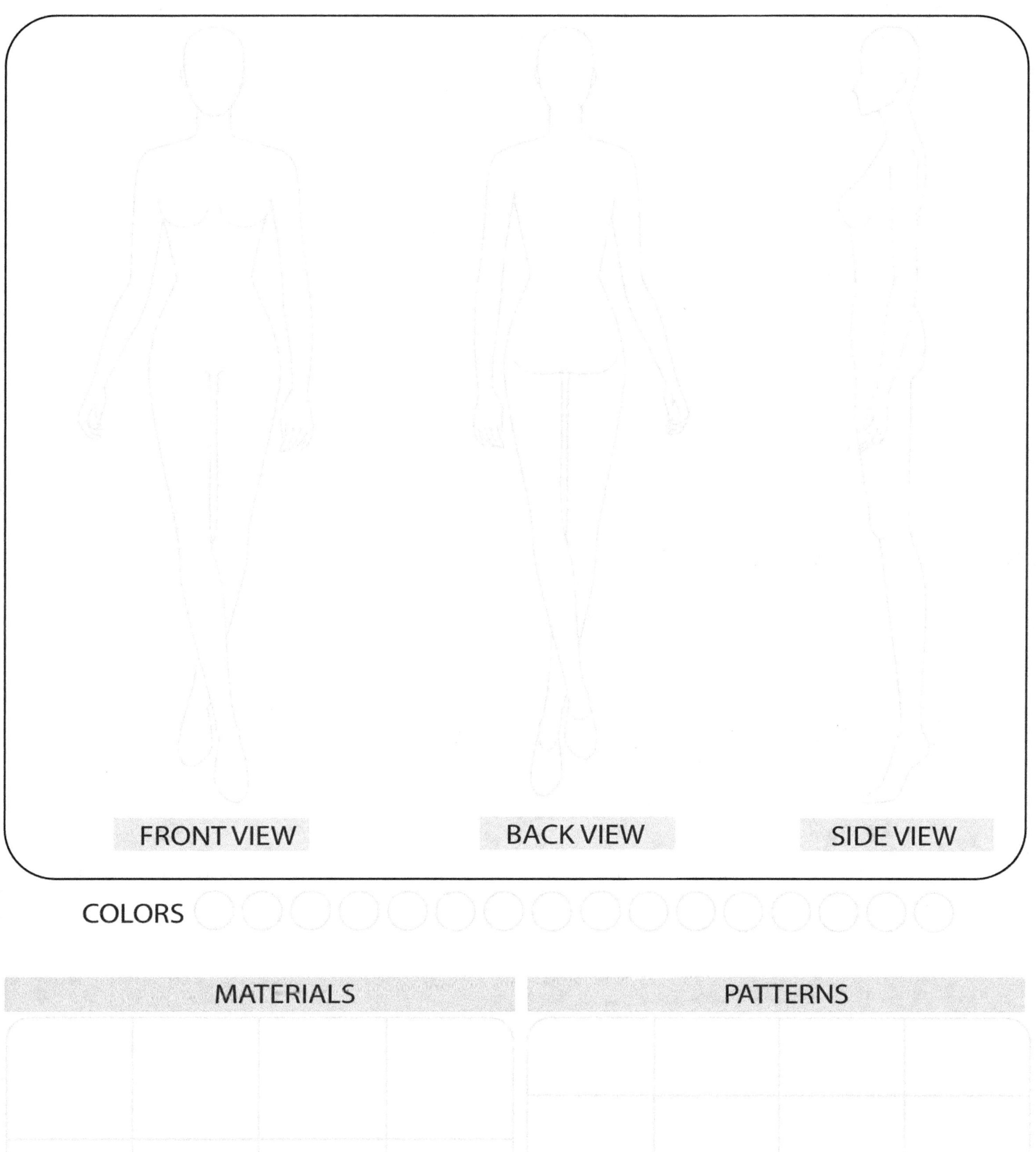

FRONT VIEW
BACK VIEW
SIDE VIEW
COLORS
MATERIALS
PATTERNS
ACCESSORIES

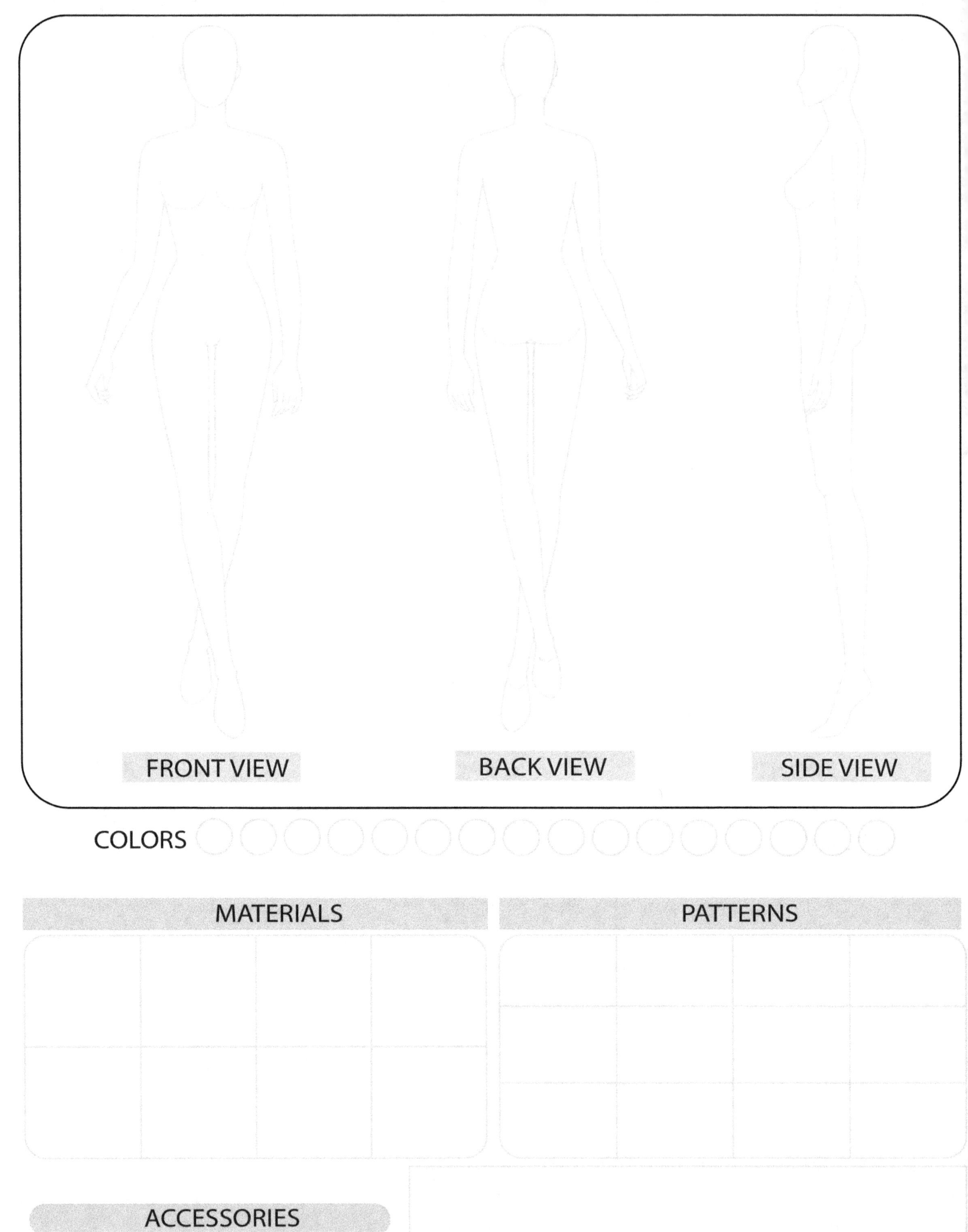
FRONT VIEW
BACK VIEW
SIDE VIEW
COLORS
MATERIALS
PATTERNS
ACCESSORIES

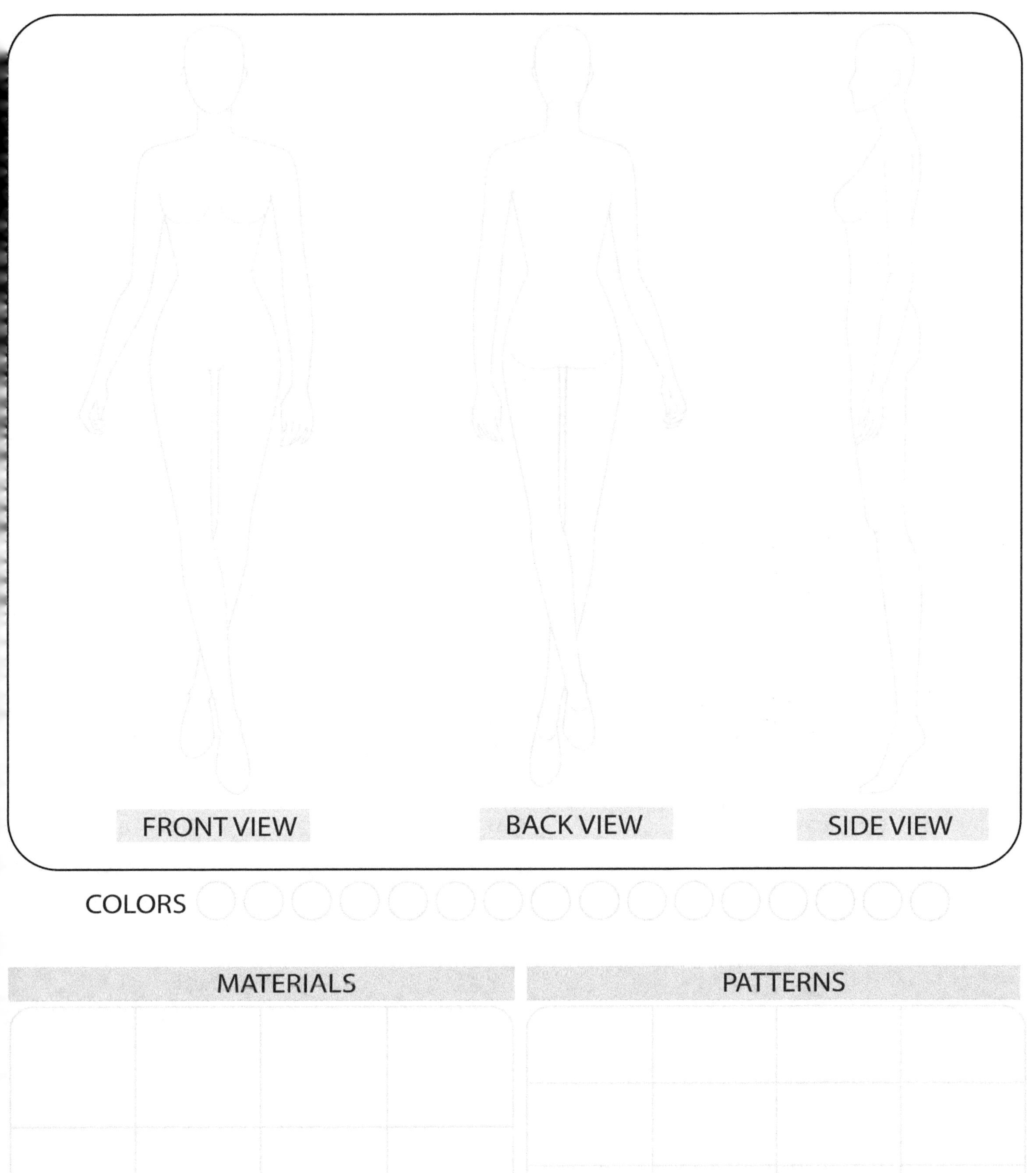

COLORS

MATERIALS

PATTERNS

ACCESSORIES

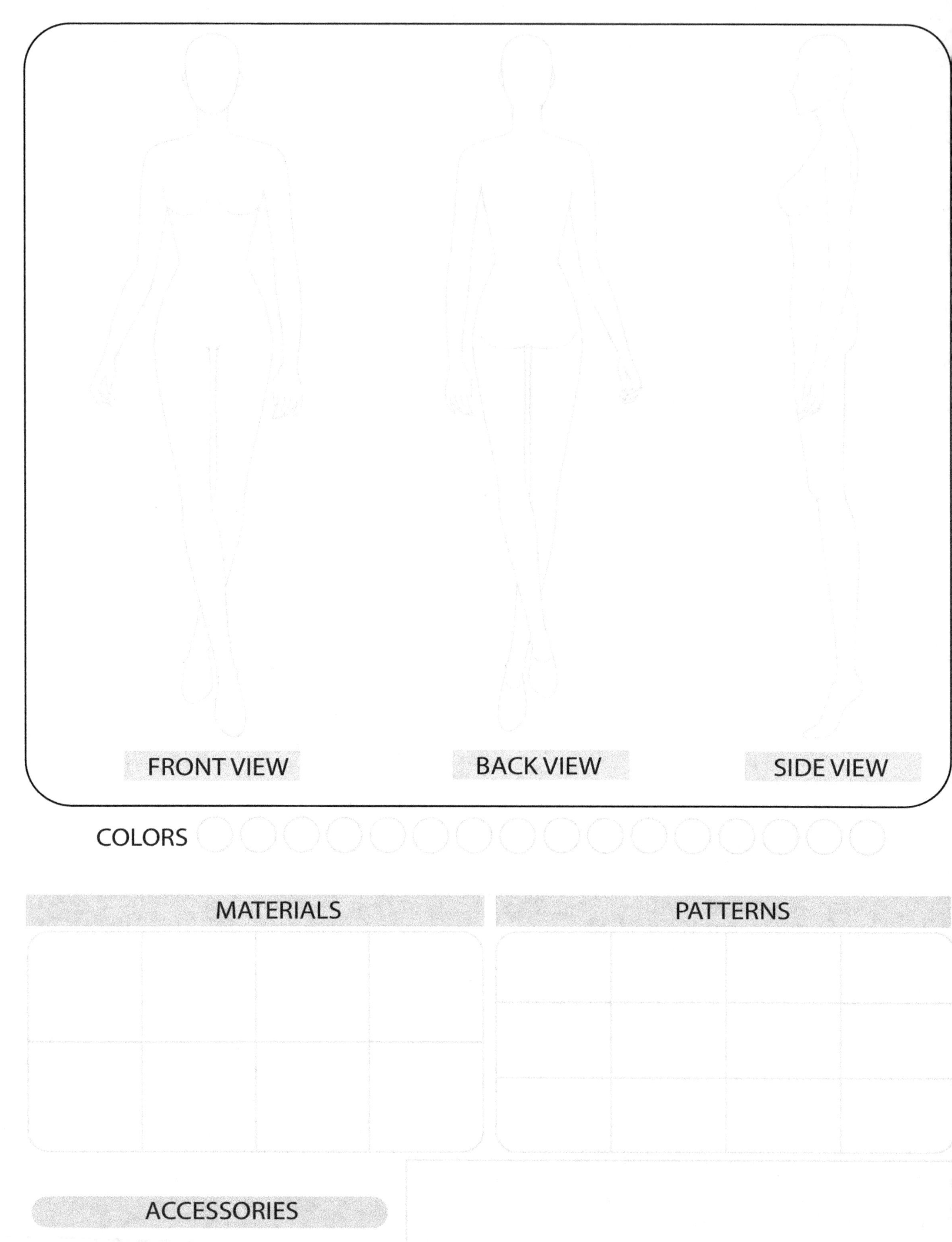

FRONT VIEW
BACK VIEW
SIDE VIEW
COLORS
MATERIALS
PATTERNS
ACCESSORIES

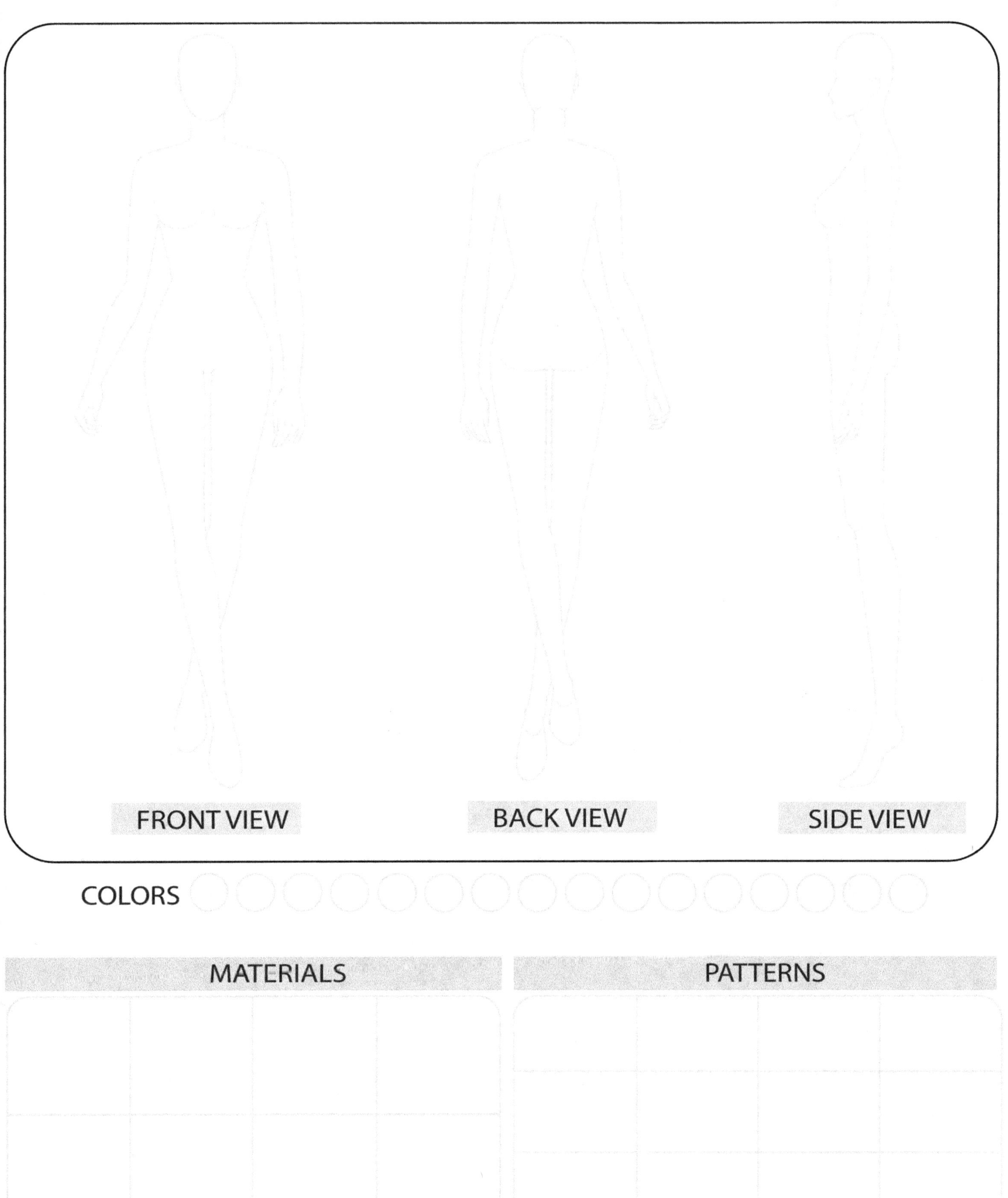

FRONT VIEW
BACK VIEW
SIDE VIEW
COLORS
MATERIALS
PATTERNS
ACCESSORIES

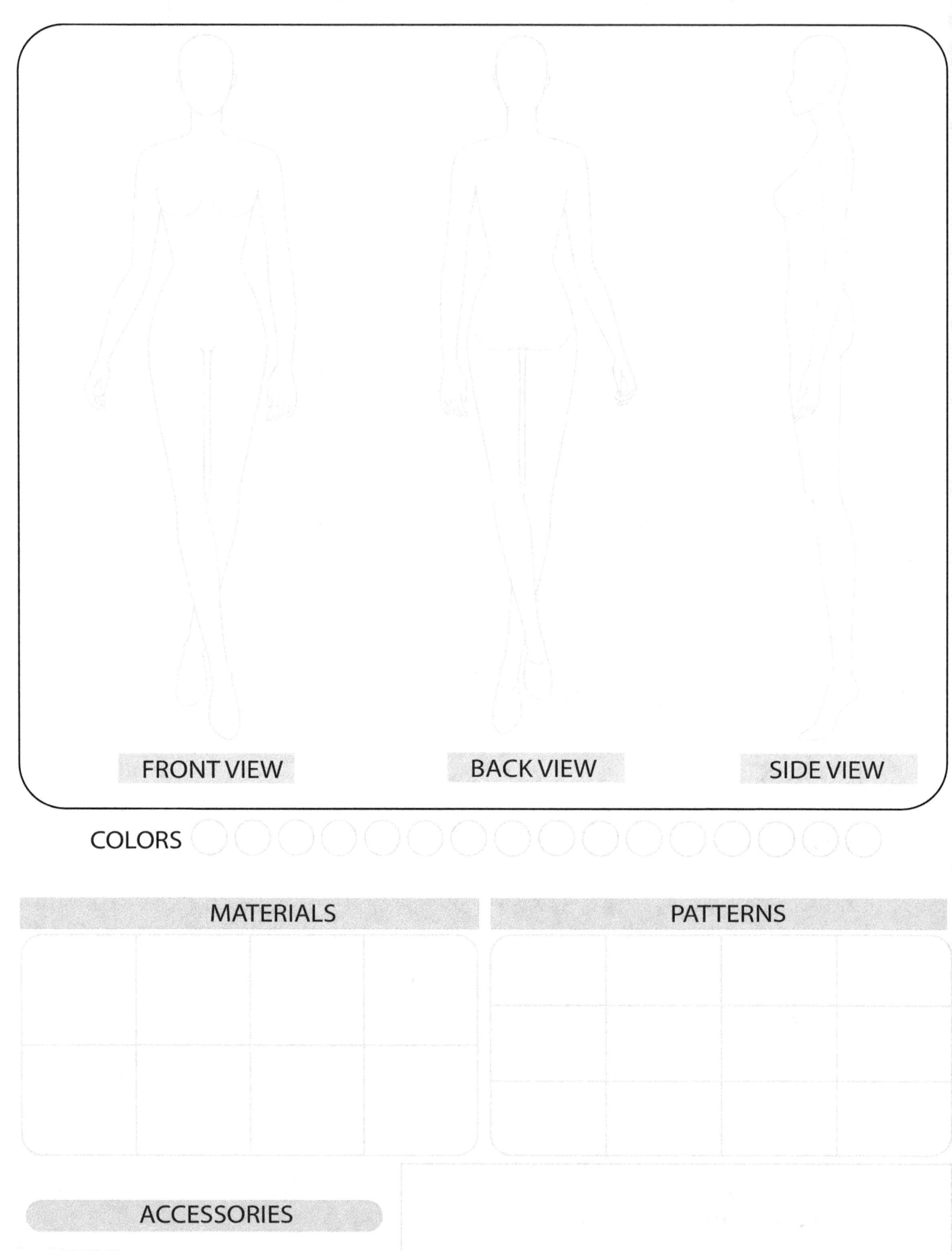

FRONT VIEW
BACK VIEW
SIDE VIEW
COLORS
MATERIALS
PATTERNS
ACCESSORIES

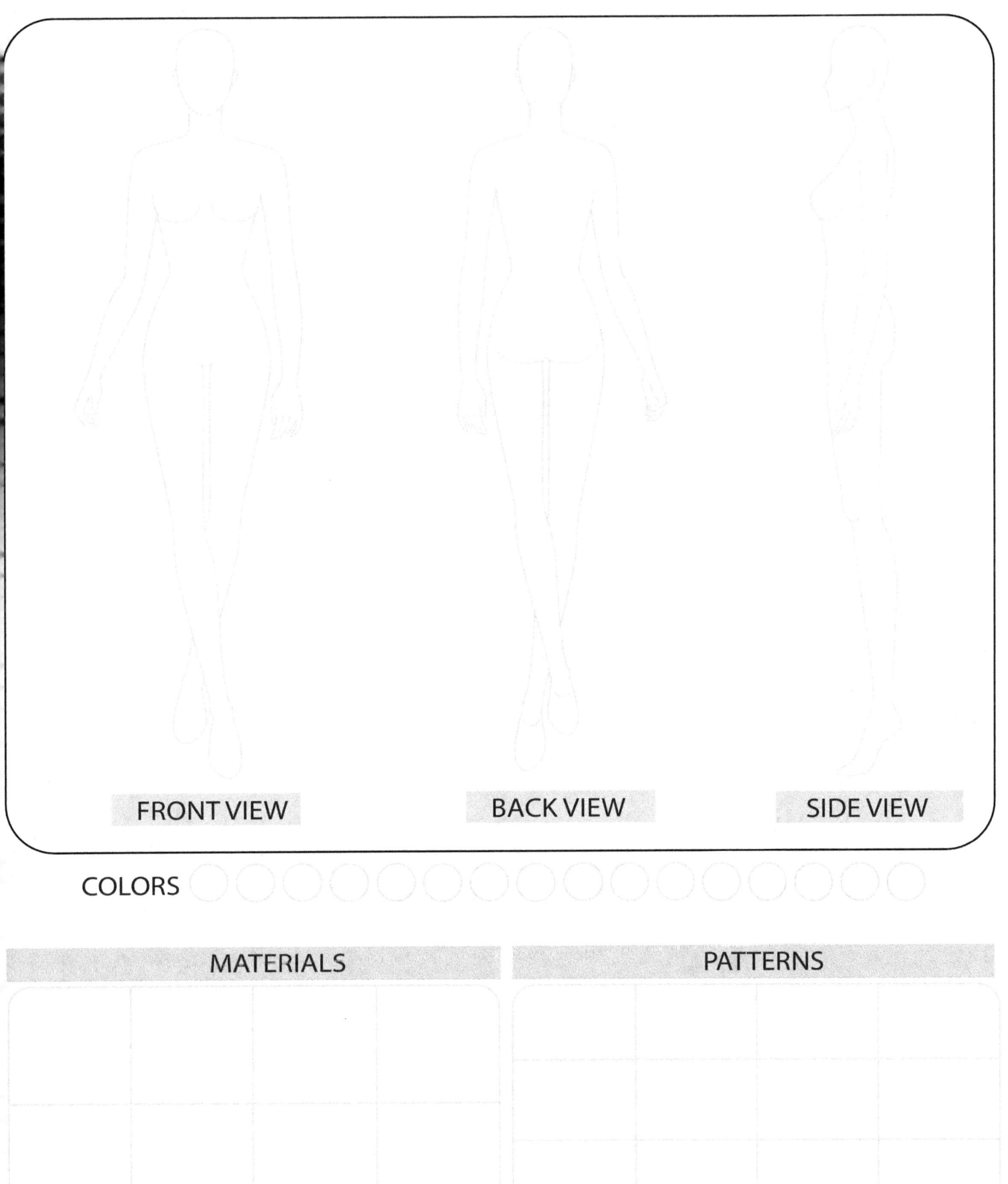

COLORS

MATERIALS

PATTERNS

ACCESSORIES

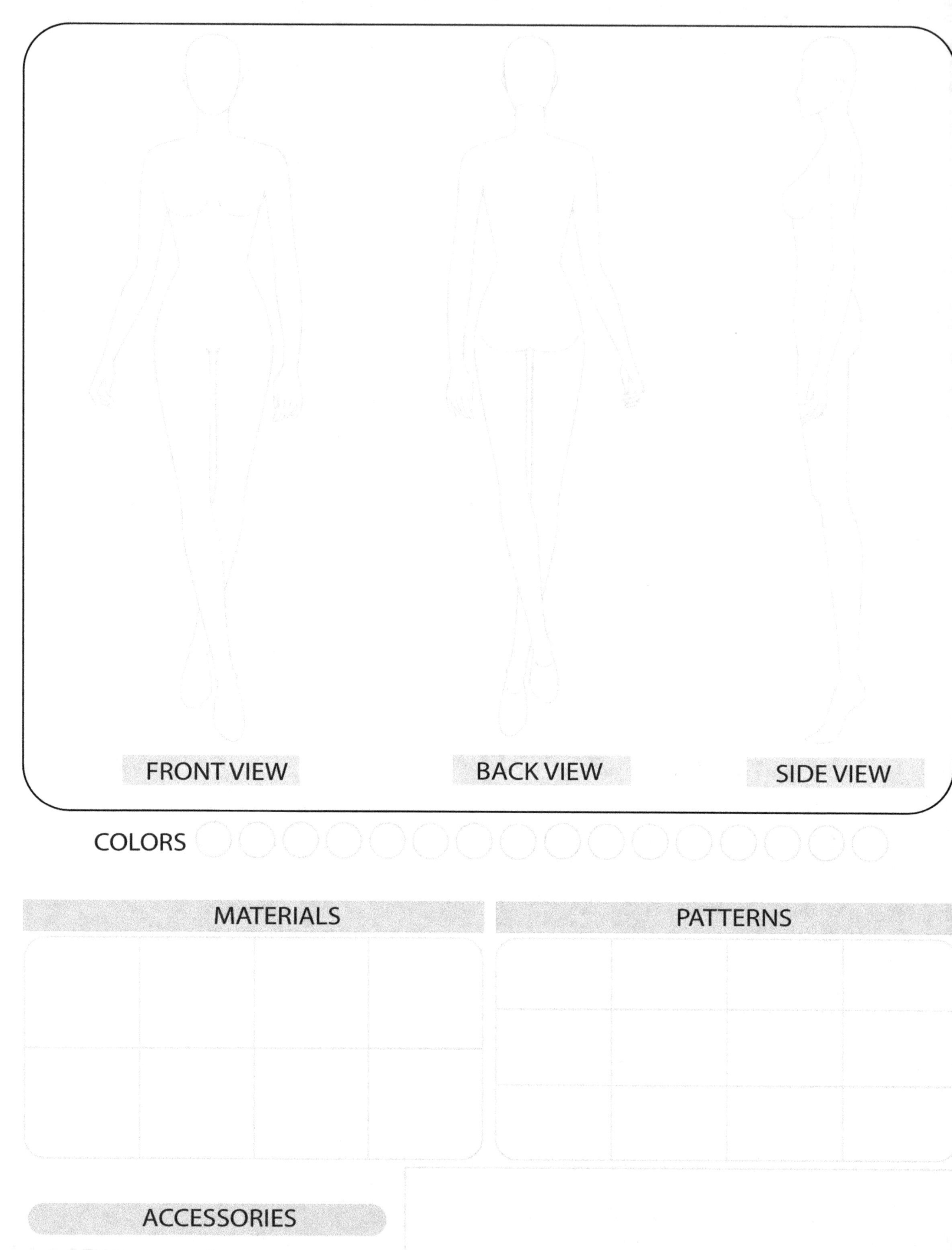

FRONT VIEW
BACK VIEW
SIDE VIEW
COLORS
MATERIALS
PATTERNS
ACCESSORIES

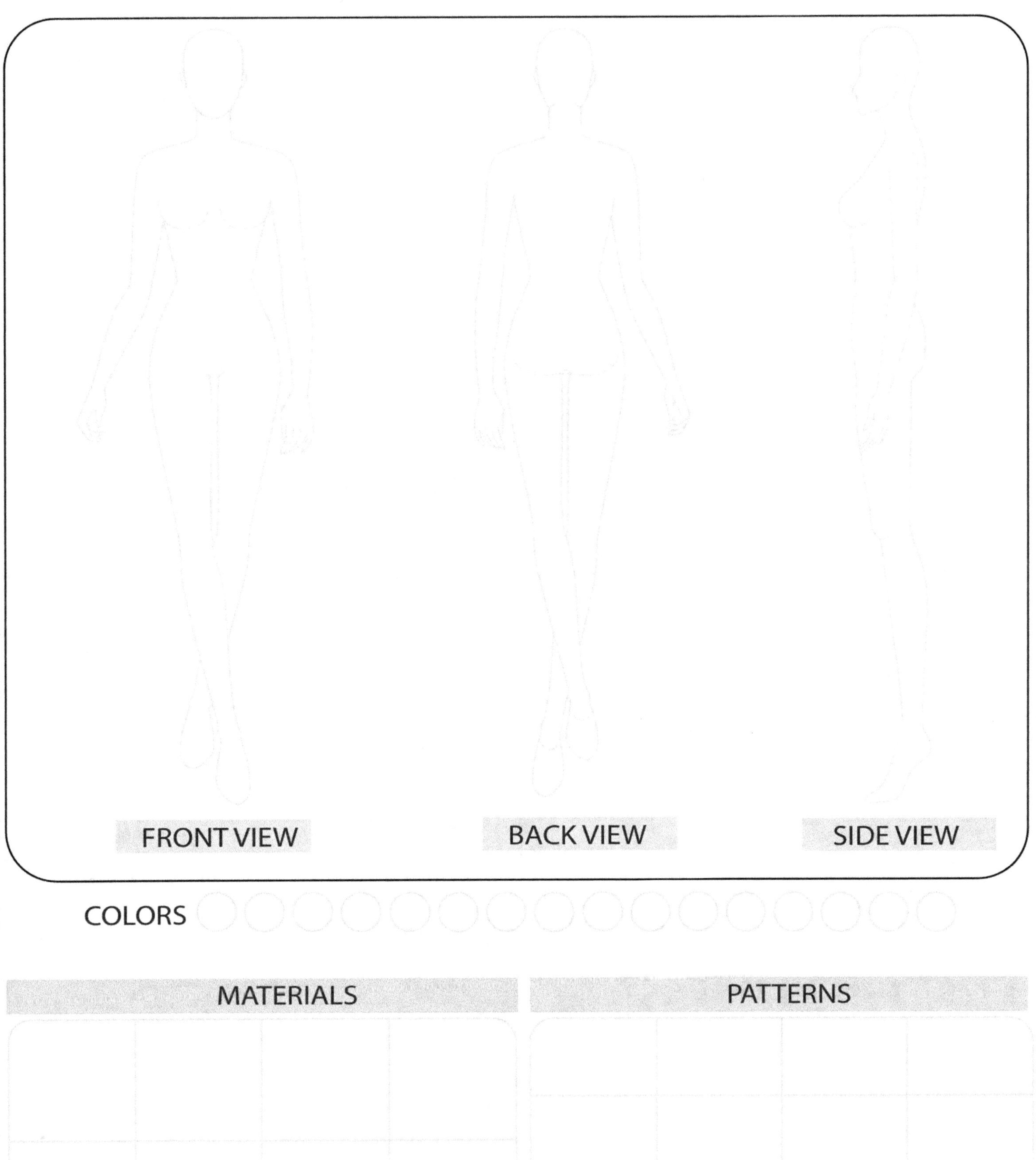

FRONT VIEW
BACK VIEW
SIDE VIEW
COLORS
MATERIALS
PATTERNS
ACCESSORIES

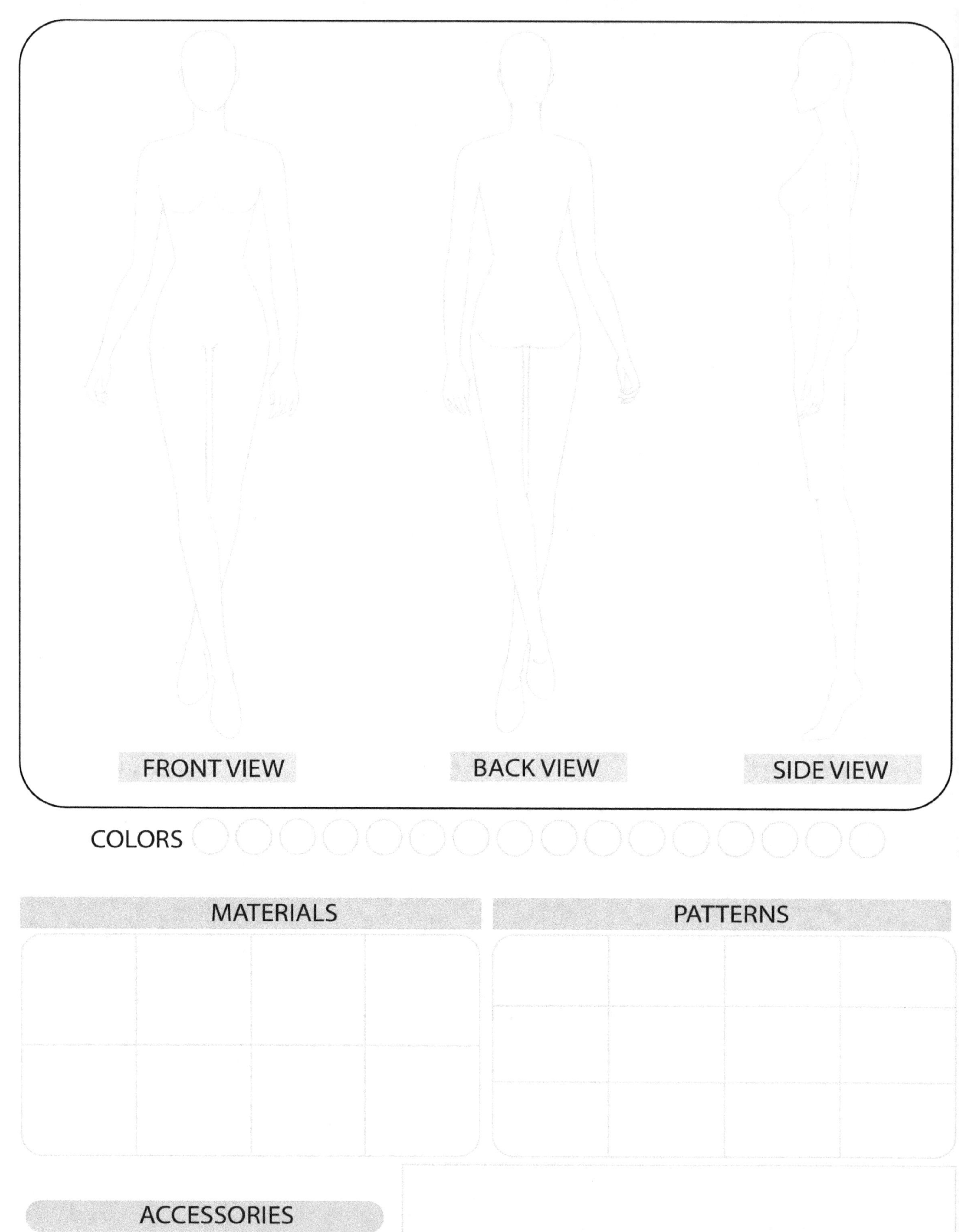

FRONT VIEW
BACK VIEW
SIDE VIEW
COLORS
MATERIALS
PATTERNS
ACCESSORIES

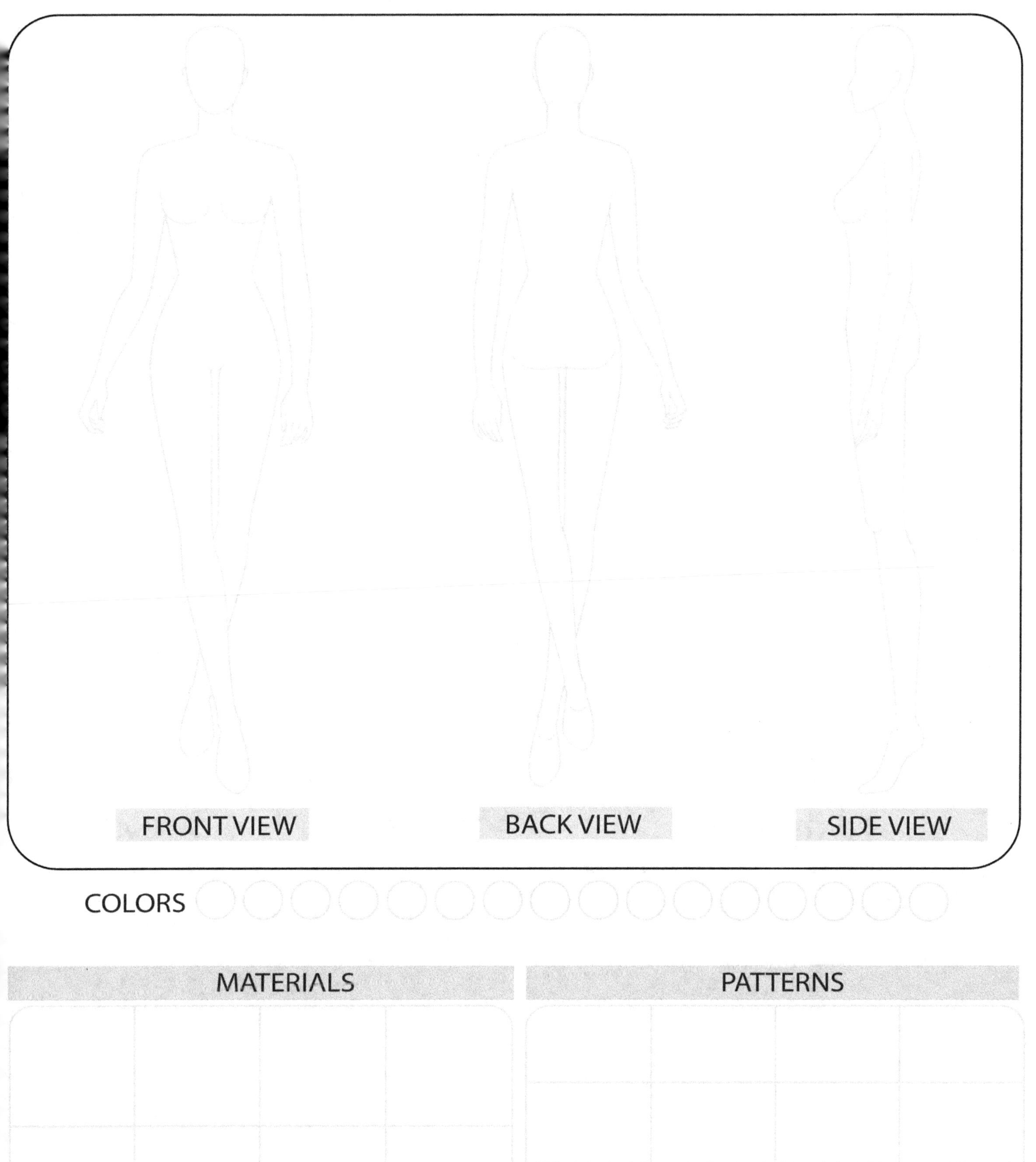

FRONT VIEW
BACK VIEW
SIDE VIEW
COLORS
MATERIALS
PATTERNS
ACCESSORIES

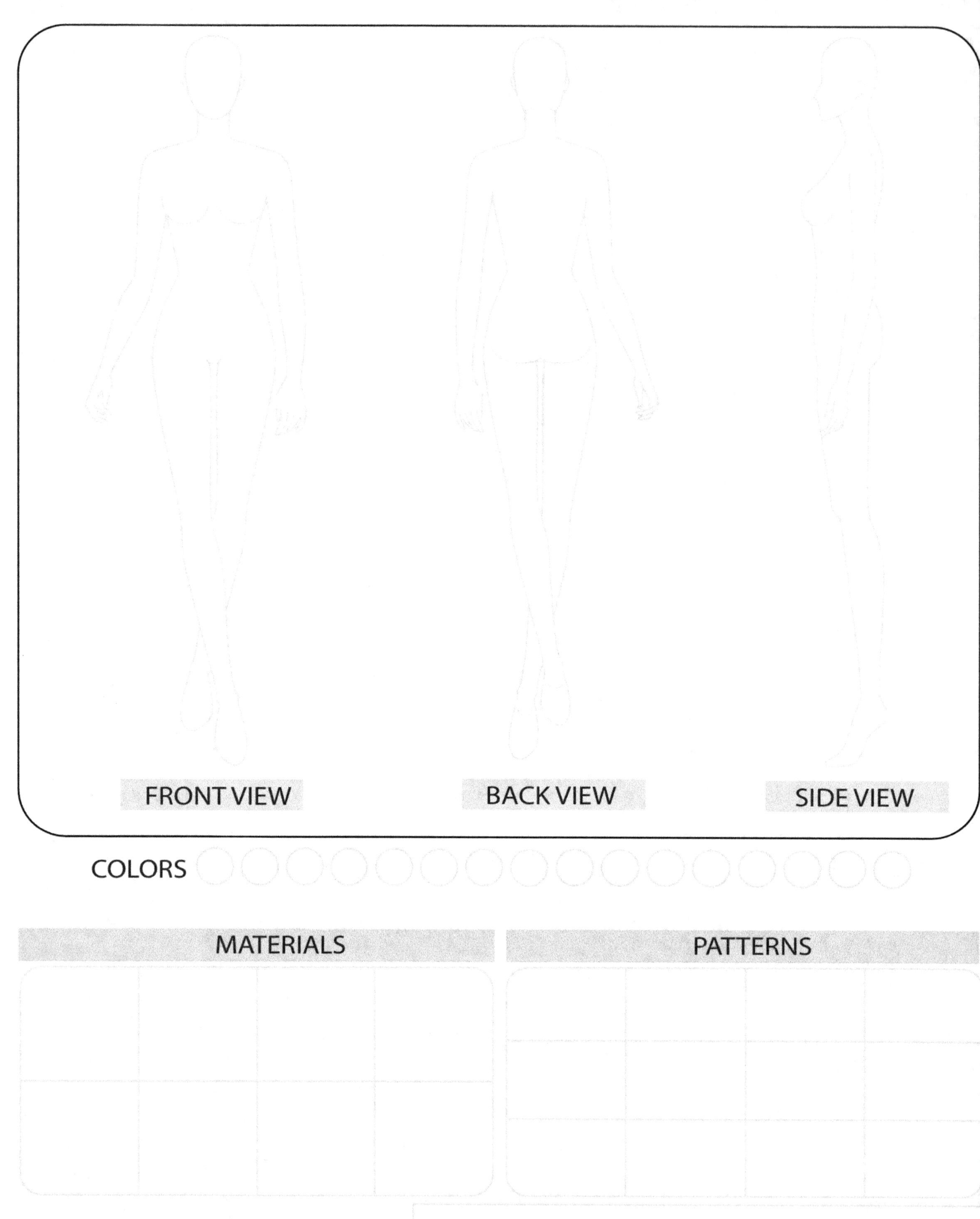

COLORS

MATERIALS

PATTERNS

ACCESSORIES

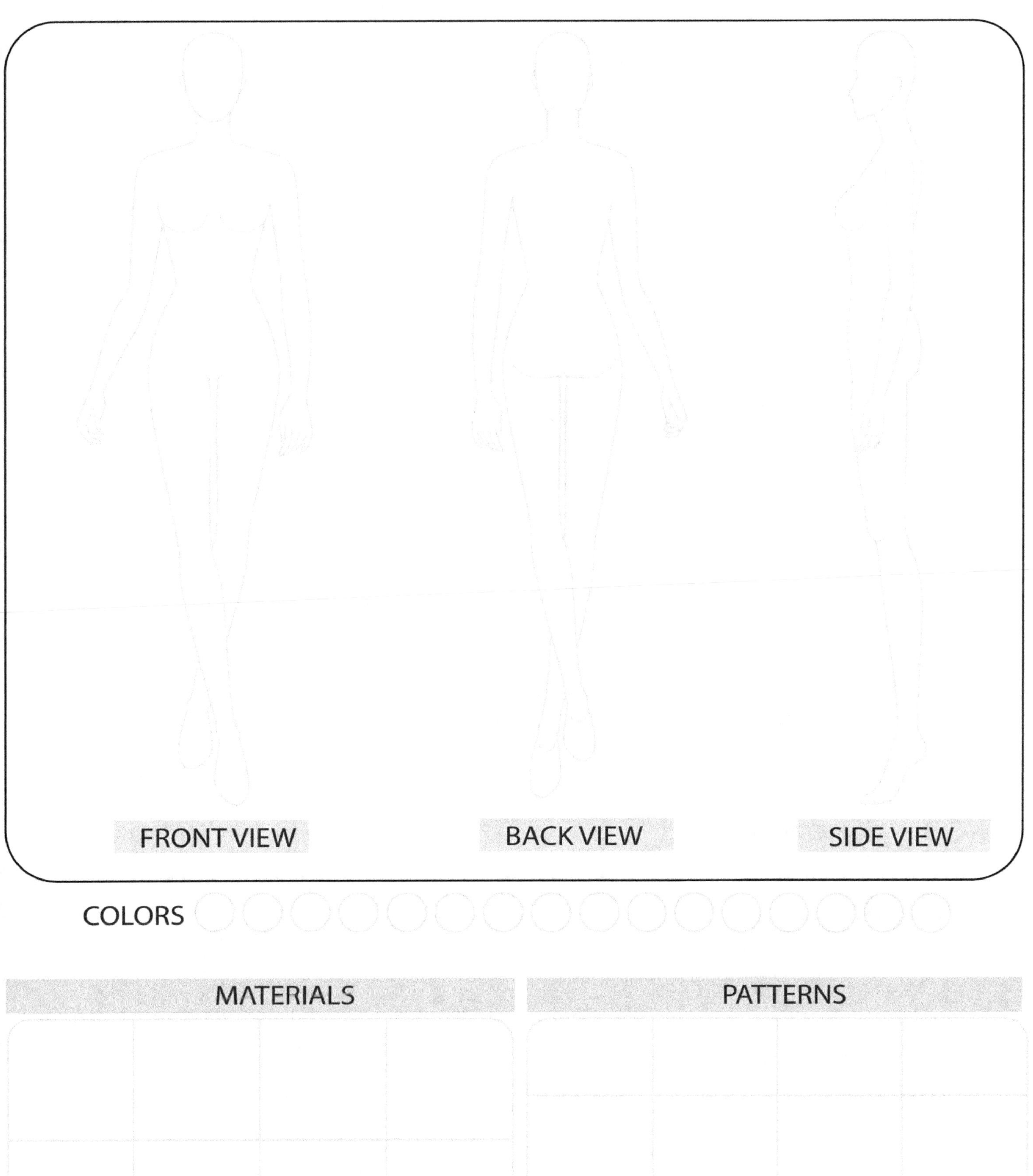

FRONT VIEW

BACK VIEW

SIDE VIEW

COLORS

MATERIALS

PATTERNS

ACCESSORIES

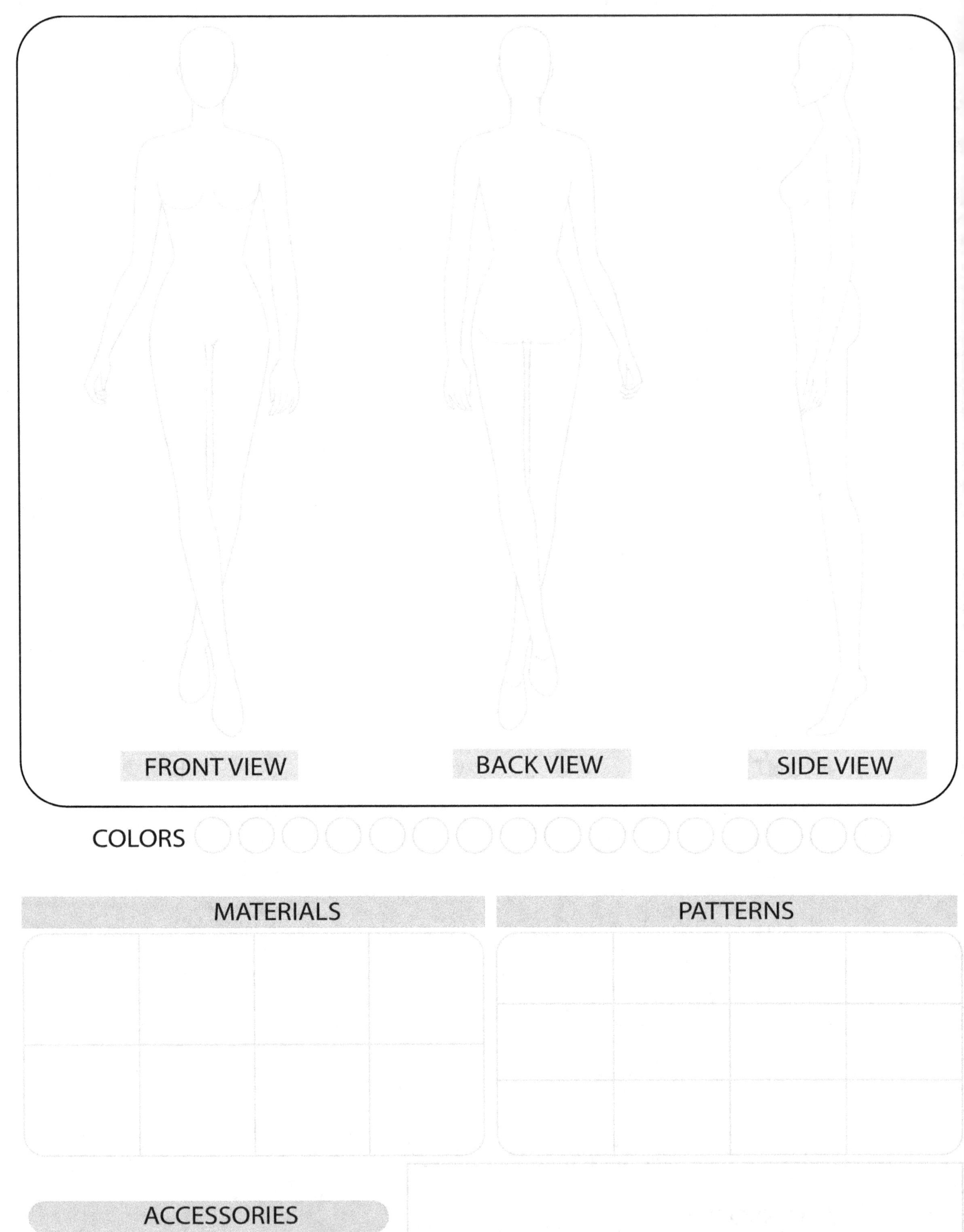

FRONT VIEW

BACK VIEW

SIDE VIEW

COLORS

MATERIALS

PATTERNS

ACCESSORIES

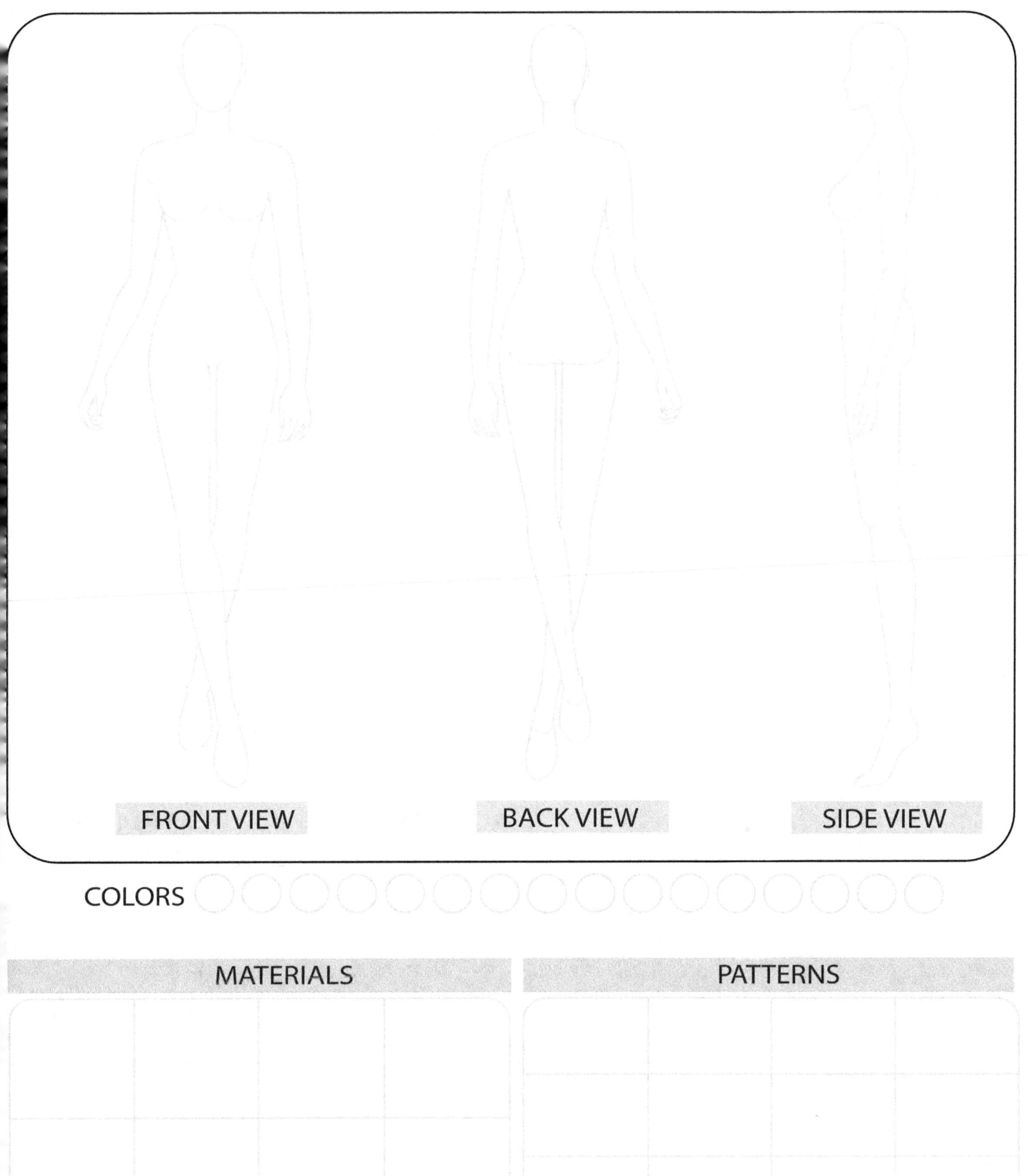

COLORS

MATERIALS

PATTERNS

ACCESSORIES

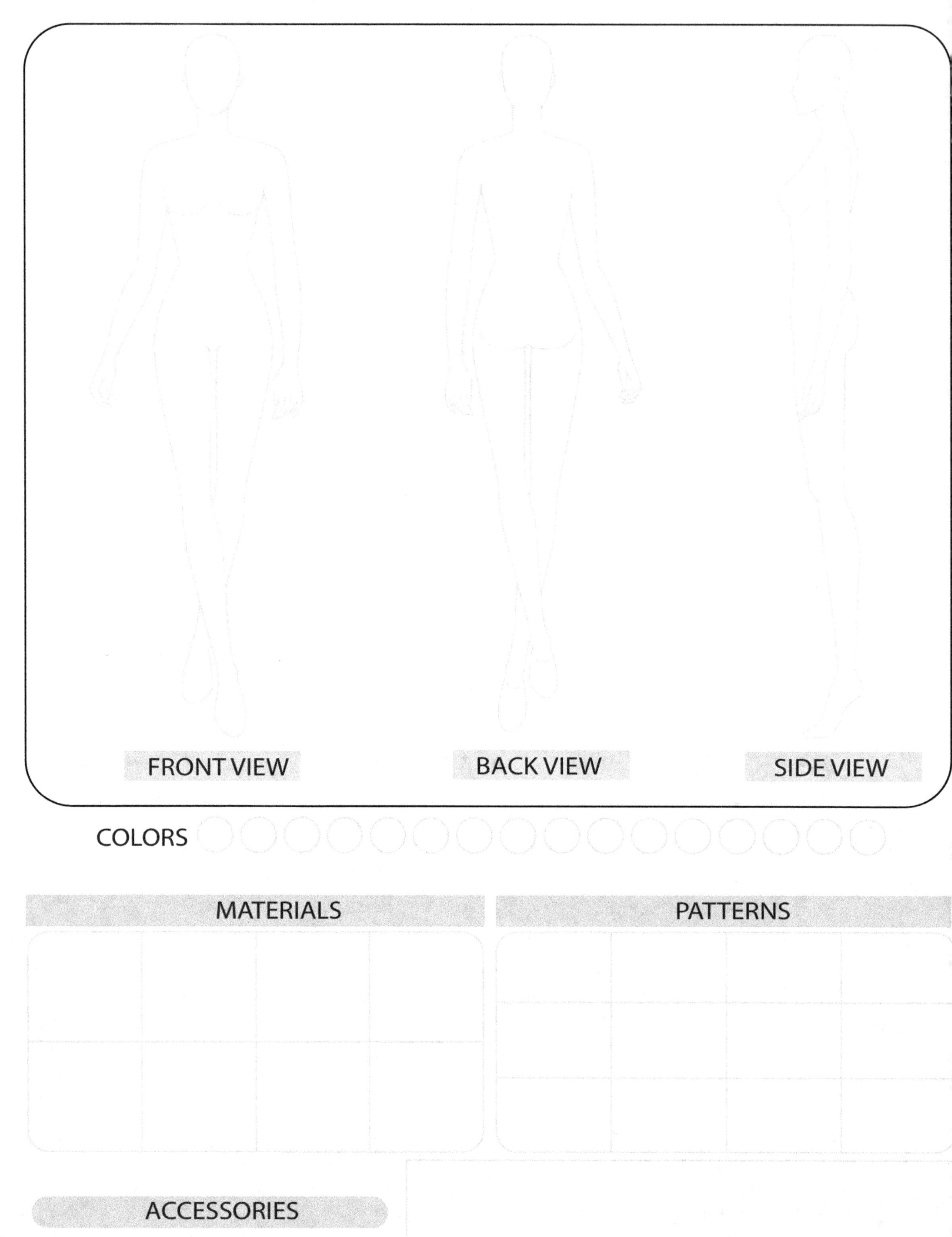

FRONT VIEW
BACK VIEW
SIDE VIEW
COLORS
MATERIALS
PATTERNS
ACCESSORIES

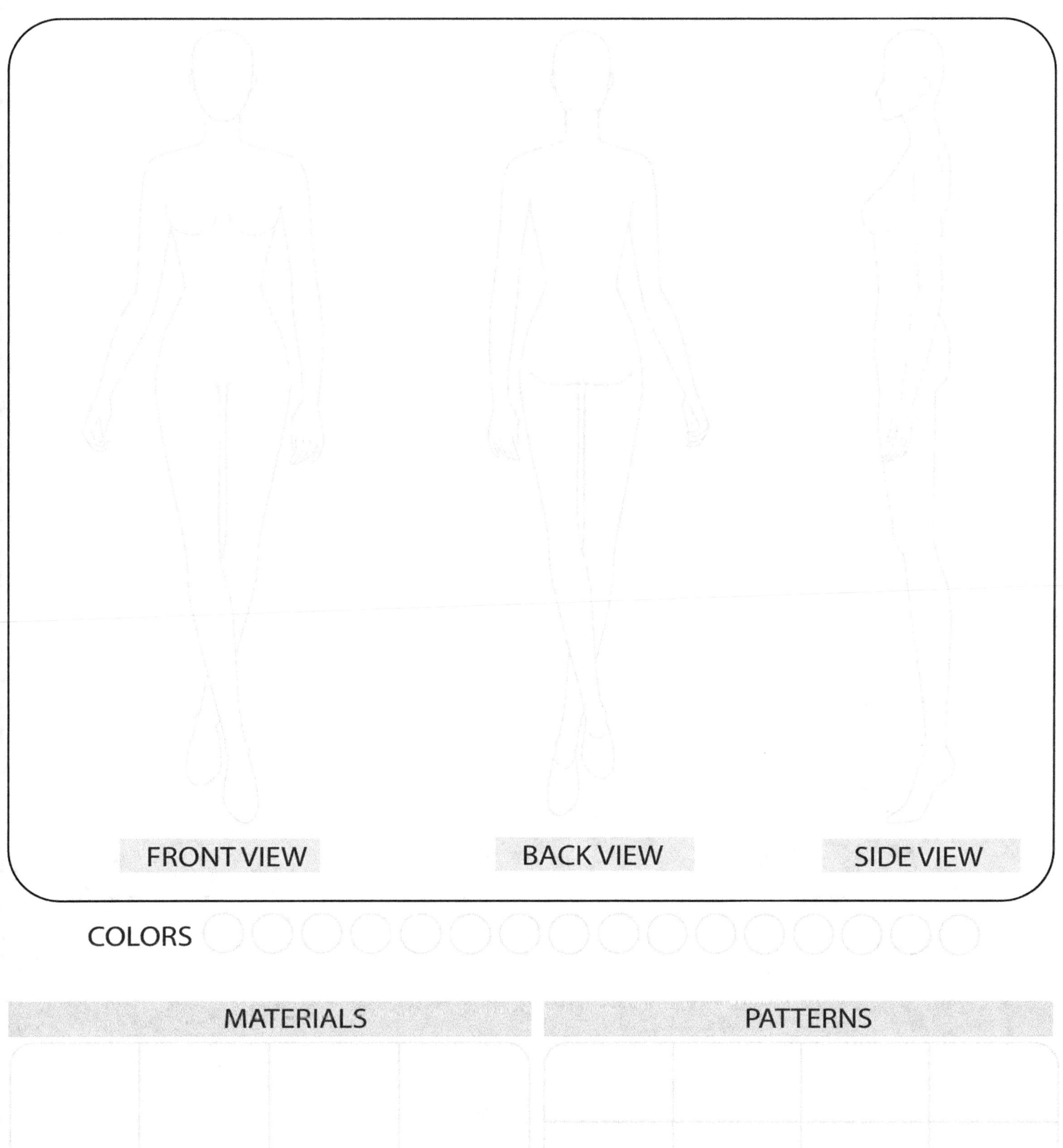

COLORS

MATERIALS

PATTERNS

ACCESSORIES

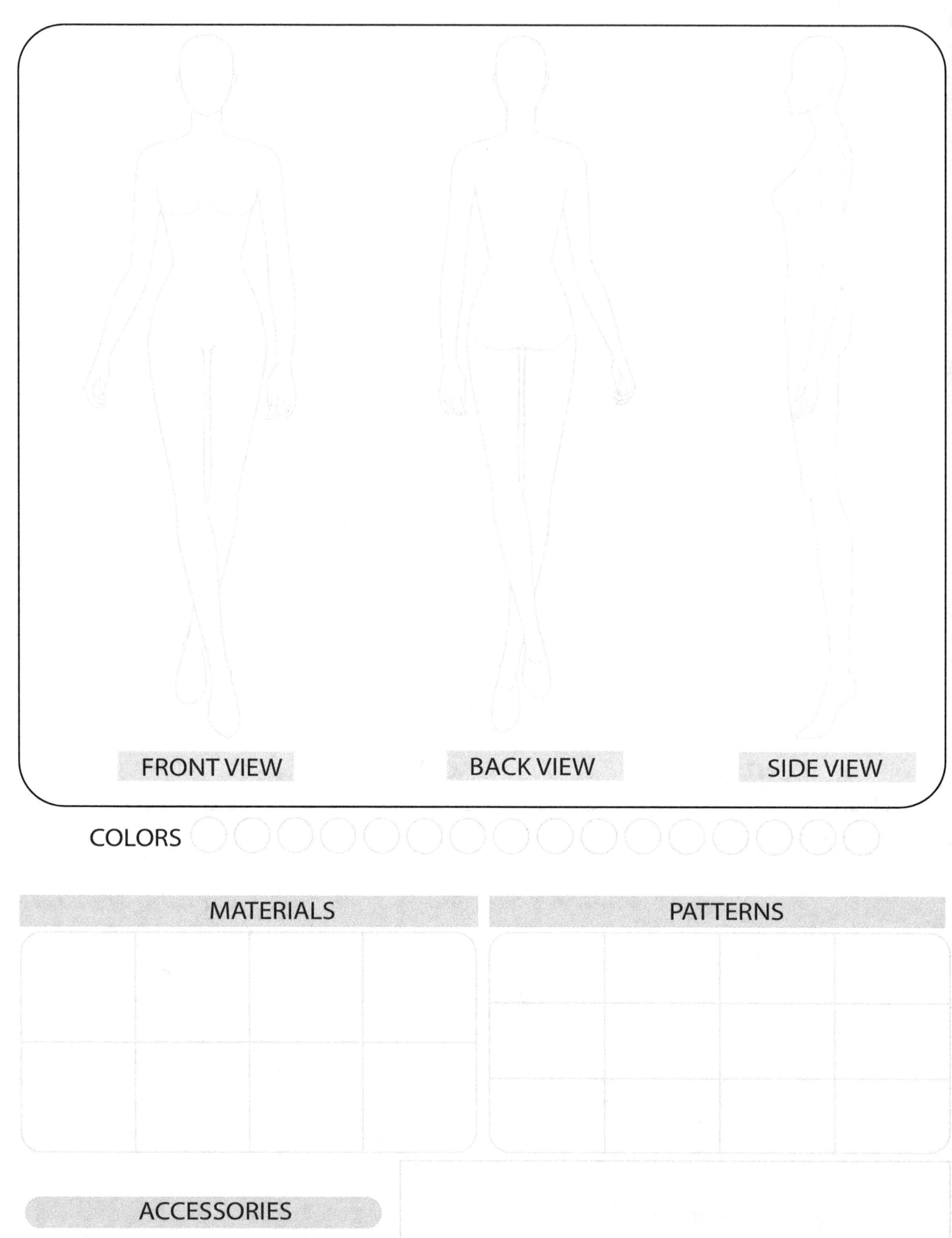

FRONT VIEW
BACK VIEW
SIDE VIEW
COLORS
MATERIALS
PATTERNS
ACCESSORIES

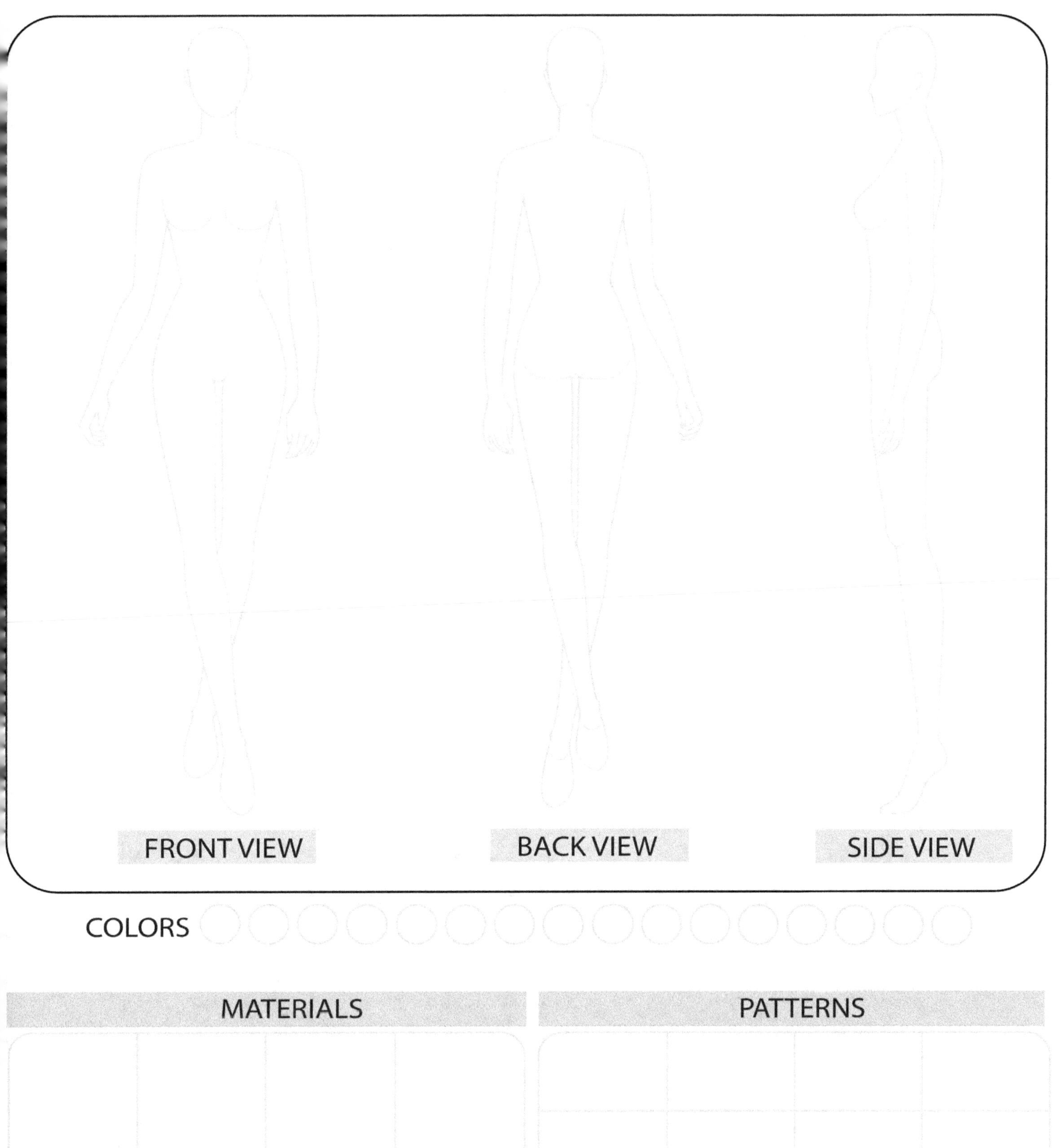

FRONT VIEW
BACK VIEW
SIDE VIEW
COLORS
MATERIALS
PATTERNS
ACCESSORIES

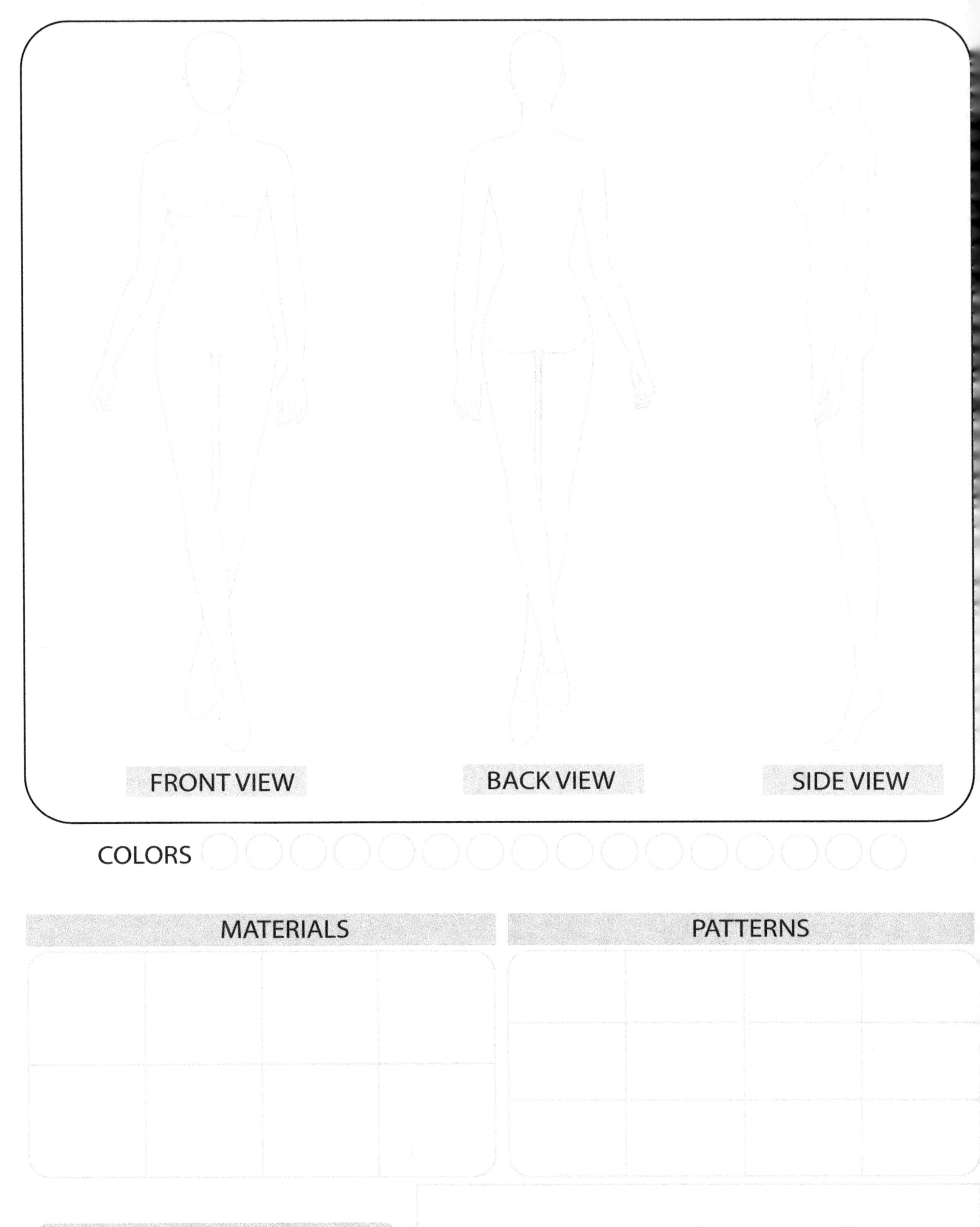

FRONT VIEW
BACK VIEW
SIDE VIEW
COLORS
MATERIALS
PATTERNS
ACCESSORIES

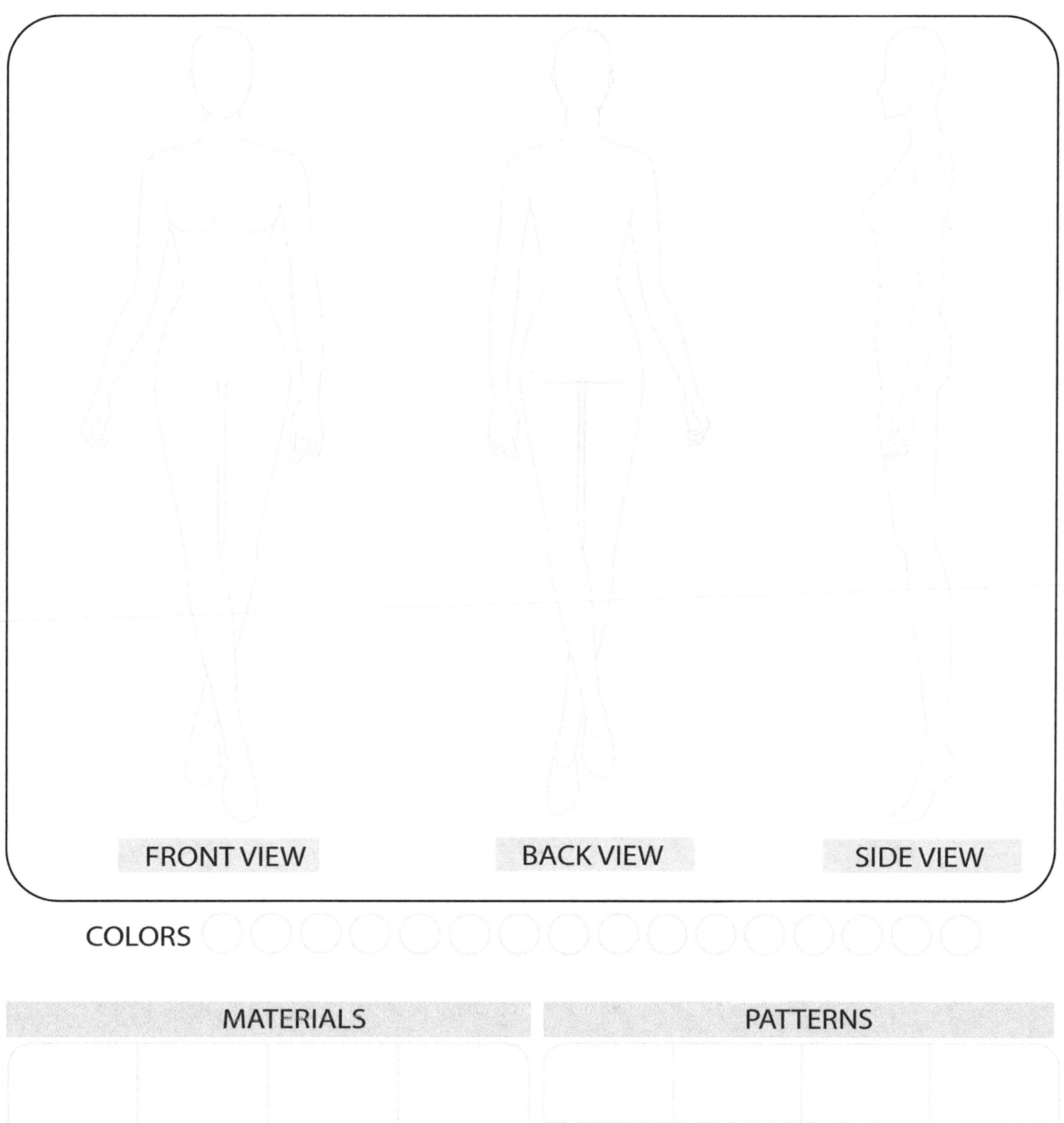
FRONT VIEW
BACK VIEW
SIDE VIEW
COLORS
MATERIALS
PATTERNS
ACCESSORIES

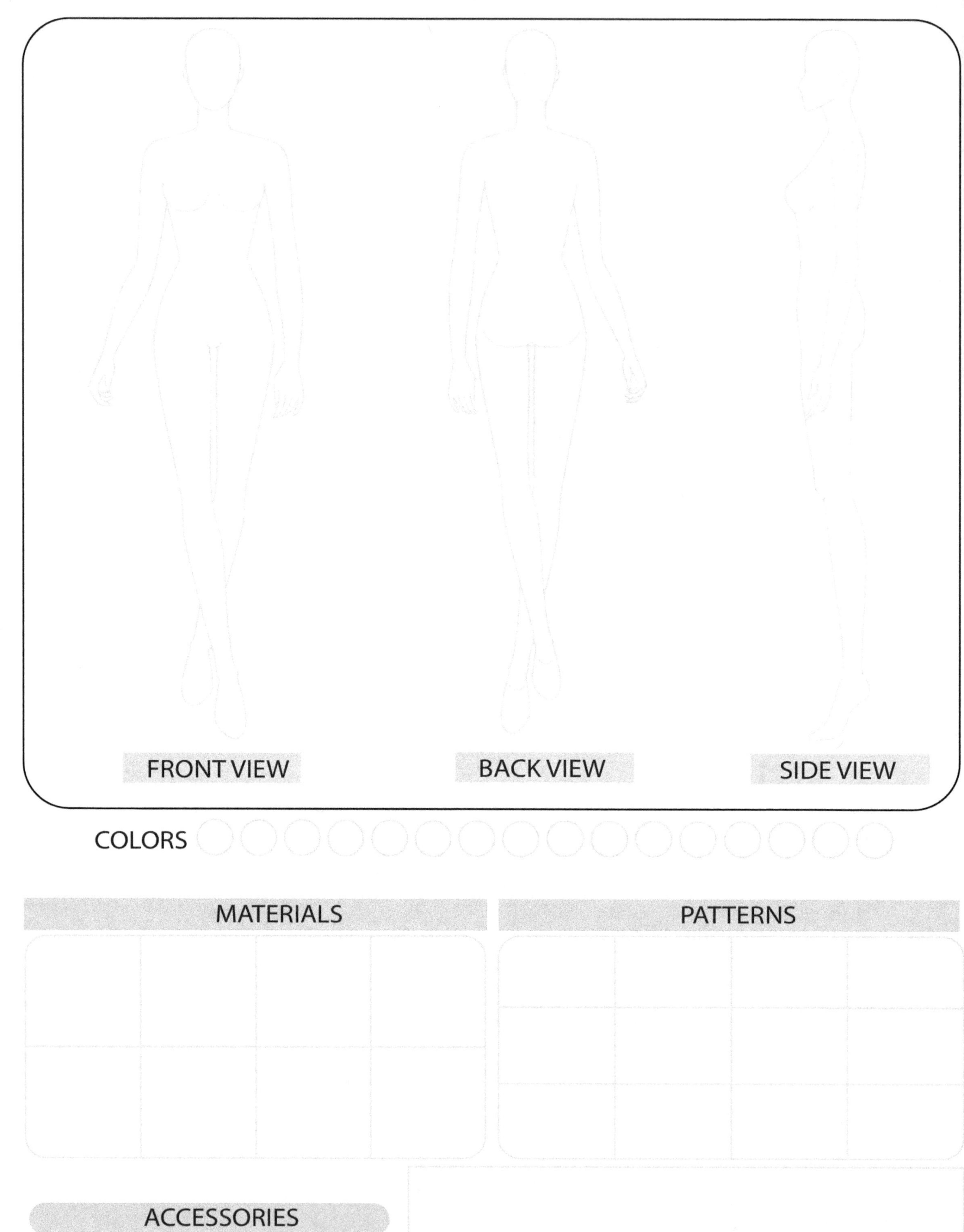

FRONT VIEW

BACK VIEW

SIDE VIEW

COLORS

MATERIALS

PATTERNS

ACCESSORIES

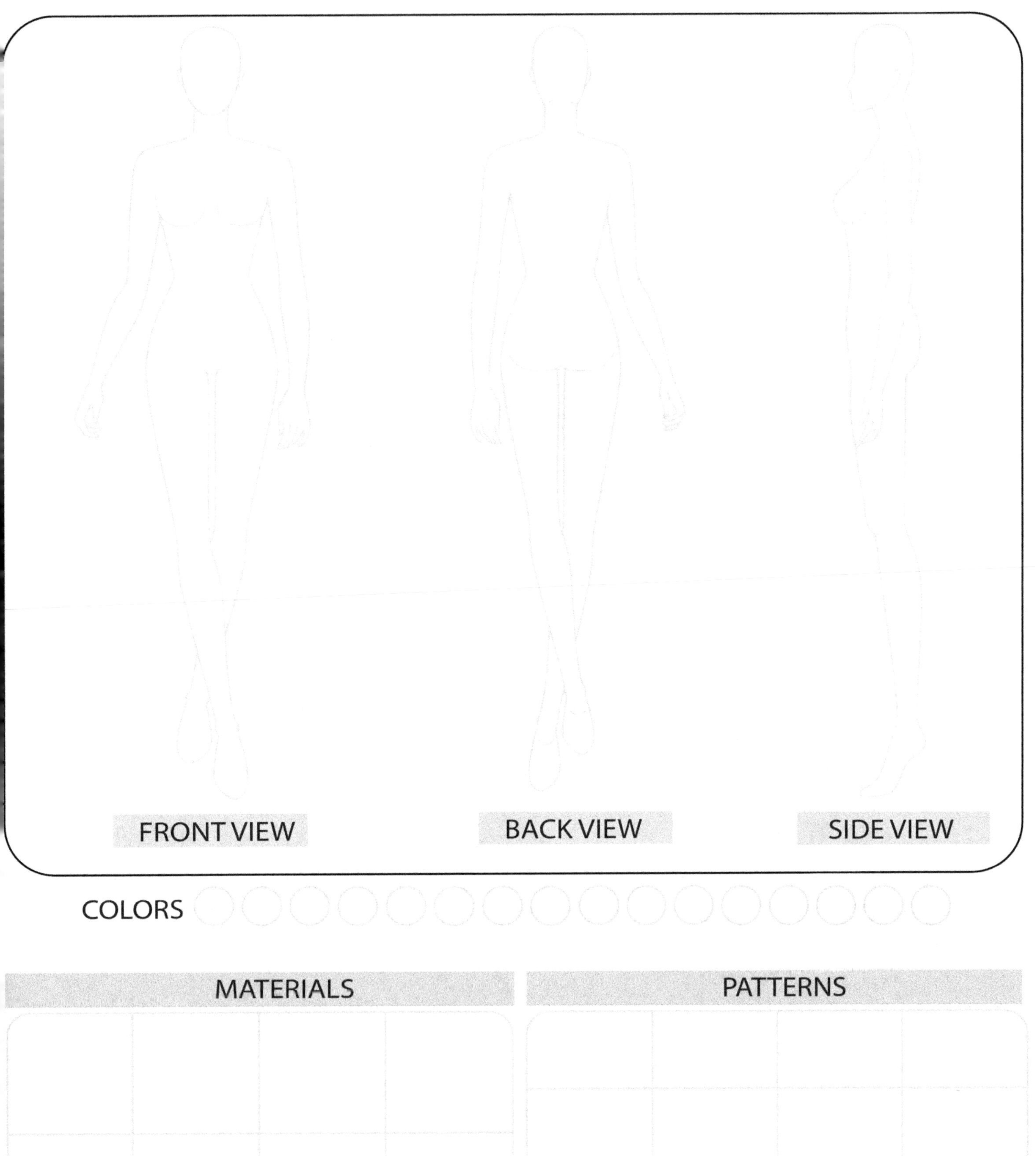

FRONT VIEW
BACK VIEW
SIDE VIEW
COLORS
MATERIALS
PATTERNS
ACCESSORIES

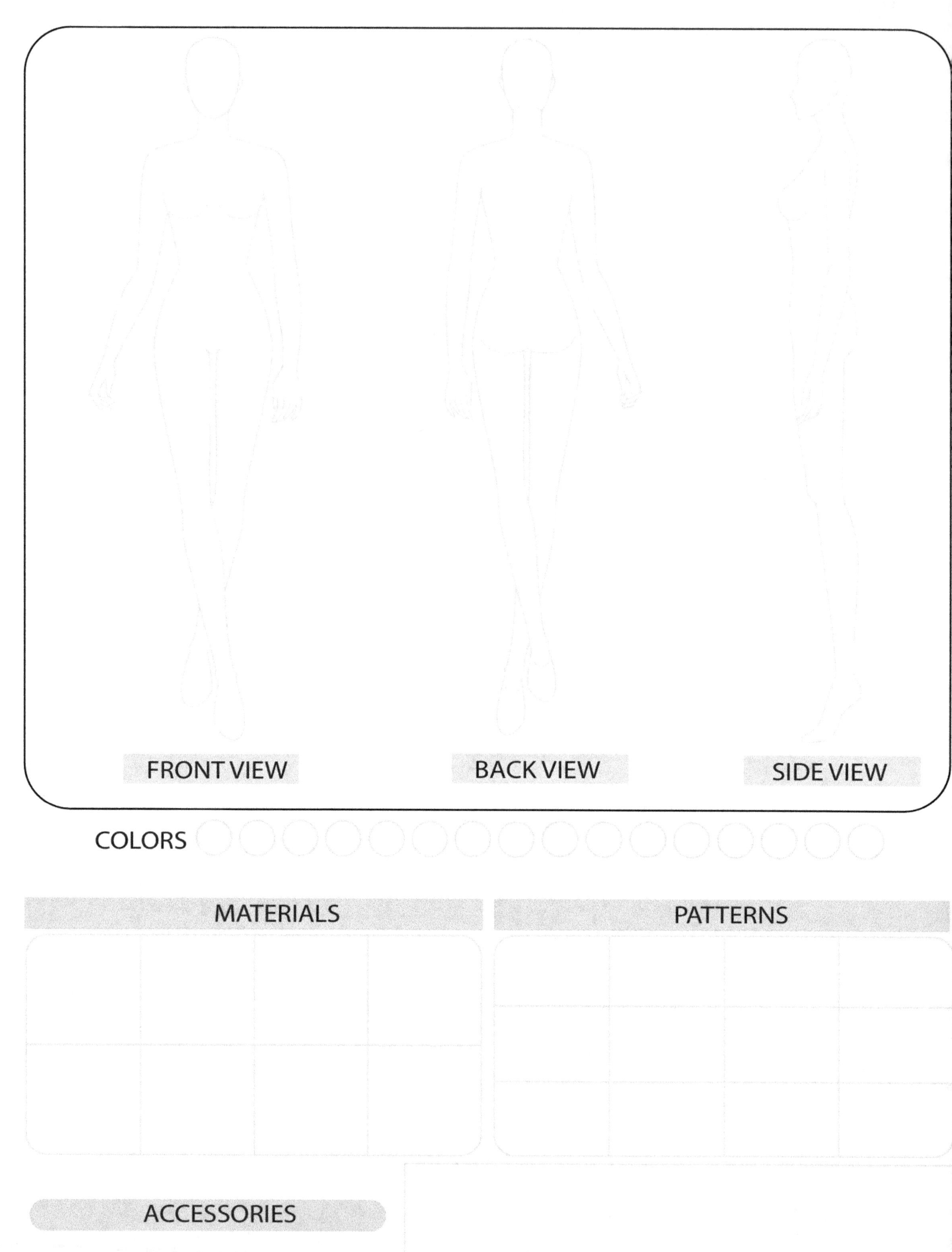

FRONT VIEW
BACK VIEW
SIDE VIEW
COLORS
MATERIALS
PATTERNS
ACCESSORIES

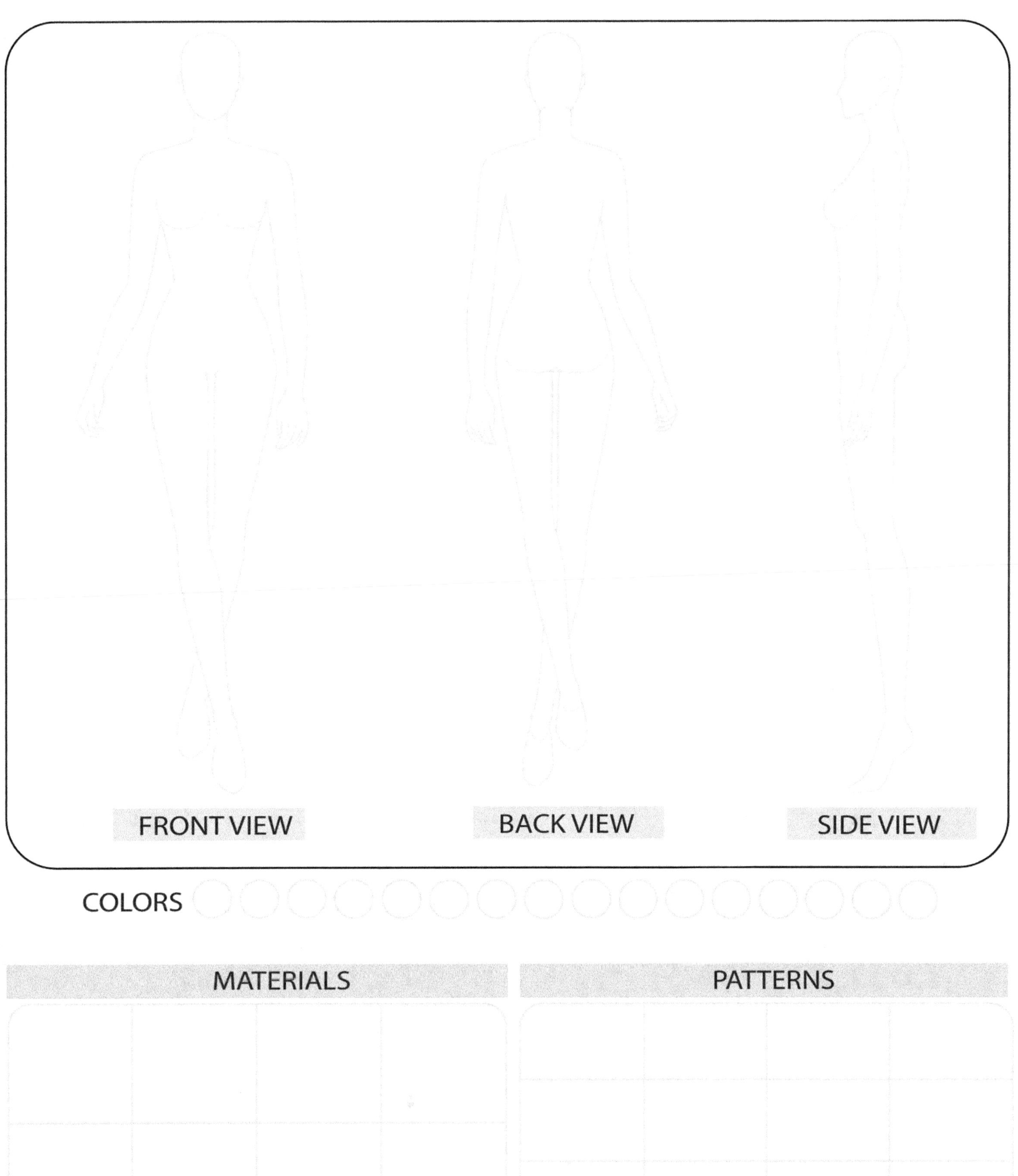

FRONT VIEW

BACK VIEW

SIDE VIEW

COLORS

MATERIALS

PATTERNS

ACCESSORIES

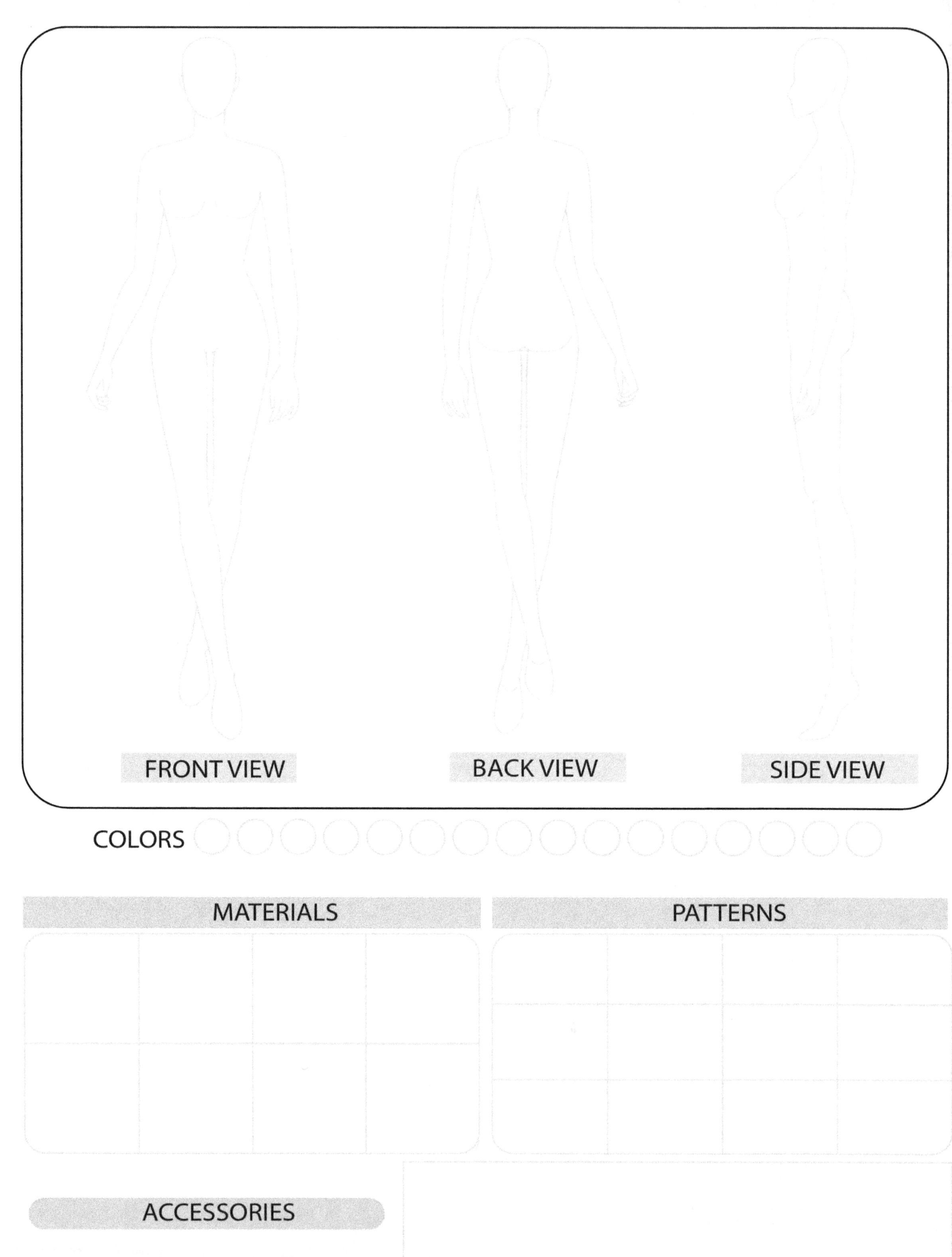

FRONT VIEW
BACK VIEW
SIDE VIEW
COLORS
MATERIALS
PATTERNS
ACCESSORIES

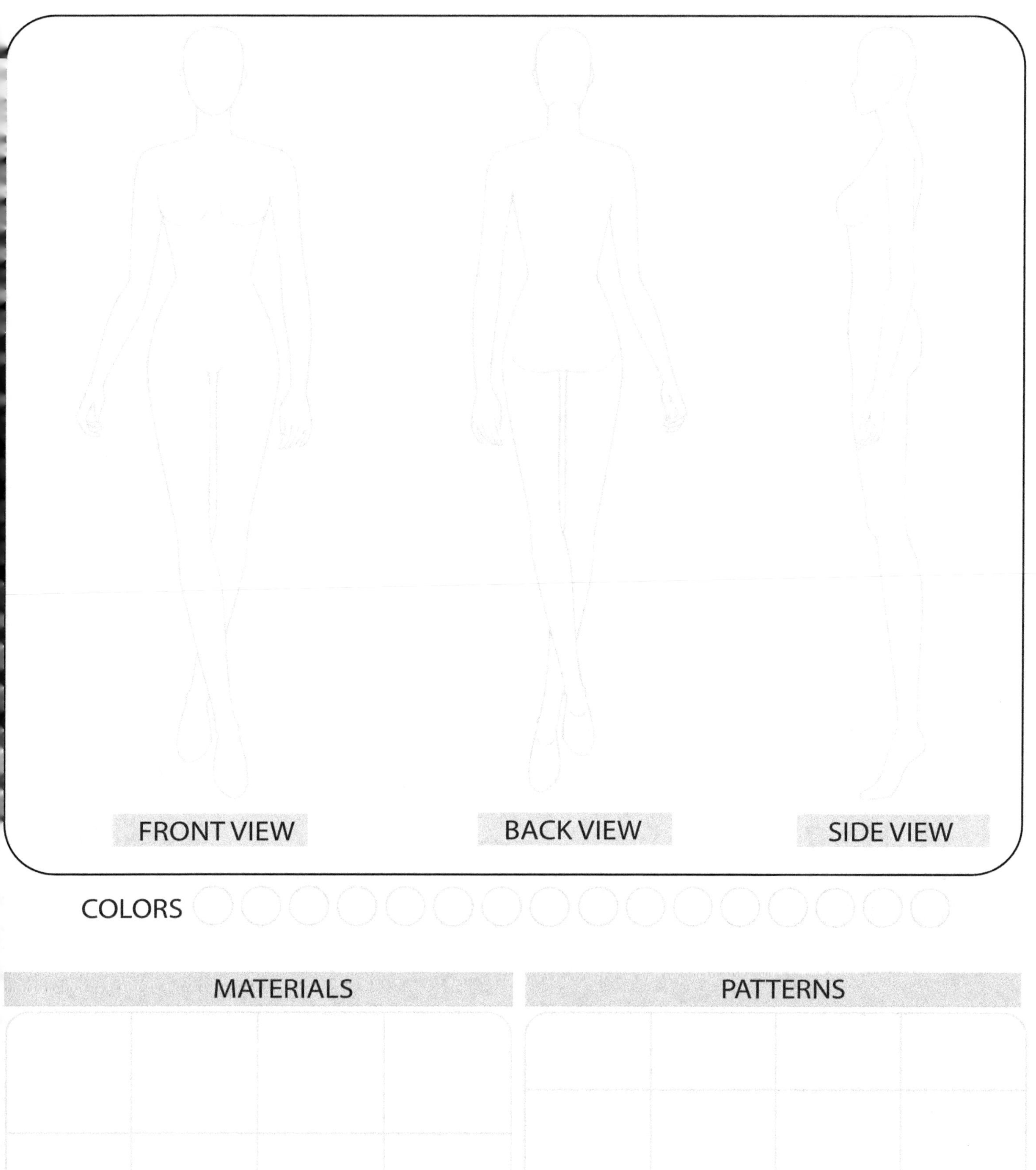

FRONT VIEW

BACK VIEW

SIDE VIEW

COLORS

MATERIALS

PATTERNS

ACCESSORIES

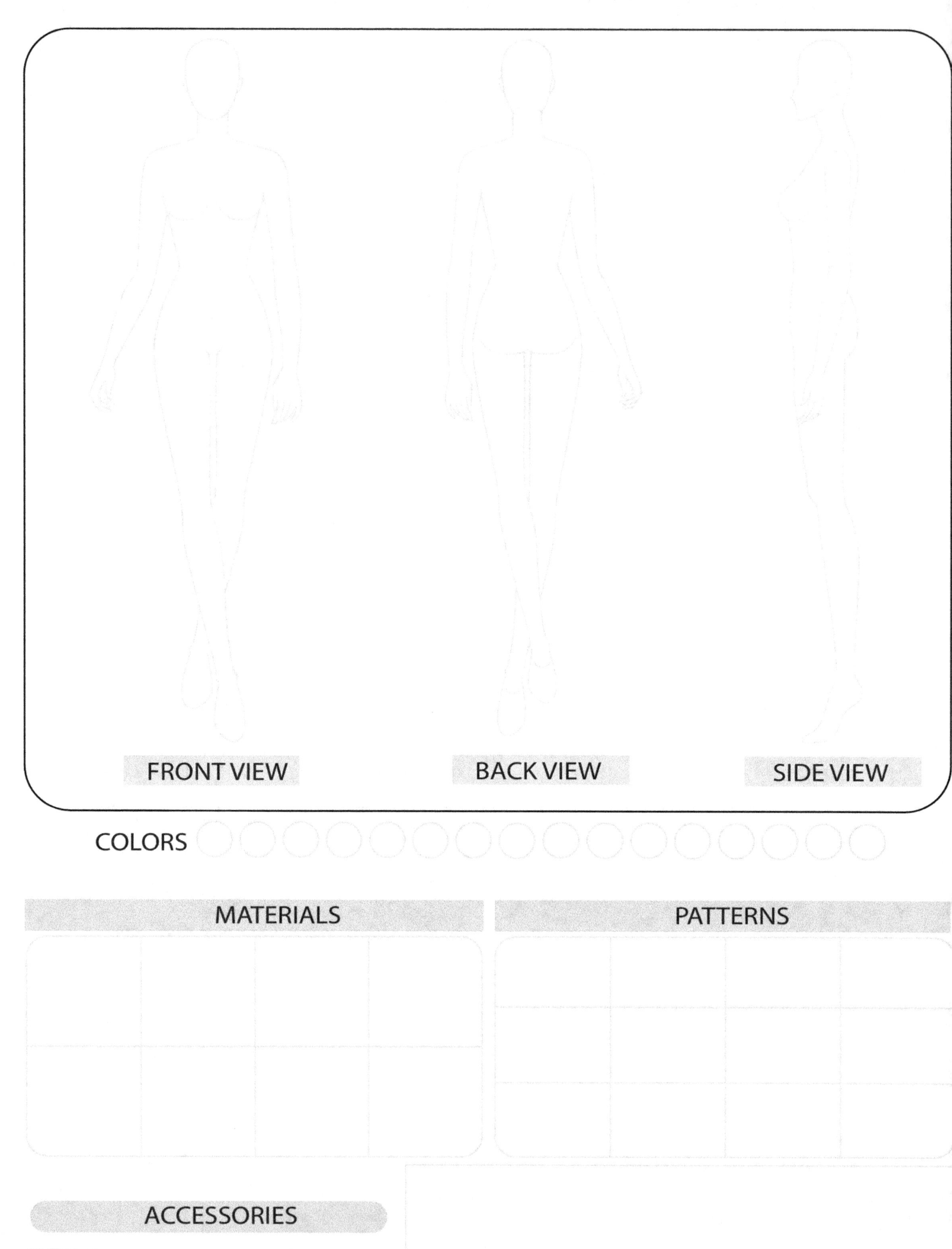

FRONT VIEW
BACK VIEW
SIDE VIEW
COLORS
MATERIALS
PATTERNS
ACCESSORIES

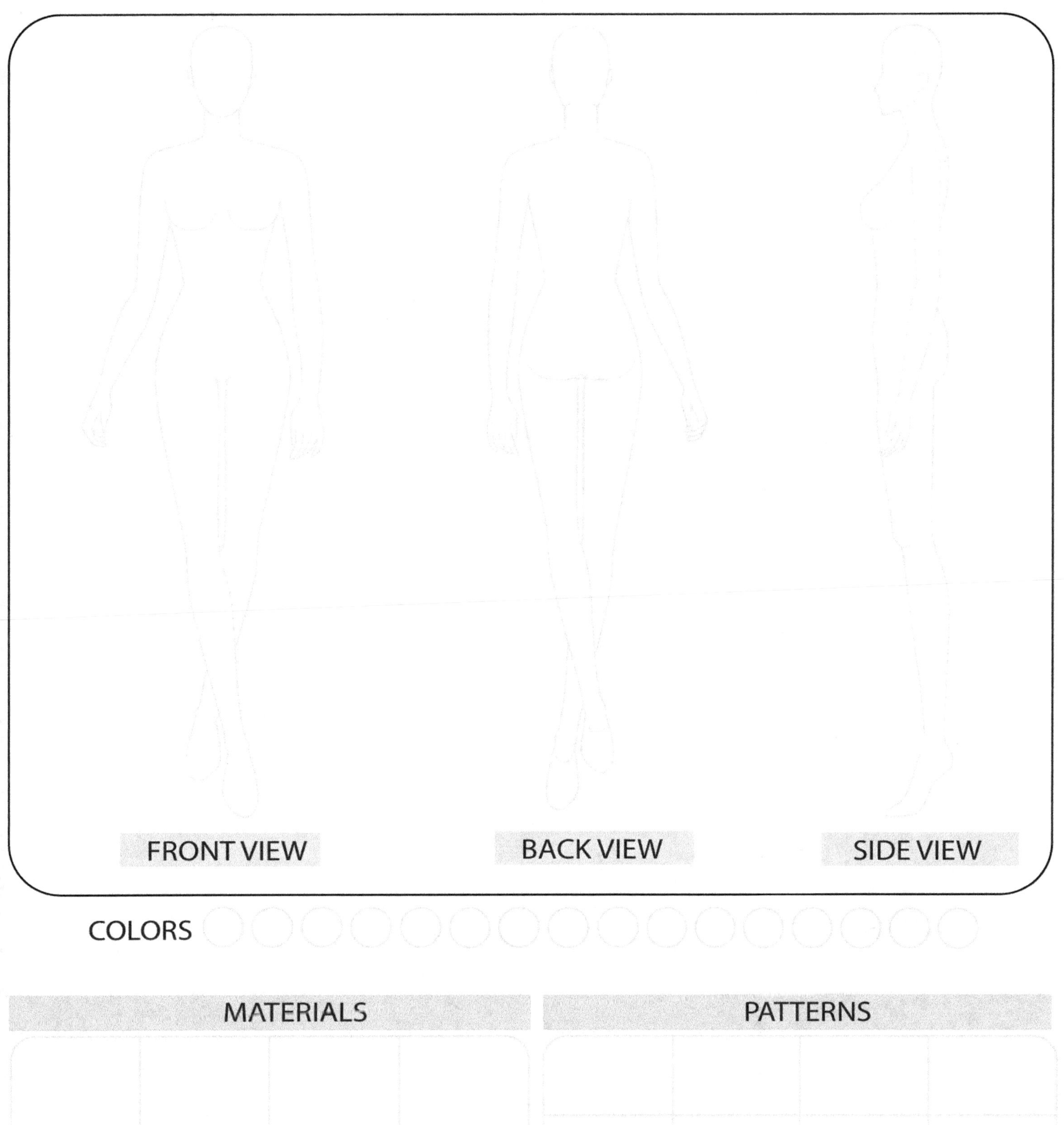

FRONT VIEW   BACK VIEW   SIDE VIEW

COLORS

MATERIALS

PATTERNS

ACCESSORIES

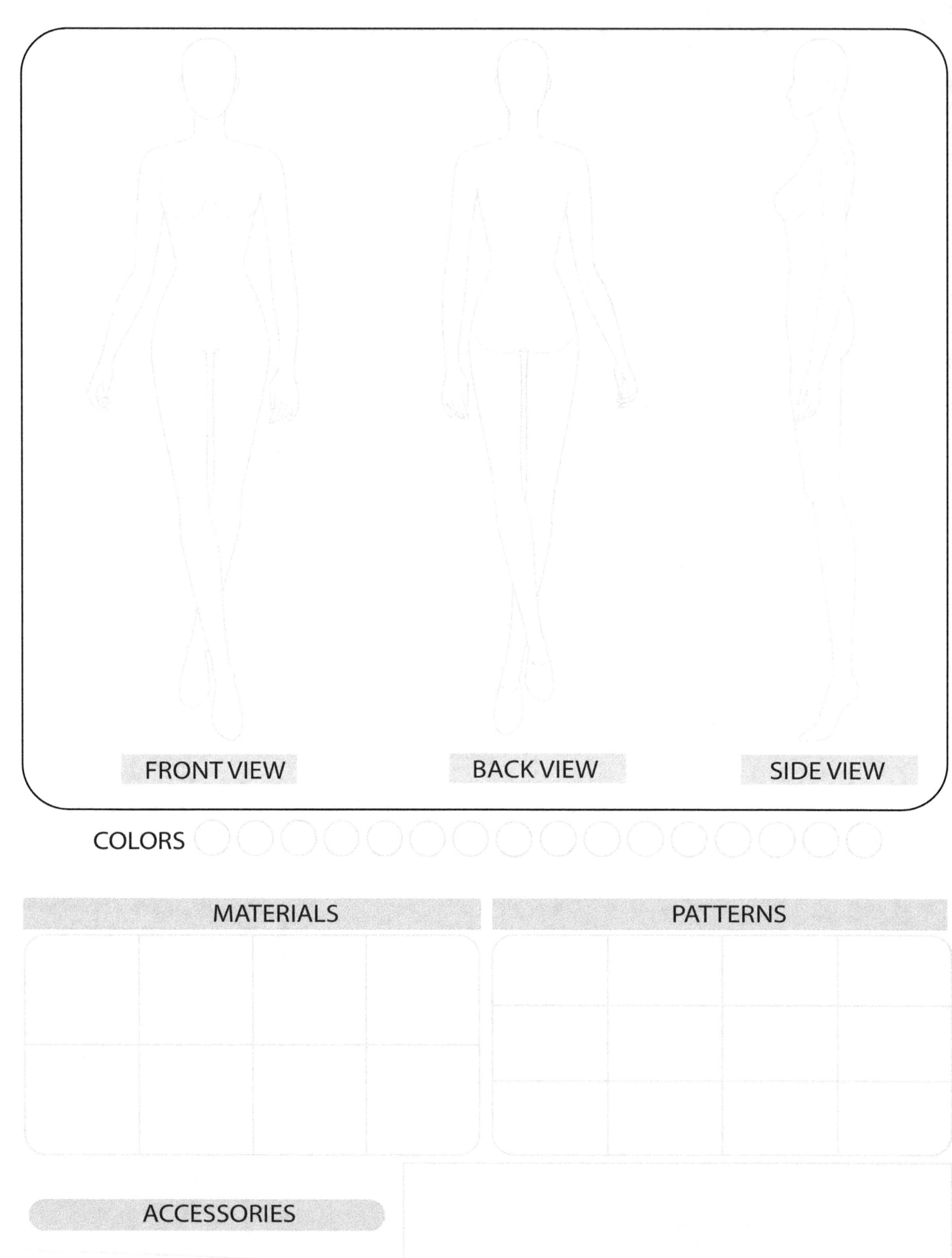

FRONT VIEW

BACK VIEW

SIDE VIEW

COLORS

MATERIALS

PATTERNS

ACCESSORIES

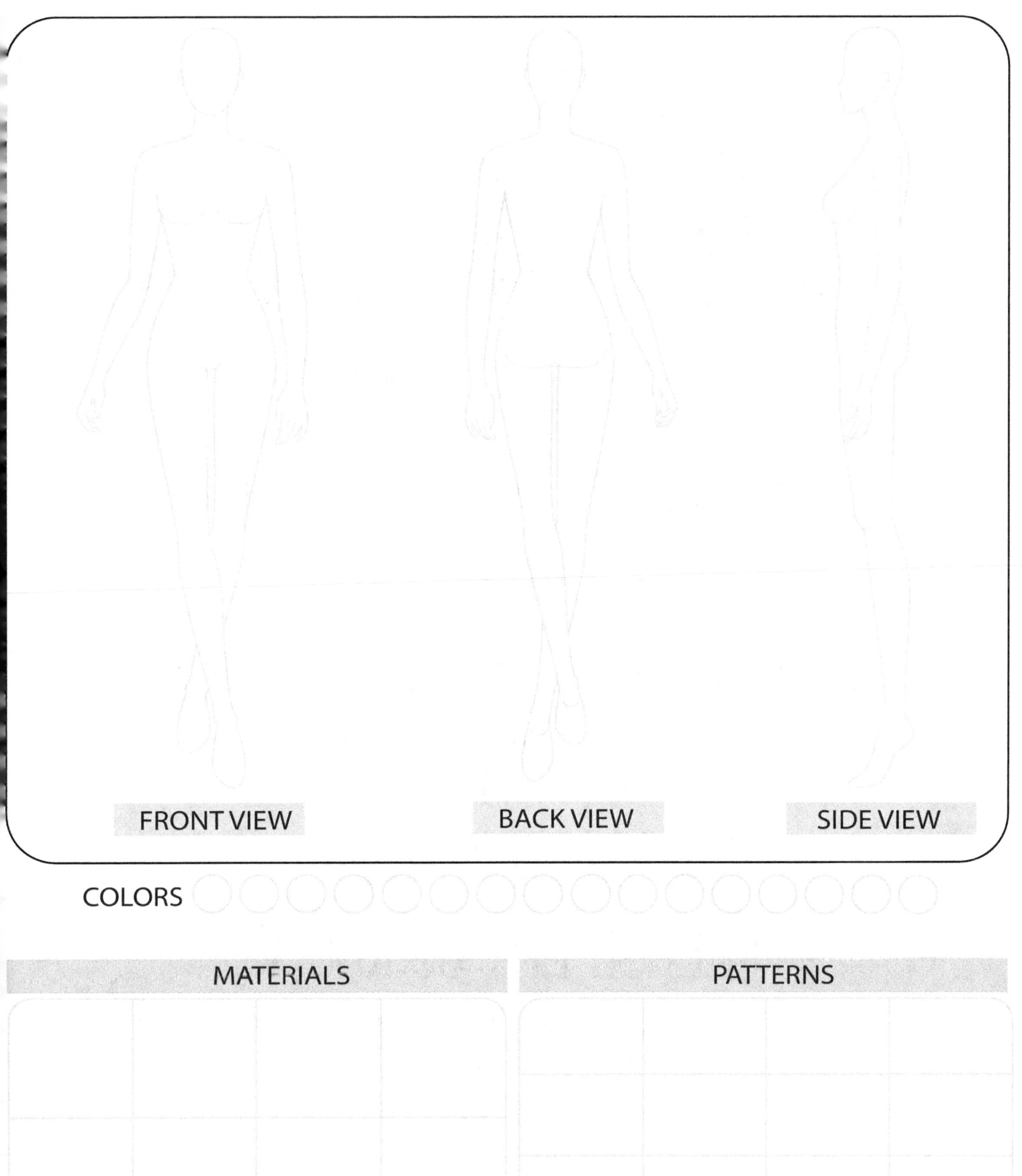

FRONT VIEW

BACK VIEW

SIDE VIEW

COLORS

MATERIALS

PATTERNS

ACCESSORIES

Thank you

WE HOPE YOU ENJOYED OUR
BOOK
AS A SMALL FAMILY COMPANY,
YOUR FEEDBACK IS VERY
IMPORTANT TO US.
PLEASE LET US KNOW
HOW YOU LIKE OUR
BOOK AT :
PROMOBILEAMZ@GMAIL.COM

www.ingramcontent.com/pod-product-compliance
Lightning Source LLC
LaVergne TN
LVHW080607200726
843509LV00007B/266